2011 Shipwright

2011 Shipwright

The International Annual of Maritime History & Ship Modelmaking

Incorporating

Model Shipwright

Editors John Bowen & Martin Robson

Editorial Assistant Stephen Dent

CONWAY

Notes for Contributors

An information sheet detailing guidelines for contributors (for example, on house style, formatting copy and attributing references) can be supplied by the editorial team on request.

Articles should be emailed as an attachment or supplied as double-spaced typescript on single sides of paper, accompanied by an electronic version on disk, in text only format. Feature articles will normally be between 4000 and 8000 words long; the submission of shorter articles is also encouraged. If using references please use endnotes. Measurements should be given in metric and imperial.

Submissions should be accompanied by illustrations, either as photocopies of drawings and photographs to accompany the text or on disk (CD or DVD) – please do not send the originals until the article has been accepted for publication. Bear in mind that in the case of ship-model photography, clarity of detail is essential.

Pictures should be either at **300 dpi resolution**, to give a width of approximately 16cm, or if at 72dpi resolution, then the width will have to be approximately 60cm in order to allow for a four times reduction to obtain an acceptable image for reproduction. Images should be saved either as EPS, TIFF, or JPEG format. In addition, we would prefer hard copies of the images to be included, to give a fall-back option should the digital images not prove adequate.

Questions relating to any aspect of submissions should be addressed to the Editor, care of Conway:

Shipwright Editor
Conway
10 Southcombe Street
London W14 0RA

Email: shipwrighteditor@anovabooks.com
Web: www.shipwrightannual.com

First published in 2010 by Conway
An imprint of Anova Books Ltd
10 Southcombe Street
London W14 0RA
www.anovabooks.com
www.conwaypublishing.com

Pages 2–3 Deck of HMS *Warrior* 1860. (John Lee/Conway)

A CIP catalogue record for this book is available from the British Library.

ISBN 9781844861231

Printed and bound by Times Printers, Malaysia

Distributed in the U.S. and Canada by:
Sterling Publishing Co., Inc.
387 Park Avenue South
New York
NY 10016-8810

Shipwright accepts advertising. For more information please contact: modelshipwright@anovabooks.com

To receive regular email updates on forthcoming Conway titles, email conway@anovabooks.com with Conway Update in the subject field.

Contents

Editorial

We are particularly pleased to open *Shipwright 2011* with an in-depth interview with Peter Goodwin MPhil. IEng. MIMarEST., Keeper and Curator of HMS *Victory*. As the leading light in his field, Peter's written work will be familiar to many readers, but his day job is to be much envied. In fact, it is not so much a job as a way of life, as for nearly twenty years Peter has had in his care arguably the nation's finest and most precious piece of heritage. Clearly, anyone reading Peter's interview cannot fail to be struck by his knowledge, understanding, respect of and love for HMS *Victory*. Among many fascinating and pertinent points, perhaps the most important we will take away is the value of empirical testing. We can all come up with theories of how things must have happened, based on conjecture and the reading of docu-

ments. But running bags of sugar up from *Victory*'s magazines to the gun decks to understand how the system of powder supply did or did not work (and in the process dispelling the powder monkey myth) is only the most obvious example of what Peter calls 'allowing the ship to tell you how it works'.

Segueing nicely conceptually, if not in running order, with Peter's work are several other articles. 'To Learn His Art' by George Stephenson examines how the eighteenth century dealt with what we now term knowledge transfer and retention. The system, despite some faults, worked well and was dependant on the crucial personal relationship between shipwright and apprentice. For the latter there was much to learn and apprenticeships ensured continuity and the passing on of hard-learned lessons and knowledge. The

Below: '*Nautilus* and *Enterprise* war schooners in the Mediterranean, 1804, as part of an American naval force operating against the notorious Barbary pirates' by Roy Cross won the Conway Maritime Sail Prize at The Royal Society of Marine Artists Annual Exhibition, 2009.

same subject matter forms the basis of Douglas Brook's short article on *sengokubune* – the ships of Japan's coastal trade. Douglas also introduces us to Mr Tomenshin Niinuma, a remarkable modern-day Japanese shipwright who faced, yet overcame, considerable problems in building ships for which plans simply do not usually exist. Knowledge is memorised, not written down, and a shroud of secrecy still surrounds Japanese boatbuilding. These are pertinent points, for George Stephenson is a former carpenter on HMS *Victory* and worked with Peter Goodwin, and they, along with Douglas Brooks, strive to preserve and share traditional skills. Again, how this is applied in practical terms is of vital importance as is the use of skilled and knowledgeable people in the restoration process, as made evident in Wyn Davies' fascinating account of the role of a specialist Heritage Lottery Fund monitor working with the HMS Warrior Preservation Trust. Taken together their knowledge, skills and experience provide an irreplaceable and highly tangible direct link to their predecessors over two centuries ago – we must ensure the process continues for the benefit of future generations.

Hence, an integral part of *Shipwright*'s role is to pass on knowledge, skills, techniques and lessons learned in a practical fashion from which readers can directly benefit. This year specific hands-on advice on the subject of hull planking comes from John Laing, on the manufacture of miniature handrails and deck ladders from B. Baldwin, and on the practicalities of building a working model, in this case of the Tug *Nangee*, from Tom Gorman. James Pottinger supplies the Modeller's Draught of the Fishery Protection Vessel *Vigilant* (III). Though not quite hands-on advice, Jonathon Kinghorn's short assessment of the authentic colours used to paint sailing men-of-war has practical application for those working on models from this period.

Graham Castle concludes his article on Carron *No 10* with the hope his model does justice to the ingenuity, skills and sweat of the men who created the 'wee-boats' known as the Clyde Puffers – he need not worry for his splendid model serves as a fitting tribute to those oft-overlooked craft. Continuing in similar fashion, and taking over two years to construct, R. Burnham's clinker-built naval whaler is clearly a labour of love for one who served his apprenticeship on such whalers in the 1950s.

We also have three, very different, cargo ships. The *Syracusia*, built around 240 BC, was a symbol of power for Hieron II of Syracuse who intended to tour the Aegean in her doling out gifts and generally filling other Greek cities with awe. Despite some input from Archimedes, the builders overlooked one crucial factor; *Syracusia* was too large to enter all but a few harbours so instead she was sent as a gift to the Egyptians who, rather enterprisingly, turned her into a visitor attraction. Only slightly more successful in her intended role was the Ben Line Steamer *Benloyal*. Built in 1959 to carry cargo to and from the Far East *Benloyal*'s fine lines are captured in B. Baldwin's excellent carved hull model. Unfortunately for the Ben Line, *Benloyal* and many like her, were rendered obsolete with the introduction of the container – today's behemoths might be able to carry huge amounts of cargo but they will never have the allure of ships such as this. As John York points out, everyone knows the story of HMS *Bounty*, but his 1:48 model highlights a crucial and often ignored part of the story: Captain Bligh's mission to transport breadfruits from Tahiti to the West Indies. *Bounty* was specially adapted to house the plants to ensure their safe arrival and the model was built with a cut-out section of deck to allow viewers to see the plants in situ.

William Macintosh manages to cover three fishing boat models in one article. Starting in the 1940s, he outlines his empirical knowledge of the design developments in the in-shore vessels that operated out of many small Scottish harbours.

The so-called T-boats were built in the 1960s to carry various dignitaries and officials on tours of the Gilbert and Ellice Islands. They were not popular, hence were used to carry supplies and less discerning passengers around the islands. Perhaps this was one reason why John Laing found information hard to come by – that and the general difficulties of obtaining information in the atolls and coral islands of the Pacific region only overcome by John collecting several year's worth of information while actually working in the Gilbert and Ellice Islands which allowed him to build his model of the *Tautunu* described here.

Robert A. Wilson's article presents two white-hulled Norwegian ships, the cruise ship *Stella Polaris* of 1927 and the fruit carrier *Rose* of 1938. The former had a long-lasting career sinking off Japan in 2006 while the latter managed only three years at sea before being purchased by Germany and renamed the *Alstertor*. She served as a supply ship to the *Bismarck*, amongst others, and was scuttled in 1941.

In geographic terms *Shipwright* certainly covers a lot of water, but not perhaps as much as the exploration ships *Fram* and *Discovery* described by Rorke Bryan. Their histories reflect, perhaps, the last great age of maritime exploration and their success, in the case of *Fram*, or failure, for *Discovery*, as ship designs provide tangible evidence of the need to conceive and the build vessels that are fit for purpose. *Discovery*'s poor insulation is only the most obvious example of a lack of thinking about what a ship is going to have to do – a timeless lesson for all those involved in ship procurement. Yet, despite their trials and tribulations, both ships survive, and can be visited, today – *Fram* in Oslo and *Discovery* at Dundee.

Rounding off the main articles is a second contribution from B. Baldwin, this time detailing the building of a 1:192 dockyard type model of HMS *Roebuck* of 1774. I hope you will all agree that this exquisite model rounds off the annual very nicely indeed.

John Bowen and Martin Robson

Interview with Peter Goodwin

KEEPER AND CURATOR OF HMS *VICTORY*

The author of *The Construction and Fitting of the Sailing Man of War, 1650–1850*, and the *Anatomy* volumes *The Naval Cutter Alert 1777*, *The 20-Gun Ship Blandford* and *The Bomb Vessel Granado 1742*, as well as *Nelson's Ships*, and *Ships of Trafalgar*, met with Conway's Publisher John Lee in Portsmouth in July 2010.

JL: Tell us about the new Museum of the Royal Navy and how HMS *Victory* fits into the new organisation.

PG: Well, *Victory* will become part of the new National Museum of the Royal Navy albeit she will remain as a com-

Above: Peter Goodwin alongside *Victory*. (John Lee/Conway)

missioned warship in the Royal Navy. She will continue in her role as the flagship of the Second Sea Lord and the navy will have their commanding officer and staff on board as they've always done. The difference it makes will be to myself and the guides, because we are the public front for the ship, running the historical side of things, and we are to be transferred to the Royal Navy Museum staff under terms that are still being negotiated. I do think the concept of the National Museum of the Royal Navy is a good one, because it is intended to include not just ourselves here at Portsmouth Historic Dock-yard, but also the Submarine Museum at Gosport, the Royal Marines Museum in Southsea, and the Fleet Air Arm Museum at Yeovilton under its management – the whole idea is to bring the Royal Navy to the public at large.

JL: How did you become keeper and curator of HMS *Victory*?

PG: It was a little bit of luck. In 1990 there were moves to transfer the work of *Victory's* guides from naval ratings to civilians. The intention was to build up a corps of people with progressive expertise rather than naval ratings who would be there on maybe a three- or six-month basis only. Knowing this was about to happen, I came on a visit to the ship and brought some of my maritime publications with me.

JL: Were you in the navy at the time?

PG: No, I had left the navy by this time. I managed to get myself an interview with the commanding officer who was in charge of implementing the new set-up. They had also been considering the idea of a curator for the ship, and it occurred to him that I might fit the bill, especially with my technical background on ships of this type. Equally, I suppose, my being ex-navy helped in that they knew they were dealing with somebody who understood how the navy and the dockyards worked. And so they started me off as one of the civilian guides, because they needed to set it up properly with the civil service, and once I got working we started defining the curatorial aspects of the ship with advice from the Royal Naval Museum. So I actually started the job in September of 1991.

There had never been a keeper and curator for *Victory* before, so it was quite a challenge. There was nobody to turn to for advice: you had to sit there and think it out. Doing the job as a guide allowed me to see the ship through the public's eyes and to start a programme of improving the interpretation of the ship, not just what the guides do, but on the physical items, because the ship at that time was quite bland. There were neat rows of guns, neat rows of tables with nothing on them, and empty storerooms. Rarely did you have any real concept about living and fighting in a man of war.

I suppose the many books that I'd read and the various studies that I'd done enabled me to create a three-dimensional history book inside the ship. I often think of myself as a historical stage manager, because the guides go out there and tread the boards, while I, as the curator, create the scenery around them and the props that they need to tell their story – which is quite interesting because my paternal grandfather was a stage manager in Bristol.

JL: You wanted to show how the ship worked?

PG: Yes. There is a *Victory* Advisory Technical Committee that meets twice a year, which deals with the continued restoration of the fabric of the ship. In the past, interpretation was not something that was dealt with as thoroughly as just keeping the ship in one piece. So you have to spend a lot of time asking yourself questions about what is needed and what things the public might want to see. The ship is about rigging, decks and the guns, but the people who go to museums today want to know about the toilet facilities, cooking and the more domestic issues.

JL: One of my first memories of you Peter was when you talked to me about experimenting with bags of sugar from the supermarket to see if it was possible for powder monkeys to carry the powder all the way from the magazine to the gun deck…

PG: …Yes! You believe certain things from reading accounts in the public records office and in publications, but until you actually physically go and do something in the ship, only then do you appreciate that the ship actually tells you how it works. Like the powder monkeys. There was this notion of these poor lads running up and down about four decks in the heat of battle. Well, having done the run in about 35 seconds once, and reminding myself that I would have to do this for about 4–5 hours in battle, you realise that this would never

Above: Interpretation items inside the hold. (John Lee/Conway)

have worked and that there would have to have been chains of people passing things along. And so we can prove that these historical facts, which we have accepted for so long, are actually not true at all. I suppose the other thing that helps me is being an ex-engineer. You can apply an engineering mind to problems and an understanding of how things work.

JL: Where did you start?

PG: I started with enhancing the galley because people always want to know what the sailors ate. The next stage was to open up an area for the sick berth. People are interested to know about the medical side of things and how people were cared for. And then we needed to look at other parts of the ship. We developed the store rooms and the cabins down on the orlop. And while all this was going on, the other major project I instigated was the restoration of the original fore-topsail from the Battle of Trafalgar, which was very badly

Above: The port side of the ship is arranged ready for battle. (John Lee/Conway)

displayed and stored. In 1993 I had it removed from the ship and started a rolling programme of total conservation, documenting and photographing this huge great sail with its battle scars, all with a purpose to develop a new exhibition solely on that one object. We have to remember that this sail which measures some 54ft x 54ft x 80ft is the largest textile conservation plan that's ever been put into progress.

Then I turned my mind to ensuring that our magazines, the hanging magazines, were correctly fitted out. For this we used original parts of magazines from the wreck of the ship *Invincible*, which sank in 1758, as reference, so it meant trips to Chatham to photograph the objects, sketch them, and take the measurements, then start drawing them.

And from that we decided that in the empty space at the fore end of the hold level of the ship, which had been empty for years, it was time to put back the grand magazine. This took five years of research and design work until finally completed with all the materials in accordance with the specifications of the period, including all the fire precautions and materials to stop fire spreading. Having done all that, and had all the cartridge bags made and filled up, you can now walk into this magazine and it is as if you are there in battle.

I recognised that we needed to tell two stories on the ship: battle and everyday life. So I decided from the start to divide the ship in two: port and starboard. Everything on the starboard side, where we can close the gunports against the weather, would interpret the living arrangements and the day-to-day routines at sea. This left the port or larboard side of the ship open for me to then set up all the guns as if the ship was just about to go into battle.

Now when you walk around the ship, you can look from one side to the other and be aware that the ship suddenly stops being a home and is an actual place of fighting.

JL: Please tell us about your early life and career and indeed where your love of the sea and principally sailing warships comes from?

PG: The draw of the sea comes from my maternal side, who were originally from Chandlers in Great Yarmouth and men who worked in the herring trade between Great Yarmouth and South Shields – so they were basically Norfolk people like Nelson. My older brother had an interest in the sea as well and we followed similar careers. We both went into the Royal Navy; we both made model ships when we were younger. When I was 15 I finished a model of a 64-gun ship, which was valued at £75 at the time. And I can remember going to the 200th anniversary of the launch of the *Victory* exhibition in

Above: View of the ship from aft, showing some of the stern decoration. (John Lee/Conway)

Chatham in 1965. I was also lucky in that my father would take us to a lot of the museums in London because we only lived in Tunbridge Wells. I really wanted to stay on further at school and then go to Chatham dockyard as a shipwright, but my family situation and finances did not allow this to happen.

So I went into the navy and spent most of my career as a marine engineer artificer in nuclear submarines, but I did initially serve on surface ships. During that time I studied for a degree in engineering related to nuclear plant operation. I still had my keen interest in warships and during the long patrols at sea in a polaris submarine I occupied my time collating all my notes about ships and construction and started to develop material for publication. I would spend my spare time ashore researching in the Public Records Office and other places to develop my book *The Construction and Fitting of the Sailing Man of War* and then the *Anatomy* books after that. I became recognised as somebody with a skill for technical writing which served me well in putting together the technical books that I decided to write.

I realised that I had got everything that I could out of the navy and that what I really wanted to do was museum or restoration work. When I first left the navy I worked as a senior design engineer for the engineering consultants Yard Ltd in Glasgow, which was originally Yarrows Admiralty Research Department. We carried out development work for the next generations of nuclear submarines and machinery and nuclear plant. We also did a lot of work for various nuclear power stations and the Scottish Electricity Board. And we were involved with the ship lift at Faslane for the fitting of polaris and the next generation of trident submarines. During this time I also completed a MPhil degree at the Scottish Institute of Maritime Studies, University of St Andrews. While at Faslane I found out that there were moves afoot to change the way that the *Victory* was to be run and that's when I came down here with a hope that somebody might consider me for a position as curator of the ship.

JL: What can you tell us about ongoing projects?

PG: We still need to develop the afterhold of the ship, which will comprise store rooms for the fish, the spirit room and the bread room, as an extension of the tour you get through the hold. Once that is done then the major projects, I would say, are complete.

When I came here the interpretation of rigging was not historically accurate and I've managed to put up something like 35 per cent more rigging than she had when I first arrived. It's very important because the rigging, the yards and the masts, are the engine room of the ship. And also, I have to keep in mind that although a lot of the visitors are families with chil-

Above: Deadeyes. (John Lee/Conway)

dren and people that are just interested in ships, many are ship modellers and you have provide them with the visual evidence they need for their projects. And as a ship modeller myself, that is another way I've looked upon how I do my job.

When the work was undertaken to restore the ship in 1922, the only gun carriages available at the time would have been those that were from land-based installations. So most of the gun carriages that were put on the ship, and then copied, were 1845 land-battened carriages. I realised that although to the general eye it's a gun carriage, the guns did not fit square and central to the ports. So having done some calculations based on those carriages and then looking at the calculations from Muller's *Treatise on Artillery* of 1782, we redesigned the gun carriages as sea service carriages, which are different. We've now started a rolling programme, and have already done about 14 or 16 carriages on the upper and middle gun decks, and of course the quarterdeck of the forecastle as well. We still need to complete the upper and middle gun decks and start on the lower gun deck.

JL: Your remit is very much to display *Victory* as she would have been in 1805, as opposed to the earlier part of her career. How do you achieve this?

PG: Most of the things you see on the ship are researched from primary sources held here in the Royal Naval Museum. Major items being investigated are the expenses books for the carpenter, the boatswain and the gunner, which tell you exactly what was going on in the last six months of 1805. There is a wealth of the information you can glean from the National Archives, but equally I have to look at what is being undertaken in the archaeological world, the things being brought up from the seabed, if they're of a similar date. And, of course, you also need to look at publications of the period – specifications written by Steel and earlier writers. I've had to write instructions to the dockyard here on how to set up deadeyes and the sizes of deadeyes, because they haven't got all that information or the information may not be as true as it should be. At the moment I'm investigating a series of documents that are detailed reports on the refitting of ships in 1803 at Plymouth dockyard and uncovering a lot that myself and other historians perhaps did not realise because the evidence wasn't there previously. It is certainly going to stir things up when this information enters the public domain. But this is all part of an ongoing process that as a historian you accept, and our aim is always to disseminate information as we find it to the public for the benefit of all.

JL: What do you believe are your most interesting and important achievements to date with the ship?

Above: Peter Goodwin has added 35 per cent more rigging to the ship since becoming curator and keeper of *Victory*. (John Lee/Conway)

PG: The most interesting and important achievements, I would say, are the grand magazine and the fore-topsail mentioned previously. The other one was two years ago when, following some research I undertook, we moved the exact position of where Nelson died within the ship based on plans in the National Maritime Museum, letters at the time of the battle, and examining the famous painting *The Death of Nelson*, working out where the artist actually sat onboard while he was sketching. After corroborating all that evidence we decided that Nelson died 25 feet further forward on the orlop deck than originally thought. In fact that there was no solid evidence to back up the original position. One of the things we have to be very careful about is that sometimes the Victorians' interpretation of history can lead to misconceptions and send people in wrong directions, and that, I think, reflects in a lot of earlier books about the Georgian navy which sometimes put it in a bad light. My task is to strive to eliminate the errors made in the late nineteenth and early twentieth centuries.

JL: How important is the use of authentic materials and indeed how do you go about sourcing such materials and the skills that are needed to create the objects that serve as interpretation pieces?

PG: If we take the ship's construction – the masts and the rigging – although we want things to look exactly right, sometimes it is more cost effective to revise what materials we use. It would be great if we could actually rebuild parts of the ship in oak, but unfortunately oak has a tendency to attract death watch beetle and other problems, so we have to think about using materials that will last longer. Teak proves very suitable for this kind of project, and the sourcing is generally done by the Ministry of Defence. The use of traditional skills and techniques becomes considerably more difficult as the years pass, especially as we don't hold the same number of skilled shipwrights here in the dockyard and we may have to contract in those particular people in the future. I advise on techniques where I can based on the historical evidence of ship construction in the eighteenth and early nineteenth centuries.

When I'm having items made for interpretation, I do seek to find particular skills, especially those people who can work in metal – iron, copper, brass or steel – and likewise if I need somebody to make me wooden bowls or small domestic items, I will look for a small business or one-man band who will provide me with perhaps 50 of the same item but each of those 50 will be unique. Back then nothing was produced in a factory: you wouldn't get bowls all looking identical. If I can get objects put in the ship that are all slightly different in detail, the visual effect to the public actually looks more true. We have used the expertise of a local ironworker who has also studied design and art, and this comes through in the things he produces. This is a man who can make you a lantern hook or a grapple iron on his forge in a small workshop. The end product always looks as if it's real and how could it not be real if you have used a real blacksmith?

JL: I understand you had some involvement in Yinka Shonibare's 'Nelson's Ship in a Bottle', the recent instalment on the fourth plinth in Trafalgar Square. Could you explain what that was and indeed what you think of the end result?

PG: I thought this was a wonderful project. As for my part in it, they naturally came to me as the keeper and curator of the *Victory* for details and information and we were able to set them off in the right direction to use such books as *The 100-Gun Ship Victory* in the *Anatomy* series, which is a common maritime publication, for the basic plans. Obviously, since that book has been written some things have changed in the ship, but for the purposes of a conceptual model the information there was sufficient. Because they wanted to ensure the authenticity of the colour scheme for the model, they came down here to look at the colours that we use on the ship and we provided them with samples of the paint so they could ensure that the model would look as authentic as possible.

I was one of those invited to the unveiling of 'Nelson's Ship in a Bottle' on 24 May 2010. I was very impressed, and I also found it quite fun, because a lot of people make ships in bottles, but I never would have thought that somebody would make a model of *Victory* on that scale, inside a bottle. And I think the finished product did the ship considerable justice, especially where Nelson can keep an eye on it on a day-to-day basis!

I was also interested in why the model was made. What was it supposed to represent? And I must admit that when I realised that Yinka was talking about ethnic groups and the differences between people living in London and working together, I found that quite a valuable idea, because it's very much the same to what happened inside these ships. The crews were not entirely English or Scottish. They were made up of people from all over the world who fought on and manned our ships. I thought that his concept conveyed that quite well in the way he used the fabrics for the sails. It gives lots of colour to the object – but equally it's nice to see that somebody's actually made a model that has a full set of sails on it – which is not always the case.

They had to build an air-conditioning system in the bottom of the bottle, which is why it stands relatively high on the plinth. That was an ingenious idea, put in I suppose at the last minute, because when you think of the heat generated within the bottle, it could be rather detrimental to the finished object.

JL: What maritime books have you been reading recently?

PG: I'm looking at two books at the moment. One is a biography on the life of Sir William Hamilton, who was a very intriguing person – archaeologist and vulcanologist. And I've just started reading a book produced in France on the building of the replica ship *Hermione*. This is another way in which we can learn and pass on information – by building replica ships. I have sailed on a few, including the *Endeavour* and the Russian ship *Shtandart* and I think we need to get young people to appreciate it is probably good for them to get on replica ships and sail-training ships to reconnect with their maritime heritage. In fact, I was only discussing the concept of building a ship a few days ago with a well-known designer, Colin Mudie, to see if there is any way of building a replica of the *Alert* cutter of 1777. One of the thoughts behind our discussions was that these ships would make very good sail-training vessels, especially in reinvigorating the concept of the sea to our youth.

Peter Goodwin can be contacted through the *Victory* website, www.hms-victory.com or by calling the ship to speak with the Captain's PA or the Visitor Services Manager.

'Nelson's Ship in a Bottle' has been created for the Fourth Plinth in Trafalgar Square by leading Anglo-Nigerian artist Yinka Shonibare. With sails made of richly patterned Dutch wax fabrics and known as African textiles due to the Dutch trade in West Africa, the work considers the complexity of British expansion in trade and Empire made possible through the freedom of the seas that Nelson's victory created. For the artist, the piece is 'a celebration of London's immense ethnic wealth, giving expression to and honouring the many cultures and ethnicities that are still breathing precious wind into the sails of the United Kingdom'. The work will remain on the plinth until the end of 2011.

Below: Yinka Shonibare's 'Nelson's Ship in a Bottle' on the Fourth Plinth in Trafalgar Square. (Conway)

'A Proper Puffer'

THE CARRON COMPANY'S STEAM-LIGHTER *NO 10* (1871)

by Graham Castle

Some models are just 'meant to be'. The subject virtually suggests itself; research data flows effortlessly from numerous unconnected sources and the project develops in a succession of satisfying stages to become a delightful miniature replica of the original craft. Sound familiar? Well not in my previous model-making experience – but there is a first time for everything and this unpretentious little Scottish 'Puffer' proved to be that occasion. *Carron No 10* represents the pinnacle of the development of the Forth and Clyde Canal's steam-lighters before they evolved into the sea-going craft that retained, and mythologised, the term 'Clyde Puffers'. Their revolutionary combination of an iron hull, non-condensing steam engine and a propeller transformed the economies of earlier forms of bulk-transport and, as this example demonstrates, produced some elegant vessels with fine lines.

This article briefly explains the background to the development of these craft together with the research that attracted me to this particular vessel, and then describes the materials and techniques used to construct a 1:32 scale ship-model presented in the 'museum-style'.

THE CARRON COMPANY

The Carron Company was established in 1759 for the purpose of smelting iron-ore and casting, or otherwise processing, pig-iron into the tools, utensils and weapons of the period. In addition to its many unique and patented designs for everyday commodities such as pots and trivets, railings and pillar boxes, laundry-irons, fire-surrounds and cooking-ranges, the company is probably best known as the eponymous 'Carron' in 'Carronade', a small muzzle-loading cannon that became an integral part of late eighteenth-century naval warfare.

For over two hundred years the company prospered as the Industrial Revolution, and numerous wars, created an appetite and ready markets for their innovative products. With its large iron-works situated on the banks of the River Carron near Falkirk in Scotland the company was to become the most important industrial employer in the region until its demise due to changing technological practices and market requirements in 1982.

In addition to operating a fleet of sea-going vessels transporting the company's products to London and further afield, a canal was built connecting the works to what would become the trans-Scotland 'Forth and Clyde Canal'. With access to Glasgow's markets and imported bulk commodities it was logical that the company would own and operate craft suited to this unique highway, initially using the horse-drawn scows and lighters that in time evolved into steam-powered lighters that puffed their way along the canal.

THE CANAL'S 'PUFFERS'

Trials with steam-powered craft on the Forth and Clyde Canal can be traced back to William Symington's wooden paddle-wheeled *Charlotte Dundas (I)* in 1801 and a compara-

Above: Carron Company Crest.

Above: SS *Raven* at Windermere.

ble iron-hulled catamaran, the *Lord Dundas*, during the 1830s.

Wrought-iron hulls were gradually being adopted throughout this period after the successful introduction of Thomas Wilson's horse-drawn passage-boat *Vulcan* in 1819. It was not until the virtues of the propeller, or screw-propulsion, were fully appreciated in the mid-1800s that all three features were harmoniously united to produce the steam-lighter or Clyde Puffer.

In the 1850s it was recorded that 'there are five screw-steamers belonging to different traders, daily at work on the main line, and one belonging to the Canal Company'. This latter craft, the *Thomas* (*c.* 1856), began life as an iron horse-drawn lighter which was then modified aft to accommodate a haystack (vertical) boiler, two-cylinder inclined steam engine, and a propeller; presumably as an evaluation by the Canal's owners of the viability of this form of propulsion and its potential to increase the canal's traffic and revenue.

The success of this experiment was such that other barge conversions followed and thereafter steam-lighters were purpose-built for use on the canal. Given the ready availability of fresh water it was logical to exhaust 'used' steam from the cylinders directly through a blast nozzle into the funnel in order to improve the gas flow past the fire-tubes before venting it up the 'lum' (funnel) with a characteristic 'puff'.

The commercial activities of the Carron Ironworks paralleled these evolutions in maritime technology and, given its requirement to import raw materials and export manufactured items along the canal, their fleet of canal-craft would have reflected these changes.

Their unique system of giving these vessels numbers provides no indication of those that may have been horse-drawn and I have no record suggesting how many craft they may have owned in total.

THE CARRON COMPANY'S STEAM-LIGHTER *NO 10* – RESEARCH AND DRAWINGS

Much of the data required to build *No 10* had been gradually accumulating over a number of years during the course of researching other projects, largely through happy coincidences.

It coalesced whilst looking for a suitable subject to represent the Steam-lighters' stage of development between the iconic 'first Puffer', *Thomas* (1856), and the early sea-going Clyde Puffer *Ballydoon* (1878) as part of my collection of ship models depicting how these vessels evolved over nearly two centuries.

Initially a very small reproduction of the General Arrangement drawing for *No 10* had been found in *Song of the Clyde*, Fred Walker's comprehensive and entertaining account of shipbuilding in Scotland, together with an

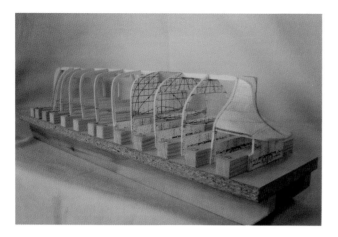

Above: Hull frame.

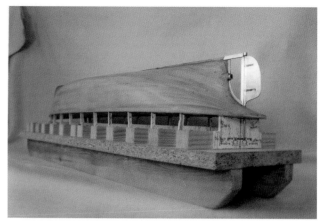

Above: Hull planked, plus brass inserts.

acknowledgement for the drawing to The National Maritime Museum, Greenwich.

I had used this drawing previously to build a small waterline model for a diorama which in due course suggested just how attractive the vessel would be if the entire hull was visible, and built to a larger scale.

After a telephone call to Greenwich, followed by some e-mails, a copy of the original drawing for Ship Number 217 was ordered from the 'Historic Photographs and Ship Plans Section' of the Museum. What unexpectedly arrived was the invaluable 'Floor Plan' consisting of the Half-breadth and Body Plan for *No 10* but not the anticipated 'General Arrangement Drawing'.

After further correspondence the 'Deck Plan' (GA) was located in the 'Awaiting Repairs' folder, copied by the Museum and duly delivered. Both sets of drawings were supplied at 1:24 scale and then reduced to 1:32. Extra copies of the Body Plan were photocopied for the model's frames as required.

Photographs of contemporary Carron lighters had been acquired over the years from a variety of sources. That of the comparable *Carron No 12* was used as a reference for the proportions of the mast and derrick, and the rigging

Above: Hull coppered.

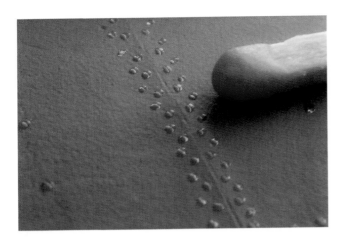

Above: Rivet work.

Above: Hull in dry dock with deck-supports/painted/ceiling boards.

arrangements, which are not shown on the original ship's drawings. Others provided clues to specific areas of interest such as deck fittings and the boiler casing but more valuably they conveyed something of the character of these little craft both to inform, and subconsciously influence, the modelling process.

RESEARCHING CONTEMPORARY PRACTICES – THE SS *RAVEN* AT WINDERMERE

Reproducing the smaller constructional features not shown on ship's drawings usually relies upon having photographs of

the vessel, access to comprehensive documentation (or the ship) or first-hand experience of the techniques involved. The older the subject then the fewer of these options are likely, particularly when the vessel concerned is a small, 'unglamorous' working-craft.

An alternative source of data is a comparable preserved vessel and I was fortunate to have had access previously to the SS *Raven* at the Windermere Steamboat Museum in Cumbria. Notwithstanding many modifications over the years, and re-plating externally, the interior of this delightful

Above: Deck ready for the guardrail.

Above: Boiler and engine room casing.

little vessel still retains the rivet, strapping and plating detail of her era.

Her relevance to this project is that the *Raven* was built in the same year as *No 10*, at an adjacent Glasgow ship-builders, fitted with a non-condensing steam engine, and to all intents and purposes to the same specifications. In essence the *Raven* is a contemporary Steam-lighter or Clyde Puffer built a few feet longer to suit her purpose on Lake Windermere.

STEAM-LIGHTER *NO 10*
Built: 1871.
Owners: Carron Company, Falkirk.
Builders: Barclay, Curle and Company, Glasgow, Scotland.
Length OA: 65ft 10in.
Beam: 14ft 2in.

SS RAVEN
Built: 1871.
Owners: Furness Railway Company.
Builders: T.B. Seath & Co, Rutherglen, Scotland.
Length OA: 71ft 10in.
Beam: 14ft 9in.

Above: Guardrail template.

THE HULL – TIMBERWORK
The hull was built, initially in the conventional manner, by planking an inverted framework. The frames were made from Liteply for easier profiling later, with stem and stern blocks laminated from balsa wood. Main bulkheads were left solid but the inside of what were to become frames was removed at this stage.

Planking was done in 5mm x 1.5mm lime with a view to achieving sweet lines rather than following conventional shipwright's practice. This hull is so fine and graceful that the planks required very little persuasion to lie nicely. Considerable care was taken when sanding and filling the hull in order to achieve a strake free finish on what was to represent the smooth lines of an iron hull.

At this stage the 1.0mm brass keel, stem and rudder-post were pinned and glued into appropriate grooves cut into the false framework; where sections of the keel and stem and rudder post met their joints were bevelled and then soldered in situ. Two brass tubes were fitted through the keel into glued blocks to accommodate the threaded rod that would form part of the turned mounting pedestals.

The propeller tube and brass rudder together with its lower bearing were similarly fitted and soldered where appropriate.

With the objective of achieving a long-lasting and very smooth hull for the plate work the hull was coated with several applications of Polyester Finishing Resin, this produced a superb finish while further filling and sealing the basic planked hull. The inside of the hull was similarly treated to seal and further strengthen it.

At this stage the hull was given several coats of primer,

making good where necessary. Frames conforming to those of the original vessel and the position of the plates' butt joints were pencilled in.

THE HULL – PLATEWORK

The quarter-inch iron plate work of the original vessel, together with its riveting pattern, is a feature of interest and well worth replicating at this scale.

Above: Guardrail lining up/shaping.
Left: Casting master, mould and hatch cover.

Above: Windlass unpainted.

Above: Stove and windlass in position.

The plates were represented with appropriate sections of Glaziers copper foil, the 'in' strakes being cut over wide and the resulting 'troughs' packed out with foil strips to provide a level surface. The 'out' strakes could then be superimposed to represent the correct lines of plating with their visible butts spaced midway between the previously marked scale frames.

Small sheets and narrow rolls of self-adhesive copper foil are available for artistic glasswork, the adhesive is excellent and of course able to withstand soldering temperatures. I have used it previously to represent copper sheathing and at 0.2mm thick it is to scale.

The pattern of plate work, and subsequent riveting, conformed to the practices used to build the *Raven* as mentioned in 'Research' and the resultant photographs; the hull's timber rubbing strakes with their angle-irons were fitted at this stage. The deck-edge strake was formed in styrene and its iron fendering simulated by 'D'-section styrene-strip bonded in place.

Once the hull was fully copper-plated the graceful lines of this vessel were evident and stunning. The resulting shape is a credit to her designer. At this stage the model's hull was again sprayed with primer and its scale frames re-drawn to provide a reference for riveting in due course.

The inverted hull could now be removed from its building cradle by cutting through the Liteply frame extensions and then much of each frame was removed with the aid of a small drum sander. What remained would be hidden behind the hold's ceiling boards.

Detailing a hull presents the ongoing dilemma of supporting the model if 'glued' rivets and the finishing paintwork are applied before the interior and upperworks are addressed, at which stage it becomes difficult to re-invert and support the hull in order to work accurately on it once again.

Consequently, I opted to complete as much of the interior and deck work as practicable, making the majority of deck-furnishings removable, and then re-inverted the hull on to a well-padded support cradle for final detailing. Rivet work was eventually simulated by applying drops of PVA glue dispensed from a disposable syringe with reference to the *Raven*'s photographs and contemporary shipbuilding technical manuals. The hull was finally sprayed with gloss-black paint and over-coated with matt varnish before reinstating the weather deck's fittings.

FITTING OUT THE HULL – CEILING BOARDS AND DECK PLANKING

As many of the building frames' deck beams were to be removed where they spanned the open hold, and eventually be replaced by two scale iron deck beams, the model's hull required support until its deck was fitted. This was achieved by converting the building board into a form of padded dry dock with a snug fit such that it braced the hull athwartships. The model's sheer-strake stringers and weather-deck carlines were added to provide strengthened deck apertures where

necessary for the hold, companionways, boiler casing and other deck structures. These were reinforced with fillets or glued dowels as appropriate.

To add interest to the model and convey a sense of purpose the hold's interior was to be visible, revealing the sump pipe, mast mounting, forward ballast tank and some cargo. This made it necessary to line the hold with its ceiling boards. These were simulated by 5mm x 1.5mm lime strips laid in a reversed form of plank-on-frame construction and then stained. The two double angle-iron deck beams were fashioned from 1/8in brass angle, soldered together and cambered, before being securely attached across the hold.

Deck planking followed my usual practice of laying a 0.4mm plywood sub-deck and then edging it with oversize (combined) covering boards/margin planks before cutting in the nibs as planking progressed. The planks are 5mm x 1.5mm lime strips cut from sheet material, with artists' card being used to represent the caulking. The laid decks were treated with a water-based fence stain, and then further toned and sealed with a floor finish called Bourneseal before being brushed with matt varnish.

With the deck still flush and unencumbered by any fittings other than the brass stem and rudder shaft, a sheet of 0.4mm plywood was laid over it such that the deck-edge could be

Below: The finished model.

marked around to produce a template for use later when fabricating the guardrail. The position of each stanchion was marked on this template and drilled through into the deck's covering boards so that, once made, the guardrail and its stanchions could be fitted and aligned correctly.

SUPERSTRUCTURE AND DECK FURNITURE

The boiler and engine-room casing was made as a one-piece removable structure so that it could be worked on away from the model. The boiler casing was built up from laminated lime, turned to shape and then detailed with copper plating and turned brass fittings. The steam and waste-steam pipes are aluminium formed around annealed brass rod.

The engine-room casing is a styrene structure built down to below deck level so that the tops of two simulated engine cylinders with their steam supply/exhaust pipes could be incorporated and visible through the skylight.

Contouring the cylindrical boiler casing to the deck's camber, and similarly mating the casing's domed covers, was done by taping 0.25mm styrene sheet to the cambered surface and then compressing Milliput between it and the matching face. When set, the Milliput was worked back and the styrene trimmed to leave a clean flanged joint.

Companionways and the hold's coaming are styrene boxes, detailed appropriately with the companionways laminated using pear wood to represent timber structures. They

Above: Port quarter view of finished model showing propeller.

have been let into the deck to give an impression of depth and a commercial (Britains) scale figure mounted on the forecastle access steps to convey a sense of scale.

The hold has been similarly furnished, but deliberately not obscured, with a few barrels, ladder, crates and a bilge rat to encourage the observant viewer.

Smaller deck fittings such as the steam valve, coal hatches and eyebolts have been fashioned from brass, either turned on a small lathe or soldered and profiled to suit. The propeller was wrought with rectangular brass blade-blanks being soft-soldered on to the boss in a turned jig, then trimmed, trued in a lathe and finally shaped before being mounted on its dummy threaded silver steel propeller shaft.

GUARDRAILS AND STANCHIONS

The guardrails presented an interesting project being prominent, having fine proportions and demanding structural integrity. Being totally visible the thirty guardrail stanchions had to be identical and induce a smooth sheer that paralleled the deck.

The stanchions were formed in a simple turned production tool that consisted of a bored cylinder and a matching piston with depth stop that together could be held to the face of a disc-sander; with square-section pear wood pushed through the cylinder by the piston until it could go no further. Thirty matching stanchions were readily formed to within 0.02in.

As the face of this little tool wore during use the piston was shimmed backwards to maintain the required overall dimension. Once made the stanchions were held in a four-jaw lathe chuck and drilled axially to accommodate fixing pins.

Using the template created while decking the hull a complete all-round rail was made by attaching scarfed scale-length timbers of pear wood to it with double-sided tape, and then laminating another set above with offset scarfs for strength. The stanchions attachment holes drilled previously could then be transferred from the template and, after trimming and sanding, the guardrail could be separated from its template and was ready to fit, lining up with the deck-edge attachment holes.

The stanchions were fastened to the deck by integral pins and the one-piece guardrail attached to them with lace makers' brass pins shaped as common bolts (square-headed). Two timberheads were slotted, shaped, drilled axially and similarly attached forward. The rails were then stained.

The spirket plates were pegged in position under the guardrail and their forward iron wrap-around simulated in copper foil. The hawse port was formed from two brass turnings that were annealed and then compressed to shape. Its function presumably being to guide a warping line on to the windlass drum as the vessel was not equipped initially for seagoing with an anchor.

CASTINGS

A number of small items were cast in resin from brass masters, using silicon moulds. These included the distinctive mooring bitts that were a feature of nineteenth-century Forth and Clyde Canal craft, and the small bollard-shaped fairleads that are mounted on the wooden guardrails.

The principle benefit of using this technique is apparent in the nine superimposed curved hatch covers that were cast from a hardwood framework master. Each casting was then laminated with stained lime hatch boards. Replicas of the wooden barrels for the hold were similarly cast in resin, painted, and hooped with strips of vinyl tape.

Below: The model mounted on its oak baseboard.

BUILT-UP FITTINGS – CARGO-WINDLASS AND THE STOVE

The cargo windlass was built from styrene with turned brass components; for realism and practicality. When rigging the model it was made to be largely functional. In operation the cable barrel may be clutched, rotated or held locked by a pawl, or only the warping drums driven to slew the derrick by its vangs, or warp the vessel if required.

Two brass gearwheels were soldered on to turned shafts drilled to suit the proposed drive and main axles. The larger wheel was drilled and filed-out to match that shown on the drawings and create the lugs of the dog clutch.

The gearwheels were used to establish the bearings' centres within the styrene chassis members which were then progressively shaped and opened out whilst being built up to maintain strength and ultimately represent the original's cast iron framework.

The cable barrel, warping drums and axle pulley were turned, and the clutch/lever and locking pawl shaped in brass. The chassis members were located initially on a styrene base and then retained by brass-rod spacers with 16BA half-nuts at each joint.

In due course the assembly was cut from its temporary base, washed, painted and reassembled. Main bearing

grease points were simulated and two windlass handles stored adjacent.

The fore deckhand's stove was similarly built up from styrene around an acrylic carcass to represent a cast-iron item, and a brass 'Charlie-Noble' fashioned to match that of the forecastle's stove.

Although shown on the drawings I was uncertain about fitting this incongruous feature, its function being presumably to provide warmth for a permanent look-out/lock hand as the vessel plied her way along the busy canal with its frequent locks in all seasons and weathers.

Whilst not apparent on drawings of other Puffers or contemporary photographs I feel able to justify it on *No 10* if only because amongst the many successful products of the Carron Ironworks they were renowned for their fire-surrounds, cooking ranges and heating stoves.

RIGGING

Standing rigging was formed from brass picture-hanging wire, unwound from its original seven strands and re-wound as three-strand wire rope with soldered eyes to represent the splices. Running rigging was aged in spirit-based stain where appropriate, weighted and left hanging until required. It was stiffened and the hairs laid by a coating of dilute PVA glue before use.

Wooden blocks were shaped from strips of hardwood reclaimed from draughtsman's T-squares, sectioned and grooved on a small circular saw table, and bound in soft brass wire with soldered attachment eyes. Metal blocks were shaped from sandwiched blanks of thin brass sheet, drilled to suit their turned brass sheaves, and soldered to appropriate attachment eyes.

The various mast irons, gooseneck and the belaying pin rack were formed from turned brass off-cuts with soldered eyes as required.

The seizing of all ropes was done on a small purpose-made hand lathe of my own design as described in 'A Rope Seizing Lathe', *Model Shipwright* 111. Head and stern mooring ropes have been set at the appropriate mooring bits ready for use with a longer towing line aft for the frequent task of towing dumb scows and lighters along the canal's open reaches.

CONCLUSION

The model was mounted on a routed oak baseboard by means of two turned-brass pillars and 6BA threaded rods in the museum style which, I feel, shows off the fine and graceful lines of this fine little vessel.

Despite the unforeseen challenges that inevitably arise when building a model from the original ship's drawings and limited data, *Carron No 10* presented a most enjoyable and very satisfying project. Small, relatively unsophisticated, working craft such as this Steam-lighter provide the opportunity to enjoy using virtually all the craft skills and specialised techniques of the model shipwright, while avoiding the inevitable repetition associated with many of the more familiar subjects. They also encourage the individual ship modeller to give substance and recognition to a specific aspect of maritime heritage that might otherwise be forgotten.

Hopefully this model conveys something of the personality of a craft that was unglamorously known only by a number and does justice to the ingenuity, practical skills and sheer hard labour of those who created and operated the 'wee-boats' that evolved into the charismatic Clyde Puffers.

ADDENDUM – SS *RAVEN* (1871)

The SS *Raven* of 1871 provides a valuable record of contemporary shipbuilding practices. The inverted framework on a robust building-board can be held in a swivelling vice or tilted to facilitate planking. Once planked the brass keel, stem, and rudder-frame inserts were faired-in, stern gear completed, and the hull sealed with resin. As the primed and marked-out hull was plated the vessel's fine lines became evident.

Plates' butts and their attachment to the vessel's framework were riveted in accordance with contemporary practices, although few of these 'heads' would gain the surveyor's approval. The modified base-board supported the hull while constructional frames were removed and ceiling boards laid before the hatches simulated iron cross beams and structural deck bracing were in place. Assorted materials – lime, styrene, Perspex, aluminium and brass, were used in the construction of the weather deck's main features.

The dummy engine seen through its skylight, open companionways and the uncovered hold, help to create an illusion of depth and substance; the smaller deck-fittings are all turned or soldered brass items. Two thicknesses of scarfed guardrail sections were laminated together whilst taped to the deck template and the stanchions' positions transferred through from underneath. The laminates were trimmed as the template was progressively cut back and the stanchions' height and alignment adjusted before finally peeling away the remains of the template. Casting the curved hatchboards ensured that they could be stacked symmetrically; being slightly pliant when warm allowed them to be 'nested' even more precisely.

Re-profiled and re-bushed metal gearwheels allow the windlass to function correctly, either driven or braked, which eases the task of winding-on turns and rigging the cargo derrick.

The unseemly high gooseneck allows all of the hatch-covers to be stowed forward if required. Presumably the deckhand will have learned the hard way that limited deck space necessitates the taut hoisting cable impeding his route from one warm stove to the next.

BIBLIOGRAPHY AND REFERENCE SOURCES

Song of the Clyde, pp.194-196, Birlinn Ltd, 1984, ISBN 1 85976 553 9.

Robson, Neil, *Transactions of the Institute of Engineers in Scotland 1857-58*, pp.49-58, 'On the Navigation of Canals by Screw Steamers'; source The Mitchell Library, General Services Department, North Street, Glasgow G3 7DN.

Thearle, Samuel J. P., *The Modern Practice of Shipbuilding in Iron and Steel 1886*, William Collins, Sons, & Company Ltd, Third Edition.

Walker, F. M., *Carron – Crucible of Scotland*, Exhibition Catalogue, Falkirk Museums, 1998, ISBN 0 90 6568694 1.

The National Maritime Museum, Greenwich, Curator Historic Photographs and Ship Plans, tel: +44 (0)20 8312 8600, email: plansandphotos@nmm.ac.uk, Ref BF06/391, Drawing No. 217.

The William Patrick Library, Cowgate, Kirkintilloch G66 1AB, lithographs and photographs of canal craft from the earliest days including Carron's lighters.

The Windermere Steamboat Museum, Rayrigg Road, Windermere LA23 1BN, telephone +44 (0)15394 455 65 (custodians of the SS *Raven*).

Photographs that convey some details and the essential character of the Clyde Puffer may be found in the following publications:

Burrows G. W., *Puffer Ahoy*, Brown, Son & Ferguson Ltd, Glasgow, 1981, ISBN 0 85174 419 2.

Fenton R. (ed.), *Ships in Focus* RECORD 26, Ships in Focus Publications, 2003, ISBN 1 901703 72-X.

Hutton, Guthrie, *Forth and Clyde – The Comeback Canal*, Stenlake Publishing, 1998, ISBN 1 84033 034 1.

McDonald D., *The Clyde Puffer*, David & Charles (Publishers) Ltd, 1977, ISBN 0 7153 7443 5.

Parkhouse N. (ed.), *Archive Issue 30*, Lightmoor Press, 2001, ISSN 1352-7991.

Syracusia (c.240 BC)

A POSSIBLE RECONSTRUCTION

by Alan Ludbrook

The *Syracusia* was built around 240 BC for Hieron II of Syracuse (*c.*306–215 BC). Her construction was partly overseen by the famous mathematician, Archimedes, who was probably a kinsman of Hieron.

The primary source for the vessel is a passage in The *Deipnosophists* (5.206d-209b) by Athenaeus of Naucratis, a Greek rhetorician and grammarian who apparently lived during the reigns of the Roman Emperors Marcus Aurelius and Commodus (yes, the ones in Gladiator!). The *Deipnosophists*, which means dinner table philosophers, is an immense storehouse of information on all aspects of ancient life.

Athenaeus quotes from nearly eight hundred ancient writers, many who would be otherwise unknown to us; amongst them is a certain Moschion. In a section describing memorable ships, Athenaeus quotes Moschion's description of the *Syracusia*. An excellent modern translation can be found in Casson (1995).

Apparently it had been Hieron's intention to use the ship to tour the Aegean distributing gifts of grain to cities experiencing famine and also to demonstrate his power, wealth and

Below: Starboard bow view.

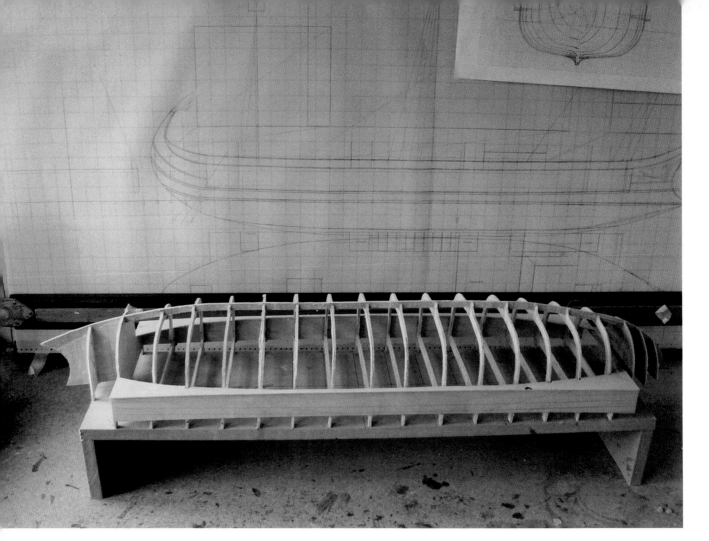

military capability. The ship proved too large to use most of the available harbours, however, and so Hieron decided to make the best of it by presenting the ship to Ptolemy III Euergetes of Egypt (reigned 246–222 BC) as a gift. The ship was sailed to Alexandria, renamed *Alexandris* and apparently remained in the harbour as a visitor attraction.

Athenaeus describes how Hieron acquired materials from Sicily and Italy and recruited an army of craftsmen. He includes details of the construction of the ship and the launch, which involved Archimedes and his screw windlass. A detailed description of the ship is given, covering its decoration, armament, cargo and crew.

In the past the description of the *Syracusia* has been dismissed as a literary exaggeration but recent historians are more prepared to accept it as an accurate account that is in part confirmed by maritime archaeology.

MAIN FEATURES

The ship is described as being built 'after the model of a twenty-er'. The term 'twenty-er' would normally imply a ship fitted with twenty oars, clearly useless on a vessel of this size. The term was apparently applied to sailing ships of all sizes and Casson compares it to the modern term 'full rigged

Ship'. However Bonino (2003) suggests that it refers to a sailing ship with a profile like a warship.

The ship had three levels or decks, the lowest level provided access to the hold and the middle level contained the cabins for the passengers. On the upper deck there were numerous structures, including a gymnasium, promenades with plant beds and arbours, a chapel to Aphrodite and next to it a library and reading room. There was also a bathhouse containing three copper tubs and a 50-gallon marble basin. Amidships were twenty stables, ten each side. There was access to a 20,000-gallon water tank in the bow and next to it a saltwater fish tank.

The ship was fitted with eight towers, in each of which were stationed four marines and two archers. There was a battlemented fighting platform on pillars carrying an enormous catapult. Each of the three masts was fitted with a bronze-sheathed top.

The upper deck was supported by Atlas figures 6 cubits (9 feet) high and reference is made to beams jutting out carrying woodbins, ovens, millstones and other services.

The *Syracusia* had an iron palisade fitted all round the ship and was supplied with four anchors of wood and eight of iron.

Above: Hull planked and bow and stern blocks in place.

Above: Interior coated with resin.

DIMENSIONS

Unfortunately, Athenaeus gives no specific dimensions but the text does contain a number of clues.

Amongst these is that the ship contained enough timber to build sixty Quadriremes. Morrison and Coates (1996) have calculated the light ship weight of a Quadrireme as 30 tons, thus allowing us to roughly estimate the weight of the hull structure as 60 x 30 to give 1800 tons. The cargo when the ship was given to Ptolemy is listed as:

60,000 measures of grain
10,000 jars of pickled fish (approx 500 tons)
20,000 talents of wool (520 tons)
20,000 talents of miscellaneous cargo (520 tons)

Below: Bow block faired in.

Above: Stern block faired in with papier-mâché shell.

The weight of grain has generated much discussion. If the measure was the Greek medimni, 60,000 measures would weigh 2,357 tons. However, this together with the other weights produces a ship of unbelievable size, which led Casson to conclude that the measure is more likely to be the Roman modii, producing a weight of 400 tons. Although this seems a very small cargo of wheat, it should be born in mind that the voyage to Alexandria was no longer being made to alleviate a famine. Egypt was at that time one of the major wheat producers of the ancient world so this gift was probably wheat of high quality. Based on the above assumptions the total cargo weight would be of 1,940 tons.

As the ratio of hull weight to cargo is very low – a ratio for wooden ships of 1:3 or even more would be normal – one could conclude that either the ship was not carrying her full capacity or, that it was due to the ship's multiple use as a merchant ship/royal yacht. It has been assumed for these calculations that the hull weight includes decoration, mosaics, armaments, stores and crew.

Weight of cargo: 1,940 tons.
Weight of hull: 1,800 tons.
Total displacement: 3,740 tons.
(3,740 x 2,240 = 8,377,600lb).

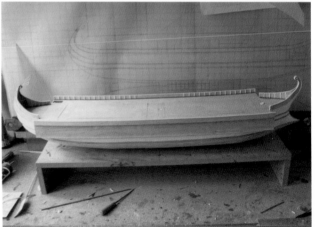

Above: Wales and bulwarks fitted.

Since a cubic foot of water weighs 64lb, underwater hull volume = 130,900 cubic feet
Using a block coefficient of 0.7, block volume = 187,000 cubic feet.
The block volume is the product of the length x breadth x draught.

Landels (1978) suggest a draught of 15 feet based on figures for Roman harbour clearances. The dimensions of the corn ship *Isis* described by Lucian suggest a length/breadth ratio of

4:1. The Madrague de Gienes wreck has a length/breadth ratio of 4.4:1. I finalised the dimensions as waterline length 230 feet, breadth 54 feet and draught 15 feet, giving a block volume of 186,300 cubic feet. In my calculations I was always concerned about making the ship unbelievably large so I have erred toward the smaller dimensions.

The largest sailing ship from the ancient world for which we have dimensions is in Lucian's description of the *Isis*, a large merchant ship on the Alexandria–Rome run. He records it as 180 feet long, 45 feet beam and the hull depth as 43.5 feet. The *Syracusia* would have to have been significantly larger than this to render her impractible. The Lake Nemi ships, though not sea going, were 230 feet and 240 feet long. In view of this, the size that I have calculated for the *Syracusia* is not unreasonable. However, in retrospect, I consider that the upper deck is quite crowded leading me to conclude that the ship could have been even larger. The size of a number of the deck structures and cabins is given as so many couches. A couch was apparently calculated as room for a couch plus access to it, approximately 25 square feet.

APPEARANCE

Many attempts have been made to reconstruct the *Syracusia*. The description of the ship is difficult to interpret as archi-tectural terms are used and it is not always clear how they apply to a ship. Adding to the problem is that there are not many representations of merchant ships for the period from the fifth century BC until the Roman period.

It has been suggested that the ship was a large, round ship with a convex cutwater (Tufa & Steinmeyer, 1999), while others suggest that it had a more military appearance with a concave cutwater (Bonino, 2003).

I favour the latter because the picture of a three-masted vessel, found in the Foro delle Corporazioni at Ostia has a concave cutwater (see Figure 1) and this is the only represen-tation of a three-masted ship from the ancient world of which I am aware. In addition, a second-century BC mosaic from Alexandria by the artist Sophilos representing the Spirit of Alexandria shows a female figure crowned with a diadem in the shape of a ship. It has been suggested that this repre-sents the *Alexandris*. This ship clearly has a ram-shaped cutwater and oar boxes but apparently no oarports (see Figure 2).

The Madrague de Gienes wreck from the south of France, one of the largest ancient wrecks of a sea-going ship with a length of 120 feet and beam of 27 feet, has a concave cutwa-ter, and the Lake Nemi ships also have a military profile.

Below: Hull painted.

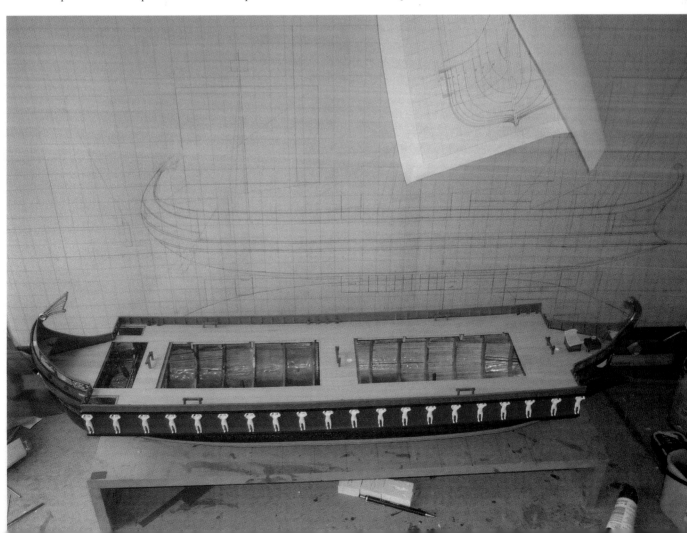

Also Atheneaus says that the freshwater tank, containing 20,000 gallons (78 tons) of water was in the bow. A ram shaped bow would provide sufficient buoyancy to support this weight.

The concave cutwater was not a true ram but may have been believed to improve the sailing qualities of the ship. Also, fitting a merchant ship with a concave cutwater and imitating the oar boxes of a large warship may have served to scare off pirates. I have assumed that the reference to jutting out beams refers to the supports for the dummy oar boxes.

Above: Deck structures complete.

The Atlas figures can then be placed conveniently on the face of the oar box and appear to support the upper deck.

Atheneaus says that the bilge was bailed by an Archimedes screw pump. This suggests that there was a low point for the bilge water to collect. So I have incorporated a

Below: Starboard view of rigged model.

rockered keel and made the ship's section the traditional Mediterranean wineglass shape to provide a suitable collection point for the pump. The wineglass shape also reduces the surface area of the bilge water, an important point when carrying grain. This cross section is seen in a number of ancient wrecks. The Madrague de Gienes wreck, a large merchant ship of the first century BC shows this profile (Figure 3). The hollow garboards would provide additional longitudinal strength to what appears quite a small keel section. Ships of this time were generally built shell first with the planks joined to each other by numerous mortice and tenons. Frames were added afterwards and nailed or spiked to the planking. Large ships like the Madrague de Gienes wreck and the Mahdia wreck were in fact double planked with each layer of planking joined by pinned mortice and

Above: Stern view.

Above: Bow view.

tenons joints. I am not aware of any decks surviving in ancient wrecks so do not know if decks were also joined on the mortice and tenon system; if they were it would give additional longitudinal strength.

The ship was sheathed in lead. Investigation of wrecks has shown that lead sheathing was nominally 1mm thick with an average size of 1 square metre but the plates were irregular and the Kyrenia ship, which was only 15 metres long, had a plate 1.23m x 2m.

Athenaeus says the whole ship was decorated with suitable paintings. I chose red as the main colour for the upper hull because marble eyes found in Greece and believed to

have been fixed on the bows of triremes have traces of red paint on their backs. The Alexandria mosaic shows the hull as mainly red and also shows the prow ornament as gold. Athenaeus, in his description of the large warship known as the 'Forty' refers to the hull having a running pattern of ivy leaves and thyrsi so I have incorporated this on the lower hull. The paint used by the ancients was encaustic, with the pigments dissolved in wax and applied hot.

The bow decoration is the typical Volute shape found on many ancient ship representations. I have shown the top of

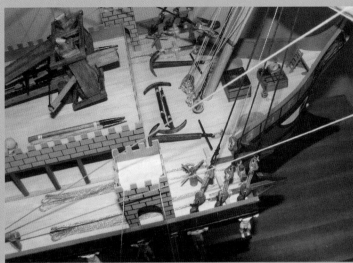

Left: Detail of after deck with stables, gymnasium, library and temple.

Below: Catapult platform with ready ammunition, stones or darts.

Above: Fore deck with anchors, fresh fish tank and top of water tank.

the volute turning aft, on some representations it turns forward and it has been suggested that this applies to ships from North Africa.

The stern decoration is the fan shape known as the Aphlaston. This was found on most ancient warships. Later Roman merchant ships often had a goosehead at the stern making them instantly recognizable, but this would have been in the days of the Pax Romana when piracy had been eliminated.

Above: Library with roof removed.

STRUCTURES ON DECK

The deck structures required a fair amount of guesswork. I have roofed them in tiles as a number of wrecks have roof tiles, probably from the ship's galley. The Temple contains a statue of the goddess Aphrodite and is a simple classical temple structure generally based on the writings of Vitruvius. The combined library and reading room contains a scroll rack on one wall and three couches. The reading room is fitted with folding doors on three sides to allow users to take the air. Athenaeus says that the Reading Room had 'in the

overhead, a circular concavity made to look like the sundial at Achradina'. As I had no idea what this would be like I fitted a simple dome. The gymnasium comprises a sanded area suitable for boxing and wrestling, with covered walk-

Below: Detail of the temple.

Above: Bath house with copper tubs and marble basin.

ways on three sides. On the forward side I placed the bath-house. The stables are much like modern stables. Originally I placed the stables next to the bulwarks, thinking that there they could be more easily cleaned. However, as Atheneaus says that an iron palisade surrounded the deck I moved the stables inboard to provide a complete walkway round the ship for the soldiers.

Athenaeus also says, 'Across the ship ran a battlemented parapet surrounding a raised fighting deck that rested on pillars; on this was set a catapult capable of throwing a 180 lb stone or an 18 foot dart; the instrument had been designed by Archimedes. Its range with either missile was 200 yards'. I placed this platform between the foremast and the mainmast as being the most convenient place, though this does mean that the catapult would have to be swiveled to fire on either bow. The fighting platform has only to support the weight of the catapult as a correctly set up cata-pult produces no recoil forces.

The anchors have been based on the wooden and iron anchors found on the Lake Nemi ships. The iron anchors have removable stocks and were encased in wood, presumably to give them more bite. The wooden anchors have lead stocks.

As the anchors are very large and heavy and would prob-ably have required some mechanical assistance, I have fitted

four capstans. The capstans positioned aft could also be used to lift the rudders if necessary.

RIG

Three masts are fitted, each fitted with a square sail. It is not thought that the triangular topsail seen on later Roman ships had been invented at this time. The foremast has a pro-nounced forward inclination. Each mast was fitted with a top and the tops varied in size as Athenaeus refers to them being manned by three, two and one man respectively. Each top required an access ladder as there is no evidence for ratlines at this early period.

Most representations show the yards being formed of two halves lashed together. The spars are supported by double halyards which appear to pass through bronze fittings on either side of the mast. Yards were apparently fitted with single braces.

Sails were fitted with sheets but apparently not with tacks. When the ship tacked the weather sheet was taken forward.

Reefing was by means of brails passing through brail rings sewn to the front of the sail. On earlier representations the

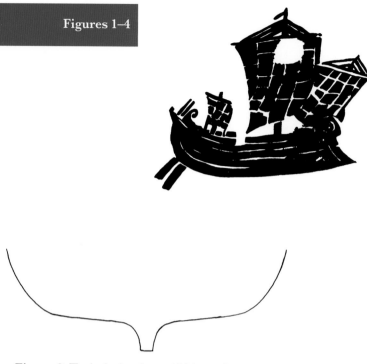

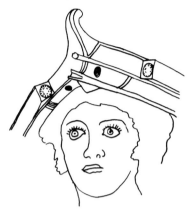

Figure 1. Mosaic in the Foro delle Corporazioni, Ostia, second-century AD.

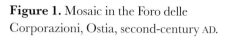

Figure 3. Typical wineglass midship section, Madraque de Gienes wreck, first century BC.

Figure 2. Detail from mosaic portraying the Personification of Alexandria by Sophilos, Greco-Roman Museum, Alexandria, second century BC.

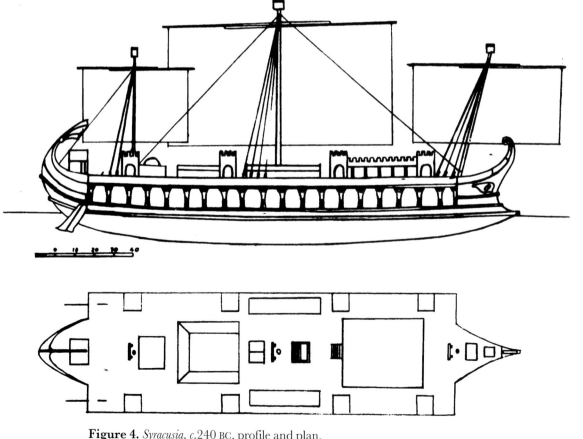

Figure 4. *Syracusia*, c.240 BC, profile and plan.

Above: Starboard quarter view.

brails pass through a fitting on the top of the yard and then run down to the deck aft. The yard is often shown bent downwards at the ends presumably by the force applied by the brails. Later representations omit the brails running aft but appear to show what have been interpreted as topping lifts and straight yards. It is suggested that as ships got bigger it became inconvenient to run the brails aft as this would mean they would have to be adjusted every time the yard was swung or left very slack. Therefore brails were now run to the masthead and then straight down to the deck and have been mistaken for topping lifts. Whether the brails were run through blocks, a mast fitting or a euphroe is unclear. I choose a euphroe as the simplest option.

ARMAMENT

The three talent (180-pound) catapult was the largest catapult recorded in ancient times. They are described in surviving technical treatises which include formulae for calculating the size of components. This was an enormous machine, about 30 feet long and 20 feet over the arms. The torsion springs were 15 feet high.

Booms for dropping missiles on to attacking boats were fitted, two to each mast and two to each tower (this also sug-

gests that the towers were next to the bulwarks). The booms on the foremast are convenient for loading the catapult though this is only a guess. Certainly lifting a 180-pound stone ball onto the catapult slider must have been very difficult. I have shown the starboard tower booms rigged.

THE MODEL

Based on the information that I had acquired I produced a rough sketch which was the basis for my model (see Figure 4).

The model is to 1:72 scale. This gives a reasonable size for possible conversion to a working model, and means that I can use commercially available figures for crew and passengers. The hull is mostly plank-on-frame with the keel and frames made from 3mm marine ply. The oar box profile was incorporated into the frames. The frames were erected upside down on a raised baseboard. This enabled me to work on the inverted hull even when the bow and stern ornaments were fitted. The hull was planked with 1.5mm ply from the aftermost bulkhead to the foremost bulkhead. The bow and stern were formed by bread and butter blocks sanded to shape. The hull was then covered in drafting tape to prevent

Above: Bow view with booms for dropping stones.

any runs and then painted internally with resin. This fills in any gaps in the planking, and allows the hull to be sanded to a smooth surface. The shape of the hull at the stern as it sweeps up to the stern ornament was very difficult to construct. In the end I carved a block of wood to represent the shape of the hull above deck level and moulded a papier-mâché shell on it. This was then glued on to the hull and subsequently planked inside and out. Next the wales were fitted. These had quite a severe curve at the stern and were soaked in ammonia to make them flexible.

The entire hull below the main wale is sheathed in lead, represented by cardboard plates scored with a ponce wheel to represent nails. Initially I cut the plates in irregular sizes but it looked so untidy that I redid the hull with plates of uniform size.

As the hull is painted above the main wale it was planked with dummy cardboard planks.

The deck was planked in lime.

The Atlas figures were cast in resin from a silicon rubber mould. The master was made from a much altered Red Indian figure.

Deck structures were constructed in 1mm ply. Much recourse was made to model railway suppliers for decorative features. Marble surfaces were made from offcuts of worktop laminate. Mosaic floors and paintings were made from suitable pictures found on the web. For the fish tank, fish shapes were cut from aluminium cooking foil and added to the tank as it was slowly filled with clear resin.

Sails are washed out tracing linen hemmed and stitched to represent horizontal cloths. Because of the absence of bowlines and tacks a wire was enclosed in the lower hem to help the sail set.

The steering rudders were constructed from brass for strength and then sheathed in wood. They run in brass bearings fitted between the two support beams which are hidden by the dummy rope lashings. Additional tillers hidden within the oar boxes are coupled together by a drive rod, enabling the tillers to be operated together if I proceed to make this a working model.

A model such as this can never be conclusive, but I have endeavoured to incorporate all the facts quoted by Athenaeus in a reasonable and sensible manner.

REFERENCES

This is not exhaustive but includes the major sources.

Bonino, M., *Un Sogno Ellenistico: Le Navi Di Nemi*, Felici Editore, 2003. It is a pity this work is not available in English. Bonino's reconstruction of the *Syracusia* strongly influenced my version.

Casson, L., *Ships and Seamanship in the Ancient World*, Johns Hopkins University Press, 1995.

Delgado, J. P. (ed.), *Encyclopaedia of Underwater and Maritime Archaeology*, British Museum Press, 1997.

Donato, G. de., 'Mare Nostrum', in *Encyclopaedia of Underwater Archaeology, Vol. 3*, Periplus, London, 2003.

Landels, J. G., *Engineering in the Ancient World*, Los Angeles, 1978.

McGrail, S., *Boats of the World*, Oxford University Press, 2001.

Morrison, J.S. & Coates J.F., *Greek and Roman Oared Warships 399–30 B. C.*, (Oxbow Monograph 62, 1996.

Rihill, T., *The Catapult, A History*, Westholme, 2007.

Spathari, E., *Sailing Through Time*, Athens, 1994.

Tufa, J. M. & Steinmeyer A. G., 'The *Syracusia* as a giant cargo vessel', in *The International Journal of Nautical Archaeology* (1999) 28.2.

Proceedings of the International Symposiums on Ship Construction in Antiquity, Tropis, Organising Committee of the Symposiums/Ministry of Culture, Athens.

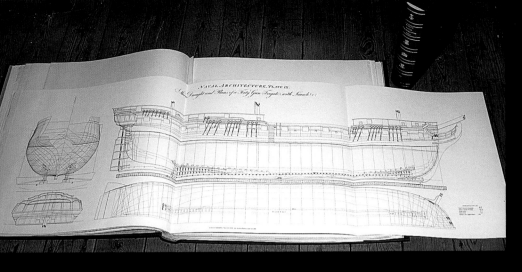

David Steel's
*Elements & Practice of
Naval Architecture*

Originally published in 1805, *Elements & Practice of Naval Architecture* was the first major publication in English to deal with all aspects of shipbuilding, whether ships for the Royal Navy, an Indiaman or other merchant vessels. The elephant folio contains 38 large ships' draughts from which the shipbuilder would take his measurements and create his moulds. Today, *Naval Architecture* is used world-wide by both ship modellers and those who care for our wooden ship heritage. The quarto text volume tells you everything you need to know to build a ship of the line. This reprint faithfully reproduces both the elephant folio and text volume and is a limited edition of 500 sets. The price for the set hand bound in blue buckram is £550 plus postage and packing. *Only 75 sets remaining.*

DAVID STEEL'S TWO GREAT WORKS ON SHIPBUILDING

First published in 1794, *Elements & Practice of Rigging & Seamanship* was the best source for young midshipmen during the Age of Fighting Sail to learn everything they needed to know about sailmaking, mastmaking, rigging a ship of the line, how to sail the ship and how to use the ship in a fight through the study of tactics. Two quarto volumes hand bound in blue buckram fully reproduce the original work including the two movable volvelles that instruct the reader in sailing a man-of-war. A limited edition of 500 sets is priced at £400 plus postage and packing. *Only 200 sets remaining.*

Hull Planking

A STEP-BY-STEP GUIDE

by John Laing

While many models with beautifully executed hull planking are seen in the pages of the *Shipwright* annual, some model makers still seem to be confused about the correct method of planking a hull.

I have seen several excellent descriptions of hull planking over the years, however, many people (including me), find complicated technical explanations difficult to understand. I therefore thought it would be helpful to produce a pictorial record of my method of hull planking, which is based on the system used by the late Harold Underhill.

The photographs show several different models, but the method of planking is exactly the same on each, and this method of planking will produce a technically accurate result no matter what the model being built.

The normal scale at which I work is $\frac{1}{8}$in = 1ft (1:96); the only difference in working at larger scales is the need to use, in some cases, heavier tools appropriate to the job in hand.

THE PROCESS OF PLANKING

Photographs 1 and 2. Very few special tools are required for planking. My entire planking tool kit is displayed in Photograph 1 and consists of a jeweller's saw, proportional dividers, 6-inch steel rule, pencil, 6-inch three-cornered file,

jeweller's barrette file, jeweller's three-cornered file, scalpel with No. 21 (curved) blade, scalpel with No. 11 (straight) blade, and emery boards. I use surgical scalpel blades rather than hobby blades, as the quality of the steel seems better and the blades retain their edge longer. Two of my tools which may be unfamiliar to some model-makers are shown in Photograph 2. The top one is a set of proportional dividers. The dividers can be set by the adjustment screw to any proportion from 1:1 to 1:10. For example, if the dividers are set at four, the distance between the small points at left is four times less than the distance between the large points at right. The tool at the bottom is a small barrette file. The body of this file is shaped like a flattened triangle with teeth being cut only on the flat front side. This means that the file can be used in very narrow spaces and against edges which don't require filing. It is very useful for removing excess glue or small irregularities from the edges of planks already fitted.

Photograph 3. Remember that in almost every case, each strake of planking will run the full length of the hull, as can be seen in the vessel under construction here. If you check 'The Lookout' in *Model Shipwright* 143, you will see that the ship in the background of the photograph shows this clearly. The only exceptions to this generalisation are vessels with an unusual hull form; for example vessels with a

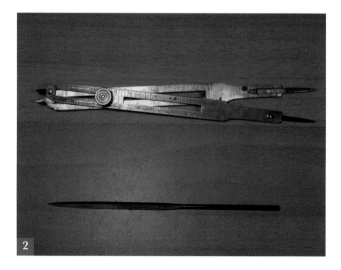

fine, long run aft or vessels with an extremely bluff bow.

Photograph 4. Before planking can begin, the frames must be true and fair in order to ensure that the completed hull will have the correct form and also to provide a good landing for the planks.

Photograph 5. Planking battens are a convenient method of determining the run of planking and also the actual width of each plank at every frame. The battens should be placed at intervals of 6 to 8 strakes of planking for ease of measurement. The next job will be to determine the position of these battens.

Photograph 6. Take a piece of light card and mark the actual length of the midships frame by positioning the card

against the keel and wrapping it around the curve of the frame. The deck edge can then be marked on the card. The distance along the card from the end to this mark is the true length along the frame. Repeat this process at several points along the hull with separate pieces of card.

Photograph 7. Lay the card for the midships frame flat on a hard surface. The true length of the frame can now be accurately measured. The midships frame is used for the following calculations as it is at this point on the hull that we know the nominal and actual plank width are equal.

Having decided on the scale width of the planks, the length of the midships frame can now be divided by the scale plank width to give the number of strakes of planking (e.g.

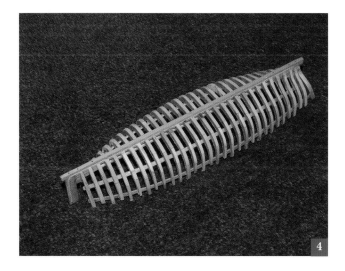

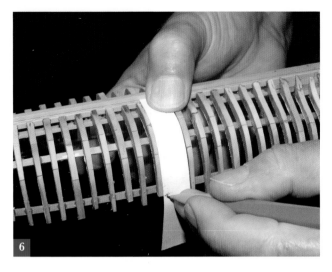

6

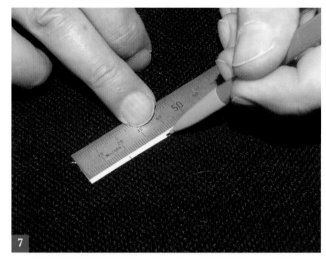

7

frame length = 144mm; plank width = 3mm; therefore number of strakes is 144 ÷ 3 = 48).

Divide the number of strakes calculated in this manner by the number of planks between each batten – 6 to 8 planks (in our example above, number of strakes = 48; batten interval = 8 planks; therefore number of batten intervals is 48 ÷ 8 = 6; therefore number of battens required = 5 (the number of battens will always be one less than the number of intervals).

Divide the length of the frame as marked on the card by the number of batten *intervals* (in our example 144mm ÷ 6 intervals = 24mm) and mark these distances along the card starting from one end. You will now have the position of the battens (5 in our example) marked evenly along the card.

Repeat this process of batten marking for each of the measured cards for your hull by dividing the length of each card by the number of batten *intervals* to obtain the distance between the battens for each card.

Photographs 8 and 9. The positions of the battens can now be transferred to the hull by simply laying the measuring cards on the frames once more and marking the batten positions on the frames on each side of the hull.

Photograph 10. The battens should now be fixed to the hull at the midships frame on each side. It doesn't matter whether they're fixed with fine cord or wire or by gluing them (the glue can easily be removed later). The main thing is that the battens are firmly anchored on the marks made on the midships frame.

Photograph 11. With the battens fixed to the midships frame, fix them temporarily on the marks at the bow and stern. Note: Do not fix the battens permanently yet.

With the battens temporarily fixed, look at the hull from all directions to see how the lines of the battens run. The aim is to achieve a pleasing run of planking right around the hull both fore and aft. Move the battens slightly if needed to achieve good smooth curves that are pleasing to the eye from whichever direction the hull is viewed.

Once happy with the run of battens, check the spacing again to ensure that no planks will be too wide or too narrow. This may be a problem at the bow or near the stern. The aim is to have no plank wider than about one foot (305mm) full size, or narrower than half the nominal plank width anywhere along its length. With a little juggling of the battens it should be possible to achieve both pleasing lines and accept-

8

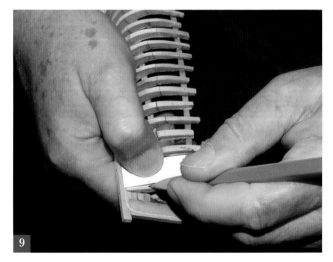

9

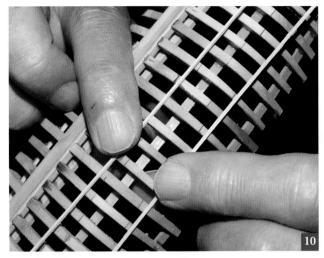

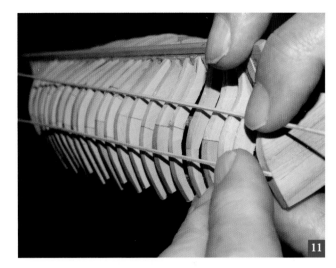

Planking Diagram
Numbers are to the right of their respective frames

A/E Forecastle

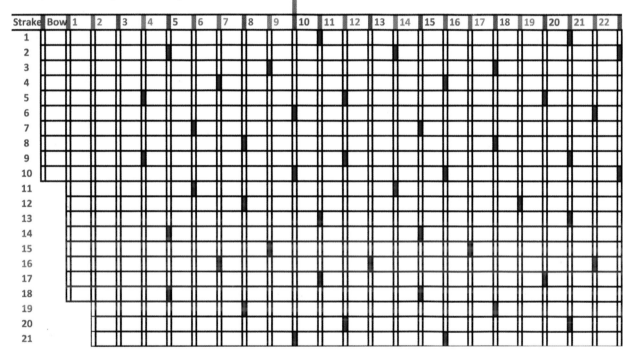

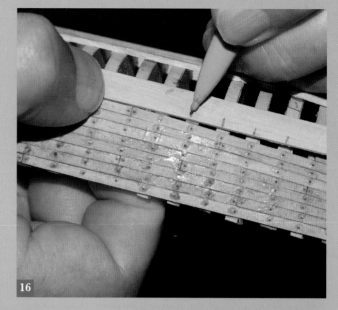

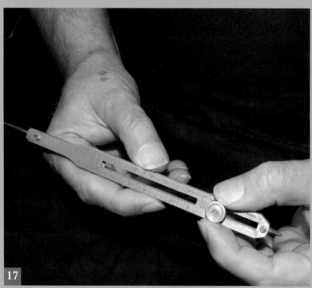

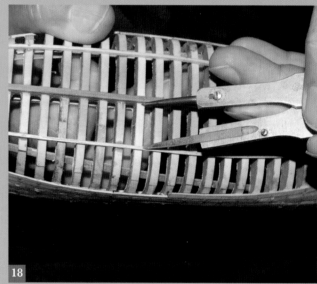

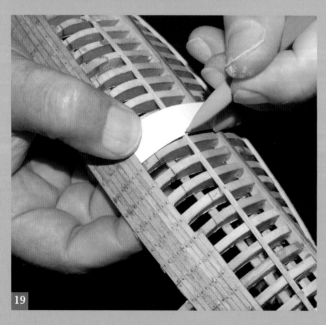

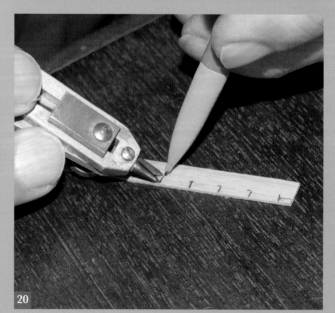

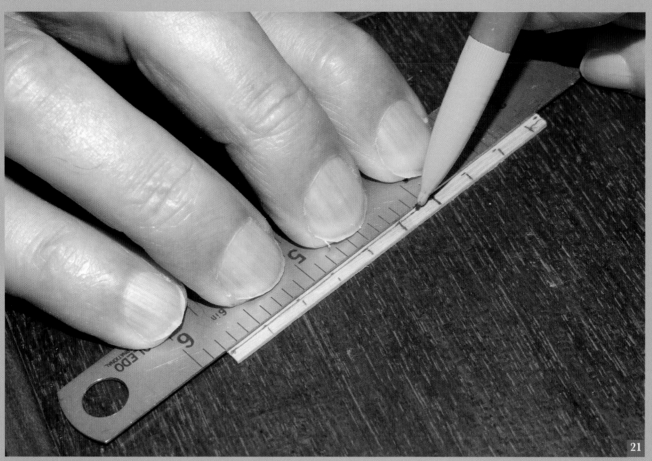

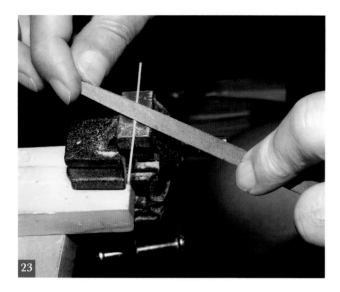

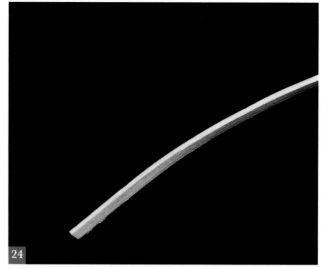

able plank widths without the use of 'stealers' on almost every hull shape.

Photograph 12. Once happy with the batten placement, a final check of the hull should be made to ensure that the spacing and lines of the battens are correct and that they are also symmetrically spaced on both sides of the hull. If everything is in order, fix the battens permanently so that they won't move during the planking process. We are now ready to proceed with the actual planking.

Photograph 13. A hull can be planked without a planking plan, but spending a few minutes to draw one up can save a lot of frustration later on. The planking plan doesn't need to be drawn to scale or be a work of art. It simply needs to show you where each plank butt is located on each strake of planking.

The plan shown is part of the one I used to plank my model of M.V. *Nareau*. It was drawn up on a Microsoft Excel spreadsheet with the cell widths adjusted to the needs of the plan. The red marks indicate the plank butts.

The plan is drawn up with regard to the rules currently in force for the vessel being built (in this case, Lloyd's rules for wooden vessels). By drawing the planking plan before planking commences, there is no chance of being 'painted into a corner' by ending up with planks too long or too short or by having butts too close to each other. It may take several attempts to get this right, but the effort is worth it.

Photograph 14. The deck line or upper edge of the planking needs to be defined before planking commences by fitting the wale or rubbing strake. The position and width of the wale or rubbing strake can be taken from the plans. If there is no wale or rubbing strake, then the deck edge needs to be clearly marked on the outside of the frames to be used as a measuring mark for the planking and the sheer strake will need to be fitted first. This will give an upper border for measuring the planking and will also help to strengthen the hull and stabilise the upper ends of the frames.

Photograph 15. Before commencing each strake of planking, carefully mark the position of the plank butts on the frames. This will save having to continually refer to the planking plan and also help to avoid confusion in constantly counting frames

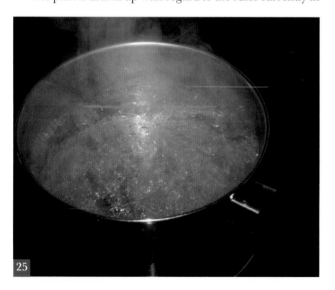

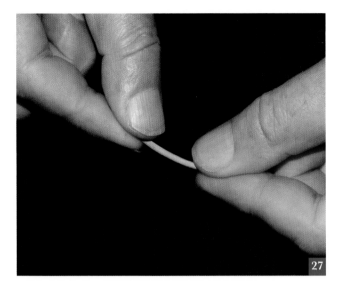

27

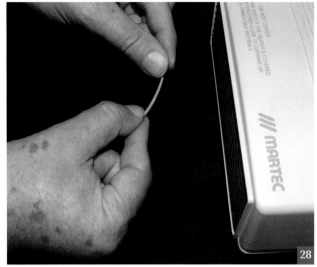

28

to find the position of the next butt as planking proceeds.

Photograph 16. Take the planking material, hold it against the hull in the position that the plank is to be fitted and mark the position of each frame on the plank.

Photographs 17 and 18. Set the proportional dividers to the number of strakes of planking left to be completed in the 'batten interval' being worked on and measure the distance remaining to be planked with the large end of the dividers.

Photograph 19. In an area of the hull where there are tight curves, it may be necessary to use a piece of card wrapped around the frame to determine the correct distance for measuring.

Photograph 20. Using the small end of the dividers, transfer the measurement to the appropriate frame mark on the planking material. This will be the width of the plank at that frame. Repeat this step for each frame along the length of the plank to determine the shape of the plank. The plank should be measured at each frame even on relatively straight lengths of hull as this will minimise any small errors that are made in transferring the widths.

Photograph 21. Once all the frames are marked for width, the full shape of the plank can be drawn. Note: It is helpful to leave the planks a little longer than required to allow for final trimming later.

Photograph 22. The plank can now be sawn to shape…

Photograph 23. …and carefully trimmed down to its final dimensions with a small file.

Photograph 24. Bend the plank to the shape of the hull where it will finally fit. This makes the final fitting of the plank easier and ensures that there are no undue stresses set up in the hull or plank as the planking progresses.

Photograph 25. Where the plank has to take a severe bend and/or twist it is best to steam or boil the wood first to make it pliable. For small planks, a few minutes boiling in a pan on the stove will be sufficient.

Caution: Some timbers contain toxic substances. Never use any utensil that will be used for normal cooking to boil your wood. Instead use a separate pan stored away from everyday cooking utensils so that there can be no room for confusion!

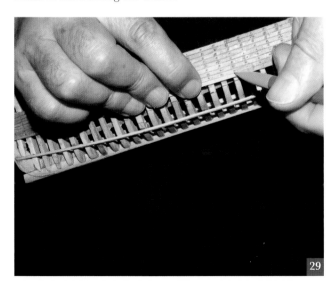

29

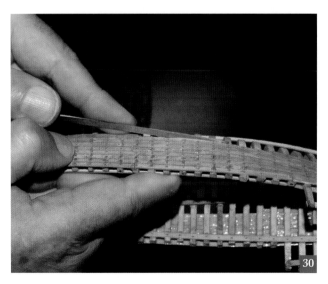

30

Photograph 26. The steamed plank can be bent to shape on a former.

Photograph 27. Or, on smaller pieces, the bend can simply be worked in by hand and held in shape.

Photograph 28. Which ever method of bending is used, the plank must be thoroughly dry before being fitted to the model. Wood expands when wet and even a very small piece will shrink slightly as it dries, leaving gaps in the planking if

fitted wet. Small pieces can be dried in the air flow from a fan heater or similar while being hand-held to shape. If drying by this method, be careful not to hold your hands in the hot air flow long enough to induce burning.

Photograph 29. Once the plank has been shaped, it can be checked for fit on the hull and the ends marked and trimmed to the final fitted length. If necessary, minor adjustments to the plank shape should be made to ensure as

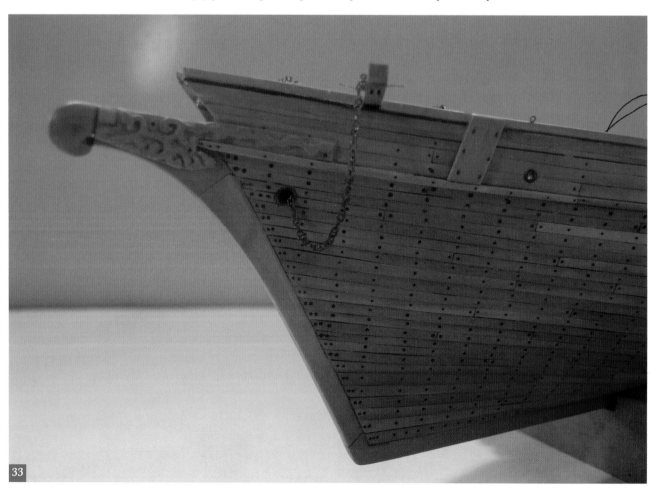

good a fit to the adjoining planks as possible.

Photograph 30. Any minor imperfections or excess glue should be trimmed from already fitted planks to ensure a good, close fit of the next plank. A small barrette file is handy for this job, as it will only cut the plank edge.

Photograph 31. After a check for fit, the plank can now be fitted in place.

Photographs 32 and 33. Take great care in cutting the end planks of each strake so that they fit snugly into the rabbet. The plank ends should form a smooth line along the stem and stern rabbets.

Photograph 34. It's a good idea to work from forward and aft towards the centre of the hull in each strake. Working in this order means that the more difficult planks at each end of the hull can be fitted first when only one end of the plank is a critical fit. It also means that the closing plank in each strake will be on a squarer section of the hull where fitting is easiest.

Photograph 35. If treenails are to be fitted, it is best to at least mark the positions of the treenails on the frames as planking progresses. By marking the treenail positions as each strake is completed the frames are right next to the plank being

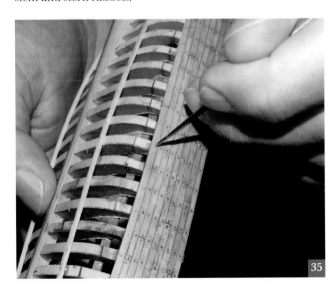

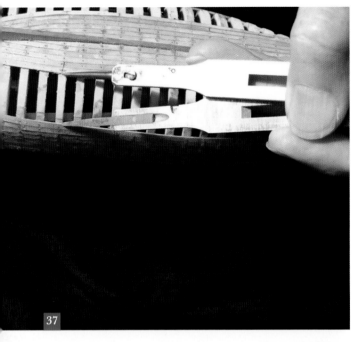

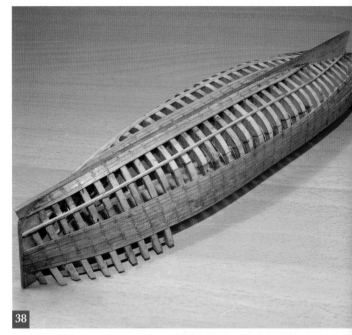

marked and the correct treenail position is easily determined.

Photographs 36 and 37. When the planking gets to within one or two planks of the next batten, remove that batten and measure to the next one (or to the planking if the last batten has been removed), taking into account the new number of strakes in the section caused by removing a batten.

Photograph 38. Work in bands of planking alternately down from the deck line and up from the keel. This will ensure that the 'closing strake' – the final stake to be fitted – will be somewhere in the middle of the hull where fitting will be slightly easier.

Photograph 39. Continue filling in the planking until only the closing strake is left to do.

Photograph 40. Great care needs to be taken in measuring and cutting the planks for the closing strake, as once they are in place they can be difficult to remove again.

Photographs 41, 42, 43. The final job is to thoroughly clean up the hull with fine files and abrasive paper, taking care to cut with the grain and not to take off too much material. After a final inspection to make sure that all marks and glue residue have been removed, the hull can be protected with the finish of your choice.

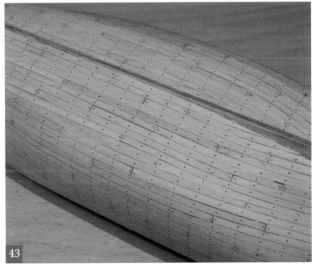

'To Learn His Art'

SHIPWRIGHTS AND THEIR APPRENTICES, 1730–1775

by George Stephenson

During the eighteenth century, Britain's first line of defence against invasion was her Royal Navy. Many of the men who manned these wooden walls have passed into legend, but the men who built them are often not recorded. When they are remembered it is personalities like Sir Thomas Slade, one of the most important Master Shipwrights of the period, who are discussed. The actual craftsmen who undertook the work are generally ignored, but this is not surprising given the types of documents that survive. Within The National Archives, Kew, London, are naval records spanning almost the entire history of England and Britain. From these, an almost complete history of the administration of the Royal Navy can be obtained. However, most archives will give a historical view from the top down and therefore leave the stories of the humble craftsmen untold.

When I was a shipwright apprentice on HMS *Victory*, between 2000 and 2006, I often wondered how my eighteenth-century counterparts' experiences compared with my own. I hoped that they had left some trace other than the great ships they had built. I had the opportunity to find out when I subsequently undertook research for my Masters dissertation at the University of Exeter. What I was looking for were records written by the shipwrights themselves and specifically referring to their apprentices. The naval department responsible for shipbuilding and repair was the Navy Board which existed between 1660 and 1832. The correspondence of this body contained most of the primary sources I was looking for. The Navy Board In-Letters (catalogued as the ADM106 series of items) consist of a wealth of material concerning the day-to-day business of the Royal Dockyards. Thanks to the Naval Dockyards Society, around two thirds of this mine of information has been catalogued. These letters, many of which were written by the shipwrights themselves, formed the bulk of the source material.

Autobiographical accounts by shipwrights are extremely rare: accounts by apprentices even rarer. One example is thought to be the sole surviving record – the account of William Chandler who served twelve years in the Navy at sea and in Portsmouth Dockyard. More will be revealed about him later. What is not recorded is what an apprentice learned during his seven years of servitude. Official apprentice schools did not appear until the nineteenth century. However, what has emerged from the records gives us a picture of what the life of an eighteenth-century dockyard apprentice was like. This article is based on the findings of my research and has produced a social history of shipwright apprentices: a history from below.

THE MASTER AND SERVANT

By 4 March 1763 William Chandler had already served nearly four years in the Royal Navy, initially as the steward of Richard Baker, Carpenter of the *Sandwich*. William was to be made Servant to Mr McClean, Acting Carpenter of the *Royal William*. He was entered in Portsmouth Dockyard as a Shipwright Apprentice for the next seven years. The previous years had toughened the young lad. William had seen service in the *Sandwich* as part of the Western Squadron off Brest and the Basque Roads. Bouts of rheumatic fever had laid him low in the verminous conditions of the sick bay and he had been among the first patients of the newly opened Haslar hospital in Gosport. He had a scar on his forehead from a wound that required three stitches. When Mr McClean presented William to the Master Shipwright in Portsmouth Dockyard, approval was given merely on the boy's appearance: 'I like him very well; for I think that he is a stout lad'. Thus began William's seven-year apprenticeship as a shipwright.[1]

At the time mentioned in the above account, the only requirements for indenturing a shipwright apprentice were that he should be at least 16 years of age and be over 4 feet 10 inches (approximately 1.47 metres) in height. They would be young men of 23 by the time they had served their time. Problems with recruitment may have caused the authorities to reduce the age restriction to 15 in 1765 and to 14 in 1769.[2] Apprentices were referred to as servants in the language of the Navy Board, the institution responsible for managing the Royal Dockyards. During this period of servitude, the

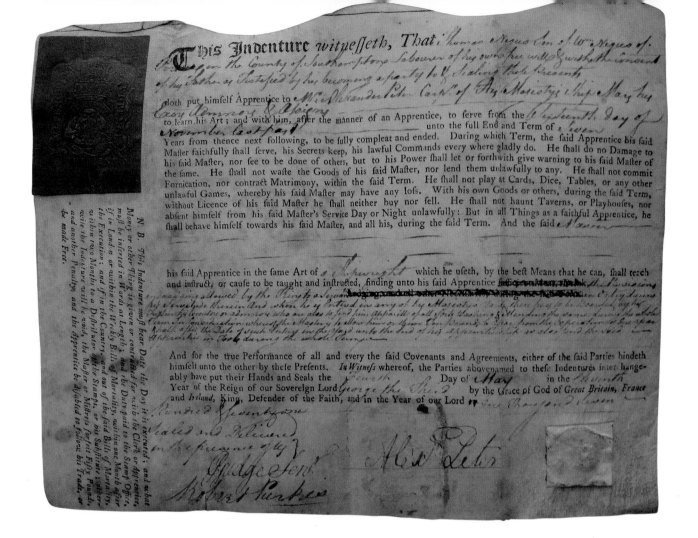

Figure 1: Apprentice indenture between Alexander Peter, Carpenter, HMS *Mars* and Thomas Negus of Portsea, 4 May 1771. Printed on vellum with manuscript insertions. Devon Records Office: 4187M/E265.

servant (as we shall now call him) would not be paid any wages; these would be paid to his master. In return the servant was required to lodge with his master and receive all food, clothing and tools throughout the whole term of servitude. If the master could not lodge his servant under his own roof, if he was a carpenter [3] on board a ship at sea for instance, then the usual arrangement was to pay the boy's father an allowance of 10 pounds per annum to cover clothing, washing and mending.[4]

Figure 1 shows an employer's half of a shipwright apprentice's indenture. This is printed on vellum with handwritten clauses specific to the terms and conditions of the occupation in question. This document is one of a pair of apprentice indentures between Alexander Peter, Carpenter of HMS *Mars*, and his two servants; John Collings, dated 31 March 1768 and Thomas Negus, dated 4 May 1771. How these have survived shows to some extent how apprentices were treated as property. These indentures were used as secu-

rity against a loan of 100 pounds Alexander Peter had taken from a Mr Line in March 1774. Mr Peter would have forfeited the boys' wages to Mr Line until the debt was paid.[5]

In transcription, the document reads as follows. Abbreviations are written out fully and original spellings have been maintained. Italics denote hand-written entries:

This Indenture witnesseth, *That Thomas Negus, Son of William Negus of Portsea in the County of Southampton, Labourer, of his own free will and with the Consent of his Father as Testified by his becoming a party to and Sealing these presents* doth put himself Apprentice to *Mr. Alexander Peter, Carpenter of His Majesty's Ship Mars his Executors or Administrators and Assigns* to learn his Art; and with him, after the manner of an Apprentice, to serve from the *Sixteenth day of November last past* unto the End and Term of *Seven Years* from thence next following, to be fully compleat and ended. During which Term, the said Apprentice his said Master faithfully shall serve, his Secrets keep, his lawful Commands every where gladly do. He shall do no Damage to his said Master, nor see to be done of others, but to his Power shall let or forthwith give warning to his said Master of the same. He shall not waste the Goods of his said Master, nor lend them unlawfully to any. He shall not commit Fornication, nor contract Matrimony, within the said Term. He shall not play at Cards, Dice, Tables, or any other unlawful Games, whereby his Master may have any loss. With his own Goods or others, during the said Term, without Licence of his said Master he shall neither buy nor sell. He shall not haunt Taverns, or Playhouses, nor absent himself from his said Master's Service Day or Night unlawfully: But in all Things as a faithful Apprentice, he shall behave himself towards his said Master, and all his, during the said Term. And the said *Master* his said Apprentice in the same Art of *a Shipwright* which he useth, by the best Means that he can, shall teach and instruct, or cause to be taught and instructed, finding unto his said Apprentice *The Provisions and Lodging allowed by the King to a Servant in Ordinary during his Servitude therein. And when he is Entered in any of His Majesty's Yards, then he is to be Boarded by his Father, or his Executors or Administrators who are also to find him Apparell of all Sorts, Washing and Mending the same during the whole Term. In Consideration whereof, the Master is to allow him or them Ten Pounds a Year from the Expiration of One Year and a half after the Date of such Entry in the Yards unto the End of his Apprenticeship, and also find the said Apprentice in Tools during the whole Term.*

And for the true Performance of all and every the said Covenants and Agreements, either of the said Parties bindeth himself to the other by these presents. In Witness whereof, the Parties above named to these Indentures interchangeably put their Hands and Seals the *Fourth* Day of *May* in the *Eleventh* Year of the Reign of our Sovereign Lord *George the Third* by the Grace of God of Great Britain, France and Ireland, King, Defender of the Faith, and in the Year of our Lord *One Thousand Seven Hundred and Seventy one.*

Sealed and Delivered
in the presence of Us:
J. Ridge Senior
Alexander Peter
Robert Parkes

N.B. This Indenture must bear date and day it is executed; and what Money or other Thing is given or contracted for with the Clerk or Apprentice, must be inserted in Words at Length; and the Duty paid to the Stamp Office, if in London or within the Weekly Bills of Mortality, within one Month after the Execution; and if in the Country and out of the said Bills of Mortality, within two Months to a Distributor of the Stamps, or his Substitute; otherwise the Indenture will be void, the Master or mistress forfeit Fifty Pounds, and another Penalty and the Apprentice be disabled to follow his trade, or be made Free.

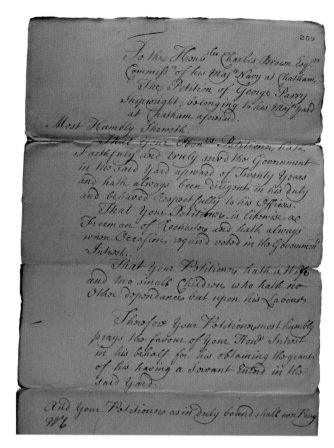

Figure 2. Petition of George Parry, Shipwright of Chatham Dockyard for a servant, 6 July 1747. National Archives, London, ADM106/1046/209.

How a shipwright or carpenter in the Royal Dockyards took on a servant as an apprentice depended on many factors. The potential master had to have the right service record: to be allowed a servant was a privilege, not a right. However, once a master had been granted a servant, this became a right for life. Only under certain circumstances was this right removed. The man was entitled to have a new servant almost immediately after the previous one had served his time. In 1742, numbers of shipwright apprentices were limited by the Navy Board to a ratio of one servant to every six shipwrights.[6] More often than not this ruling proved hard to implement as men returning from overseas, widows' entitlements and recruitment incentives boosted dockyard employment figures in wartime.

When a shipwright wished to take on an apprentice, he would write a letter in the form of a petition to the Navy Board. This letter would be submitted to the dockyard officers who would forward it to London. If the Navy Board agreed to the request, a Navy Board clerk annotated the letter accordingly and sent a warrant to the Dockyard officers. Figure 2 is an example of such a petition from 6 July 1747. In this case, an annotation appears on the front of the letter, 'W6', together with the more usual note written on the reverse, the lower right-hand corner having been folded over for the purpose. As there was no mechanical means of copying, on receipt at the dockyard offices, these warrants were copied by hand into the respective Navy Board Warrant Books.[7]

Transcribed, the letter above reads as follows:

> To the Honourable Charles Brown
> Commissioner of his Majesty's Navy at Chatham,
> The Petition of George Parry
> Shipwright, belonging to his Majesty's Yard
> at Chatham aforesaid.

Most Humbly Showeth
That Your Honourable Petitioner hath Faithfully and truly served His Government in the said Yard upward of Twenty Years and hath always been diligent in his duty and behaved Respectfully to his Officers.
That Your Petitioner is likewise a Freeman of Rochester and hath always when Occasion required voted in the Government's Interest.
That Your Petitioner hath a Wife and two small Children who hath no Other dependance but upon his Labours.
Therefore Your Petitioner most humbly prays the favour of Your Honours Interest in his behalf for his obtaining the grant of his having a Servant Entered in the said Yard.
And Your Petitioner as in duty bound shall ever Pray.

George Parry had the right to vote, and so was permitted to take on an apprentice on political grounds. According to the *List of Workmen and Apprentices in His Majesty's Dockyards 1748*, Parry was then 33 with twenty-one years' service and was described as able. His servant was Charles Dadd, 16 years of age with eleven months' service, and his ability was described as well. This made the total number of male Dadd family members serving in the yard up to thirteen: seven shipwrights and one apprentice, two caulkers and one apprentice, one joiner and one riggers' labourer.[8]

On receipt of the warrant at the Royal Dockyard, the master and servant would be sent for to appear before the Master Shipwright (also known as the Builder). If he was satisfied with the appearance of the boy, the Clerk of the Cheque (i.e. the accounts director) would enter the boy in the appropriate pay book. The new master and servant, together with the boy's father, would then draw up the indenture during the next six months. The boy's father paid a premium to the master on which duty of sixpence in the pound was paid to the agent. In the two indentures of Alexander Peter, the fathers paid four shillings and sixpence (2.5 per cent) duty and therefore paid a premium of nine pounds to Mr Peter.[9] Each indenture has been cut in a wavy line to create two identical halves. The other halves were given to the apprentices to keep as proof of identity and of their status and

Figure 3. Reverse of indenture between Alexander Peter and Thomas Negus. Devon Records Office: 4187M/E265 verso.

contractual obligations for the next seven years. Figure 3 shows the receipt for the duty paid by Mr Negus to indenture his son Thomas and that six months of the apprenticeship had already expired: It reads:

> *N.B. The Consideration within mentioned is One Year's Half passed.*
> *Received the day of 9th June 1771 the sum on four shillings and sixpence His Majesty's Duty of Sixpence in the pound on the within consideration.*
>
> *George Durnford*
> *Entered: H.A.*

William Chandler's case is unusual in that his father was not present to broker the deal with the shipwright to whom he was indentured. William was the steward of Carpenter Richard Baker, with the bosun of the *Sandwich* acting as go-between. After enrolment William was assigned to a quarterman; Mr Dunn, who then assigned him to another shipwright to be instructed; Mr Cote.[10] This may have been standard practice to ensure that boys were not trained by their masters as many shipwrights and apprentices were related to each other. In the cases of Alexander Peter's servants, both their fathers were of different trades; Collings was a mariner and Negus was a labourer. Mr Peter may have trained his two boys directly, but if he was at sea he would not necessarily have been permitted to take them with him. Different rates of ship permitted different numbers of servants.

William Chandler's training method of being put with instructors outside the household may have been the norm to avoid favouritism or abuse. However, the wages of a son who was servant to his father would boost family income in hard times. As per the laws in force at the time, all indentures were liable for a tax of sixpence per pound premium. Many shipwrights mention in their correspondence with the Navy Board that their servants' indentures were 'lodged with the Clerk of the Cheque', the senior accountant in a Royal Dockyard. This would imply that indentures were drafted, signed and witnessed in his office. Therefore, the Clerk of the Cheque may have been licensed as a 'Distributor of the Stamps'. If not, then indentures would have to be drafted by a lawyer.

Figure 4. Commissioner Hughes, Portsmouth to Navy Board, 12 March 1766. Margin notes naming ships at Portsmouth and wind direction at time of writing. Young William may have worked on these ships during his apprenticeship. National Archives, London, ADM106/1145/73

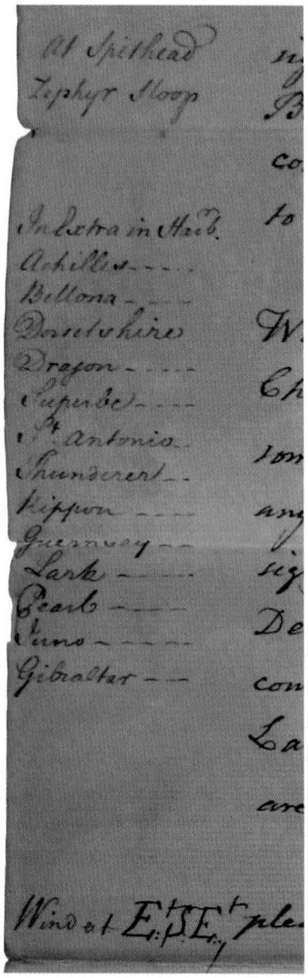

At Spithead

Zephyr Sloop

In Extra in Harbour
Achilles
Bellona
Dorsetshire
Dragon
Superbe
San Antonio
Thunderer
Rippon
Guernsey
Lark
Pearl
Juno
Gibraltar

Wind at East South East

WORK AND TRAINING

After being introduced to Mr Dunn, his quarterman, William Chandler was soon put to work. He was a cadet and worked one week in the Dockyard and the alternate week afloat, including the newly launched *Britannia*. The number of ships in Portsmouth was greater than usual so the shipwrights and their servants were put to work: 'to open up the men of war, to let air in, and keep the ships from rotting: But this did not last long, for we only went in the morning and evening; so were in the yard the greatest part of the day'.[11]

This presumably meant removing all the inside planking and thick stuff against the frames in order to ventilate between the timbers. William needed tools to learn his trade and his master soon gave him the first items for his tool kit: a saw, an axe and a chisel. They were second-hand and of poor quality because Mr Cote, his instructor, made and fitted new hafts. When working on the frigate *Niger* he had a toolbox made. William was living on board ship at first and had to be fetched by boat to work in the dockyard. Working alternate weeks ashore and afloat was limiting his ability to learn his trade. On questioning his master, Mr McClean simply retorted that if he cannot learn to build ships then he'll learn to dismantle them. After a few months, McClean was appointed to a new ship and with his lady and servant rented a house in Gosport. William could now work full time in the yard, but his troubles were only beginning.[12]

The work of a shipwright apprentice depended on to whom he was indentured. If indentured to a shipwright or carpenter, the young man could expect to be trained in that trade. In the first two years of his apprenticeship, the boy would be classed as a cadet and would undertake general labouring under supervision. After three years, the boy would be undertaking what was termed 'mens' work', i.e. he would be carrying out the duties of a shipwright, still under that supervision. Throughout the whole period of indenture, wages for the servant were paid to the boy's master. The boy would be reliant on his master for food, shelter, clothing and tools whilst the servant lived under his master's roof. If the servant was indentured to a carpenter serving on board ship, the boy would go to sea with his master. However, if the carpenter was transferred to work either ashore, or in a ship not permitting servants on board, the boy would be entered into one the Royal Dockyards. If this meant the master could not provide a roof over the boy's head, then the master was liable for the payment of 'board wages'. In most cases this was a payment of ten pounds *per annum* to the servant's father *en lieu* of boarding the apprentice himself.

The numbers of servants that were allocated to individual shipwrights varied with rank. Master Shipwrights were allowed five servants at a time and with a premium payable of 20 guineas (21 pounds sterling) each at indenture, officers' earnings could soon mount up. However, these young gentlemen could expect a different career path than the usual servant. In the absence of further and higher education on the subjects in hand, these young men had paid the higher premium for the privilege. During the final decades of the eighteenth century all the Master Shipwrights throughout the Royal Dockyards had been apprenticed to their predecessors.[13] This practice was seen as favouritism in some quarters. In November 1750, one such complaint was raised by Commissioner Brown of Chatham Dockyard against Mr

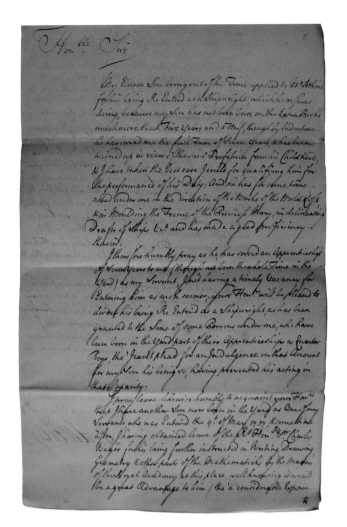
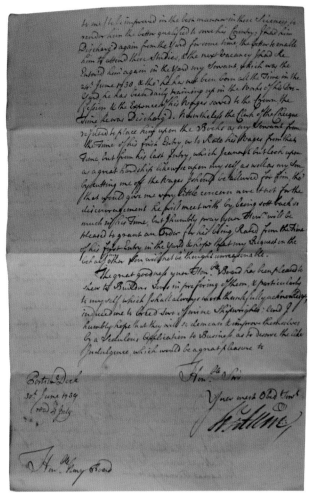

Figures 5 & 6. William Allin, Master Shipwright, Portsmouth Dockyard to Navy Board, 30 June 1739. National Archives, London: ADM106/910/7 recto & verso.

Ward, the Master Shipwright. Brown refused to sign Ward's recommendations for the promotion of newly served officers' servants directly into junior officer posts: 'if no other Shipwrights are to be preferred but Builders' [i.e. Master Shipwrights'] Apprentices lately out of their time, there will be little Encouragement left for Men of long Service and great Merit'.[14]

Clearly, the senior dockyard officers wielded a great deal of power and favour over the workforce under their command. However, there were ways these officers could provide the theoretical training these apprentices needed. Master Shipwright William Allin sent his son to the Naval Academy. His letter of 1739 (shown in Figures 5 and 6) gives a good indication as to what lengths senior technical personnel were prepared to go in training their successors for service. This letter accompanied one by Commissioner Richard Hughes in support of these claims. Although annotated on receipt by a clerk at the Navy Board, no details of any actions or decisions taken have been recorded.

Honourable Sirs,

My Eldest Son being out of His Time applied to Mr. Atkins for his being Re-Entered as a Shipwright, which he refuses doing, because my Son has not been born on the Extra Books much more than Five Years and a Half, though by Indenture he has served me the full Term of Seven Years, and has been trained up in view of the said Profession from his Childhood, and I have taken the best care I could for qualifying him for the performance of his Duty; And he has for some time acted under me in the direction of the Works of the Mold Loft, and in Moulding the Frames of the Princess Mary, in delineating Drafts of Ships etc. and has made a good proficiency therein.

I therefore humbly pray as he has served an Apprenticeship of Seven Years to me (though not born the whole Time in the Yard) as my Servant, I not having a timely Vacancy for Entering him as such sooner, your Honours will be pleased to direct his being Re-Entered as a Shipwright, as has been granted to the Sons of some Persons under me, who have been born in the Yard part of their Apprenticeships as Quarter Boys, though I can't plead for an Indulgence on that Account for my Son his being so, having prevented his acting in that capacity.

I pray leave likewise humbly to acquaint your Honours that I have another Son now born in the Yard as One of my Servants, who was Entered the 9th May 1737, and some time after, I having obtained leave of the Right Honourable Sir Charles Wager for his being further instructed in Writing, Drawing, Geometry and other parts of the Mathematick by the Masters of the Royal Academy at this place, well knowing it would be a great Advantage to him (though a considerable Expense to me) to be improved in the best manner in these Sciences, to render him the better qualified to serve his Country; I had him Discharged again from the Yard for some time, the better to enable him to attend these studies, and the next Vacancy I had Re-Entered him again in the Yard my Servant, which was the 24th June 1738, and though he has not been born all the Time in the Yard, he has been daily training up in the Works of his Profession, and the Expense of his Wages saved to the Crown, the Time he was Discharged. Nevertheless, the Clerk of the Cheque refused to place him upon the Books as my servant from the Time of his first Entry, or to Rate his wages from that time, but from his last Entry, which I cannot but look upon as a great hardship likewise upon myself, as well as my Son by cutting me off his Wages I should be allowed for him, though that would give me very little concern were that for the discouragement he will meet with by being sett back so much in his Time, but humbly pray your Honours will be pleased to grant an Order for his being Rated from the Time of his first Entry in the Yard and hope that my Request, on the behalf of my other Son, will not be thought unreasonable.

The great goodness your Honourable Board has been pleased to show to Builders Sons in preferring of them, and particularly to myself, which I shall always most thankfully acknowledge, induced me to breed Sons of mine Shipwrights; And I humbly hope that they will so demean and improve themselves by a Sedulous Application to Business as to deserve the like Indulgence, which would be a great pleasure to

Honourable Sirs
Portsmouth Dockyard
Your most Obedient Servant
30th June 1739
William Allin

Sir Charles Wager was a senior Naval Lord from 1718 to 1733 and would have continued to be a significant player in Admiralty affairs.[15] Clearly, by this time Allin and others were training their sons for a different profession than that of an ordinary shipwright. Their efforts were not recognised officially for many decades to come. Records showing what a shipwright was taught during his apprenticeship are rare if they exist at all. In William Chandler's account of his apprenticeship in Portsmouth Dockyard, between 1764 and 1771, only a few passing remarks to his work are made. No formal training school for apprentices was established until the nineteenth century after Sir Samuel Bentham's reforms. Textbooks for shipwrights were few and far between and

mostly aimed at officers' servants who were destined for a more professional career. Among the most important books were William Sutherland's *The Ship-builders' Assistant* of 1711 and *Marine Architecture: or Directions for Carrying on a Ship* of 1716. This latter was in fact the eighth reprint of Edmund Bushnell's *The Complete Shipwright*, the third edition of which was published as long ago as 1669.[16]

During the latter half of the eighteenth century, this two-tier training regime was unofficially adopted by the senior officers of the Royal Dockyards. The career path of a shipwright had changed permanently. This meant that ordinary shipwrights could only expect promotion to junior officer status. Many servants of Master Shipwrights and other senior officers were made up to quartermen or foremen immediately on completing their apprenticeship. However, their fathers had paid double the premium at indenture for these privileges. Unofficially, these boys were being trained in much more theoretical subjects. The profession of Naval Architect was unknown in Britain at that time, but steps had been taken towards its creation.

PAY AND CONDITIONS

The seven years that an apprentice shipwright served were not spent in complete penury. There were opportunities for servants to earn some money on their own account. According to William Chandler's biography, he was often able to earn a few pence here or a few shillings there. At one time, he was bosun of one of the Dockyard boats and earned a shilling a week. Also, apprentices were allowed 'chips', the daily allowance of timber offcuts that could be taken out of the yard under one arm. These could be sold for around five pence a day. On numerous occasions William took his chips to friends, or carried the chips of more elderly men, for payment of food and lodging. Wednesdays and Saturdays were 'women's chips days' when the men could take an extra allowance of wood for their womenfolk.[17]

This practice, and its associated abuses, gave rise to several expressions used in the English language today: 'you've had your chips'; 'when the chips are down'; 'a chip on the shoulder'; and is the reason why we British call French-fried potatoes 'chips' – being much thicker in size they look like chips. An incident at Chatham Dockyard, reported in a letter to the Navy Board of 17 June 1756, gives the specific origin. Due to abuses of the practice of taking chips, shipwrights were ordered by a Navy Board Warrant of 4 May 1753 to carry their bundles of timber underneath their arms instead of on their shoulders. By this means, the shipwrights could maintain their ancient rights but reduce the cost of waste material as the bundles would be smaller. The Master Shipwright and his First Assistant endeavoured to stop a large group of shipwrights from leaving the yard with their

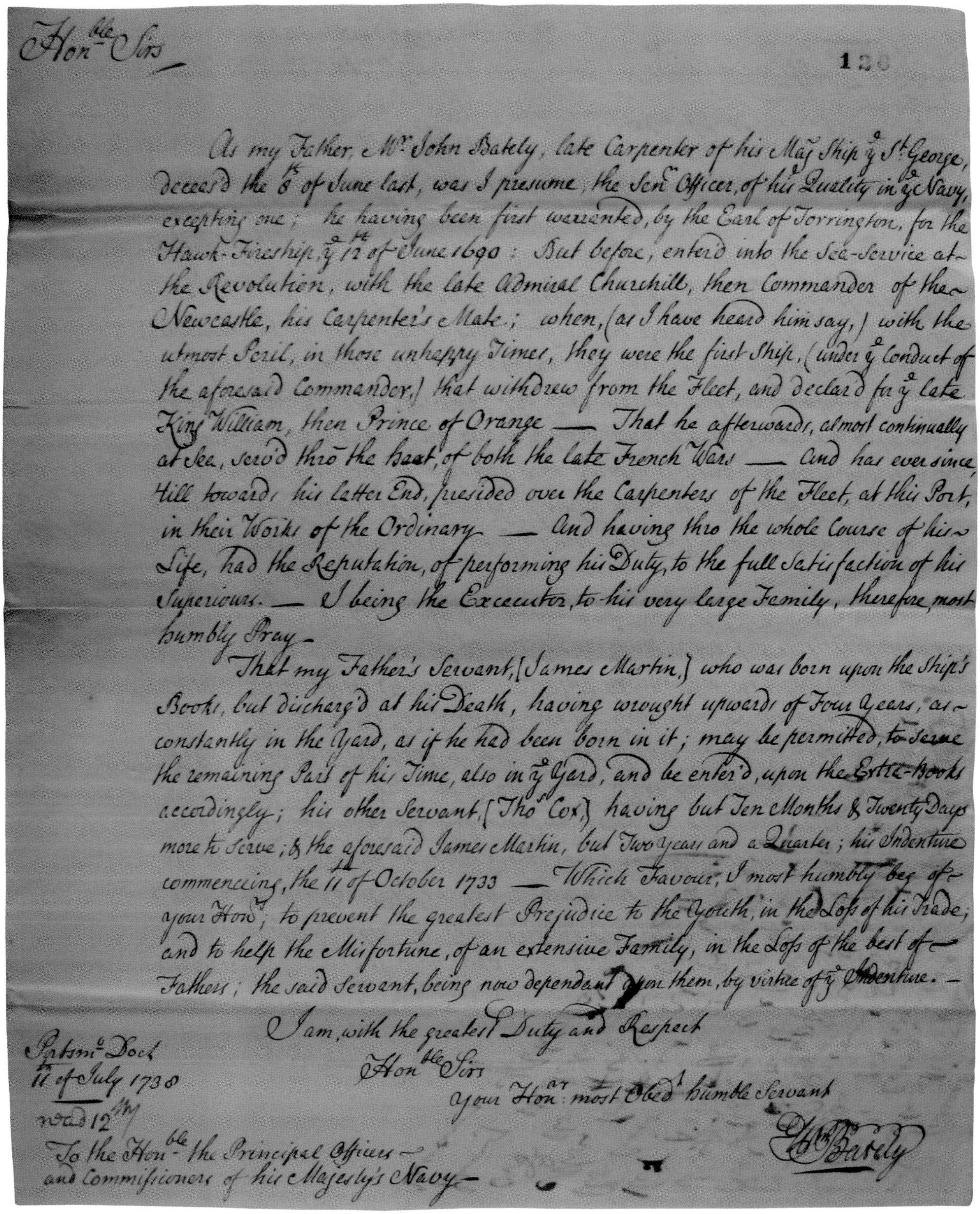

As my Father, Mr. John Bately, late Carpenter of his Maj:y Ship y:e St. George, deceas'd the 8 of June last, was I presume, the Sen:r Officer, of his Quality in y:e Navy, excepting one; he having been first warrented, by the Earl of Torrington, for the Hawk-Fireship, y:e 12 of June 1690: But before, enter'd into the Sea-Service at the Revolution, with the late Admiral Churchill, then Commander of the Newcastle, his Carpenter's Mate; when, (as I have heard him say,) with the utmost Peril, in those unhappy Times, they were the first Ship, (under y:e Conduct of the aforesaid Commander,) that withdrew from the Fleet, and declar'd fn y:e late King William, then Prince of Orange —— That he afterwards, almost continually at Sea, serv'd thro' the heat, of both the late French Wars —— And has ever since till towards his latter End, presided over the Carpenters of the Fleet, at this Port, in their Works of the Ordinary —— And having thro' the whole Course of his Life, had the Reputation, of performing his Duty, to the full Satisfaction of his Superiours. —— I being the Executor, to his very large Family, therefore most humbly Pray —

That my Father's Servant, [James Martin,] who was born upon the Ship's Books, but discharg'd at his Death, having wrought upwards of Four Years, as constantly in the Yard, as if he had been born in it; may be permitted, to serve the remaining Part of his Time, also in y:e Yard, and be enter'd, upon the Extra-Books accordingly; his other Servant, [Tho:s Cox,] having but Ten Months & Twenty Days more to serve; & the aforesaid James Martin, but Two Years and a Quarter; his Indenture commenceing, the 11 of October 1733 —— Which Favour, I most humbly beg of your Hon:rs to prevent the greatest Prejudice to the Youth, in the Loss of his Trade; and to help the Misfortune, of an extensive Family, in the Loss of the best of Fathers; the said Servant, being now dependant upon them, by virtue of y:e Indenture. —

I am, with the greatest Duty and Respect

Hon:ble Sirs

your Hon:r most Obed:t humble Servant

Portsm:o Dock
11 of July 1738

rec'd 12:th

To the Hon:ble the Principal Officers — and Commissioners of his Majesty's Navy —

[signature] Bately

Figure 7. Petition of 11 July 1738. Request for late father's apprentice to continue to serve his apprenticeship. National Archives, London, ADM106/895/126

chips on their shoulders. One particularly vocal individual refused to comply and the assembled men charged forward without lowering their chips, pushing the two officers ahead of them out through the dockyard gate.[18]

The Royal Dockyards paid lower wages than yards in the private sector, but could offer a steady income and used the terms and conditions of employment to attract craftsmen. In consequence, a shipwright in the public sector could earn more in a year than his private sector counterpart. For most of the eighteenth century, pay was fixed at two shillings and one penny a day. An extra lodging allowance of twopence halfpenny a week could be claimed. This was a left over from when most shipwrights rented their homes. The sale of chips could amount to approximately three shillings a week. The wages of a servant ranged from one shilling and twopence per week in his first year of service, to one shilling and ten pence in his last. The only deduction from dockyard wages was a payment of twopence a month for the provision of a dockyard surgeon.[19]

The wages of a shipwright apprentice no doubt boosted household income in straightened times. If a shipwright or carpenter could indenture his son to himself, then so much the better. Many of the surviving petitions within the Navy Board In-Letters ask for warrants to appoint sons, grandsons, nephews, cousins and in-laws as servants. If a shipwright became injured or incapacitated, the grant of a servant (i.e. his wages) provided a much-needed disability allowance. These rights were also extended to retired shipwrights and artificers' widows as a means of providing a pension. A typical example of this practice was that of the late John Bately, shown in Figure 7.

In the letter of 11 July 1738, William Bately, who was also his father's executor, briefly outlined his father's career. John had two servants at the time of his death and William requested that the youngest be allowed to finish his apprenticeship in order to provide for his late father's large family. An almost illegible note on the reverse granted permission. The complete letter makes interesting reading and transcribes as follows:

Honourable Sirs,

As my Father, Mr. John Bately, late Carpenter of his Majesty's Ship the St. George, deceased the 8th of June last, was I presume, the Senior Officer, of his Quality in the Navy, excepting One; he having been first Warranted, by the Earl of Torrington, for the Hawk – Fireship, the 12th of June 1690: But before, entered into the Sea-Service at the Revolution, with the late Admiral Churchill, then Commander of the Newcastle, his Carpenter's Mate; when, (as I have heard him say,) with the utmost Peril, in those unhappy Times, they were the first Ship, (under the Conduct of the aforesaid Commander,) that withdrew from the Fleet, and declared for the late King William, then Prince of Orange ____ That he afterwards, almost

continually at Sea, served through the heat, of both the late French Wars ____ And has ever since, till towards his latter End, Presided over the Carpenters of the Fleet, at this Port, in their Works of the Ordinary ____ And having through the whole Course of his Life, had the Reputation, of performing his Duty, to the full Satisfaction of his Superiors. ____ I being the Executor, to his very large Family, therefore, most humbly pray

That my Father's Servant, (James Martin,) who was born upon the Ship's Books, but discharged at his Death, having wrought upwards of Four Years, as constantly in the Yard, as if he had been born in it; may be permitted, to Serve the remaining Part of his Time, also in the Yard, and be entered, upon the Extra – Books accordingly; his other Servant, (Thomas Cox,) having but Ten Months and Twenty Days more to Serve; and the aforesaid James Martin, but Two Years and a Quarter; his Indenture commencing, the 11th October 1733 ____ Which Favour, I must humbly beg of your Honours; to prevent the greatest Prejudice to the Youth, in the Loss of his Trade; and to help the Misfortune, of an extensive Family, in the Loss of the best Father; the said servant, being now dependant upon them, by virtue of the Indenture.

I am, with the Greatest Duty and Respectfully
Honourable Sirs,
Your Honours' most Obedient and humble Servant
William Bately

There is no mention of Bately's eldest apprentice being kept on in the letter, only his youngest servant who would be most at risk from redundancy. The footnote 'received 12th' is written in another hand. It is interesting to note how quickly the correspondence of the Navy Board was handled. With despatches travelling almost daily up to London from Portsmouth and Chatham, replies were often received within two days. Plymouth correspondence was often turned round within a week. Considering the journey mail coaches had to make on unmade roads, these were remarkable achievements. In 1748 the Earl of Sandwich asked for a list of workmen in all the Dockyards to be compiled. According to this list, James Martin was an able shipwright still serving in Portsmouth Dockyard. There is no mention of a Thomas Cox of the right age at any of the Dockyards in the 1748 list and so one must presume that he was discharged either when his master died, or when this list was compiled.[20]

Injuries received at work or infirmity after long service were often compensated in the same manner. A typical example is the case of Carpenter Daniel Marsh, dated 2 October 1741. In his petition, Marsh stated that he injured a hand while serving on the *Bedford*. Three years previously Marsh had indentured a servant, Thomas Webber, while the *Bedford* was in Portsmouth for a rebuild. On being re-launched both men continued serving in the ship, during which time Daniel injured his hand. At the time of writing Daniel Marsh had been superannuated. He was probably a 'Greenwich Out-Pensioner'; a Greenwich Pensioner living in his own home instead of in the famous Hospital. However, his servant was discharged during the third year of his apprenticeship. Marsh requested that the young man would be allowed to continue in the Dockyard for the remainder of his time. A warrant granting permission was issued to that effect on 3 October 1741. Marsh would have received his superannuation payments and in addition would have continued to receive his servant's wages for the rest of the boy's time.[21] What happened to young Webber is not recorded. There is no entry for him in the 1748 Description Book, so he may have been discharged on completion of his apprenticeship.

The main problem with living in the Dockyard towns of the eighteenth century was the supply of money or rather credit. The wages of Naval Dockyard personnel were paid quarterly, one quarter on arrears. Hence, almost the entire population of the surrounding towns lived on credit and it appears it was relatively easy to let things get out of control. Throughout all of William Chandler's apprenticeship, all his masters became overstretched through running up excessive tavern or store bills. William's indentures were sold from one shipwright to another to help clear debts. None of his masters could fulfil their legal obligations and provide food and clothing on a regular basis. On several occasions he went barefoot with his clothes in rags, even in the depths of winter. Perhaps he may have fared better if his father could intervene on his behalf, but that would have risked everything for young William. Alexander Peter's two apprentices, John Collings and Thomas Negus may have had similar experiences after 1774.[22]

Mr Peter's two servants were passed over to solicitor Mr John Line of Lindridge, Devon, in accordance with the terms and conditions of a loan for 100 pounds in March 1774. The loan had to be repaid by the following September, with interest of five per cent payable. If forfeit, then the loan doubled each year or part of each year the payment was outstanding. One servant, John Collings had only ten months left to serve, while the other, Thomas Negus, had two years and eight months remaining time to serve.[23] Although both of these young men would have remained on the dockyard books as being servants of Alexander Peter, the pay due to them would have been forfeit to Mr Line. Presumably Mr Peter would have shown these documents to the Clerk of the Cheque in order to make arrangements for payment. There are no records to show if this debt was ever repaid.

When masters became indebted during the period of indenture, these times could prove difficult for their apprentices. As mentioned earlier, Alexander Peter's two boys' indentures were mortgaged against a loan for one hundred pounds. William Chandler had at least two different masters during his apprenticeship. Both of them had serious financial problems as a result of running up debt and over-stretching their credit; in fact whole communities would be living on credit in between pay days. All such artificers often found their situation untenable. An unidentified source in an article by H. E. Richardson in the *Mariner's Mirror* of 1947 states, 'Every shipwright in His Majesty's Yards that takes up his money on usury or by assignment (and it is almost impossible to avoid it) suffers a loss of at least 40s a year'.[24] Forty shillings, or two pounds sterling, would probably be the total interest and stamp duty payable on an indentured loan in one year. With a basic pay of thirty-nine pounds per annum, this is comparable with an interest rate of around five per cent – the rate Alexander Peter was charged.

Figure 8 shows the legal bond between Alexander Peter and solicitor John Line of 12 March 1774. This document, together with an accompanying loan indenture (DRO: 4187M/E266), formed the agreement whereby Mr Peter's apprentices were to act as collateral for the loan. Extending credit to a shipwright would not only enable him to pay his on-going household bills, with his job security as collateral, but it would enable any aspirational person to acquire many of life's luxuries. Apart from copious quantities of alcohol, William Chandler's masters were buying something much more expensive: tea. During his time on board the *Sandwich*, as steward to Carpenter Richard Baker, William often brewed and served tea for his master. Baker made tea for William every day the boy was ill in sick quarters. When accompanying his mistress, William would serve tea to her house guests. When Baker was in a fit of rage, he threw his best cups and saucers at William![25] The Bakers may have been living beyond their means with tavern bills and aspirational goods like tea and china to be paid for.

Mr McClean, his first apprentice master, became in debt through his partner's propensity for the bottle. McClean was forced to sell William's indentures in order to pay off debts, having been put in a debtors' prison. Mr Lambeth of Gosport, to whom McClean owed money for food and drink (he may have been a storekeeper), had refused any more credit. 'Mrs. McClean' (for she was actually married to someone else but lived with McClean) sold the furniture to the pawnbrokers in an attempt to settle the debt. While McClean was in prison, the *Africa* was ordered to sea. That ship's Carpenter was also a pawnbroker in Gosport, the small town across Portsmouth Harbour from the Dockyard where many of its workforce lived. An agreement was reached whereby McClean and the *Africa*'s Carpenter would swap ships as they were both of the same rate. After several weeks of negotiations, William's indentures were eventually sold to a Mr Aulquier.[26]

One can only assume that the Clerk of the Cheque at Portsmouth must have had a hand in these affairs. If he had not allowed the two Carpenters to change ships, then the

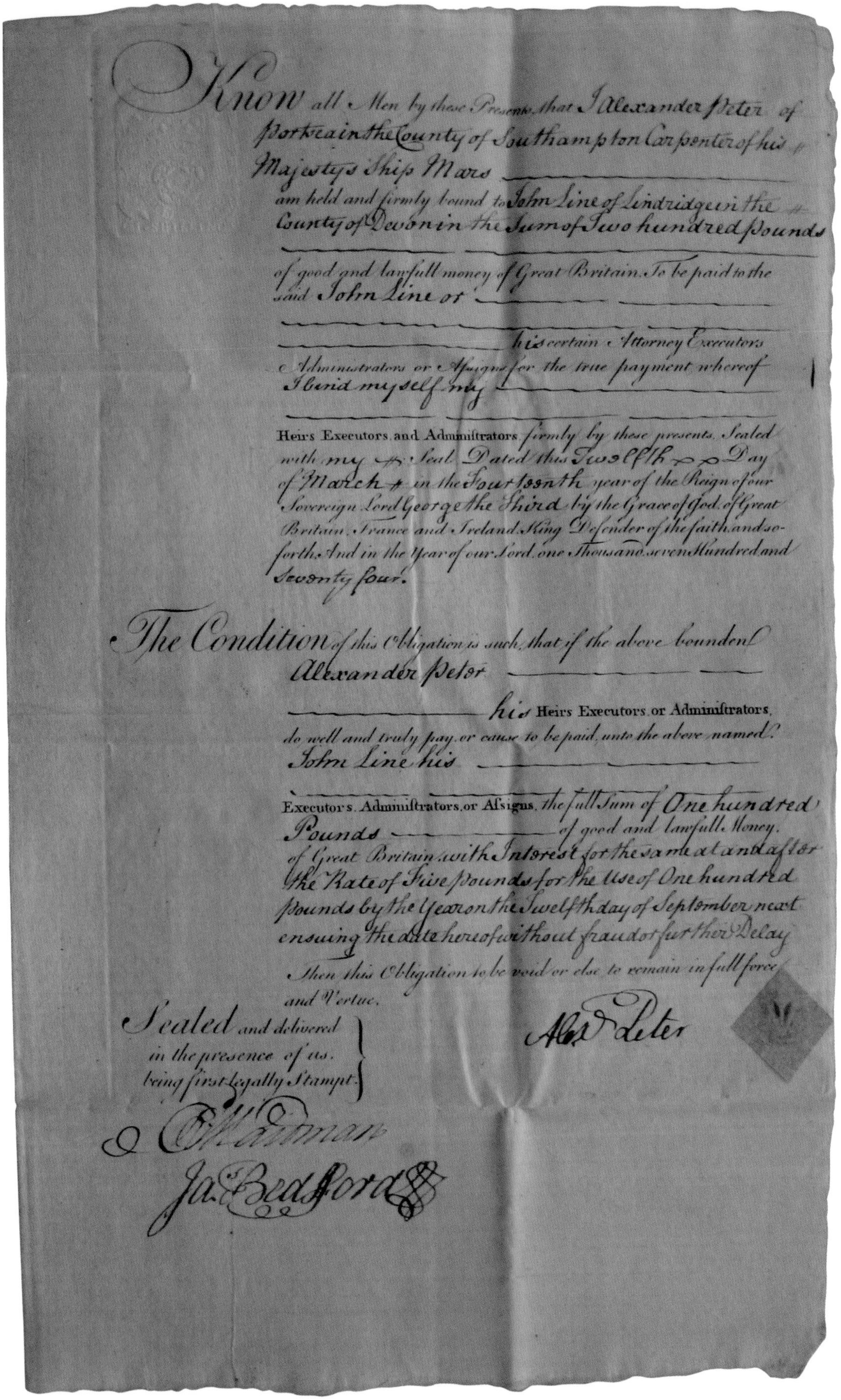

Know all Men by these Presents, that I Alexander Peter of Porkea in the County of Southampton Carpenter of his Majestys Ship Mars am held and firmly bound to John Line of Lindridge in the County of Devon in the Sum of Two hundred Pounds of good and lawfull money of Great Britain. To be paid to the said John Line or _____ his certain Attorney Executors Administrators or Assigns, for the true payment whereof I bind myself my _____ Heirs Executors, and Administrators, firmly by these presents. Sealed with my Seal. Dated this Twelfth Day of March in the Fourteenth year of the Reign of our Sovereign Lord George the Third by the Grace of God, of Great Britain, France and Ireland King Defender of the faith, and so forth. And in the Year of our Lord, one thousand seven Hundred and Seventy four.

The Condition of this Obligation is such, that if the above bounden Alexander Peter _____ his Heirs Executors, or Administrators, do well and truly pay, or cause to be paid, unto the above named John Line his _____ Executors, Administrators, or Assigns, the full Sum of One hundred Pounds _____ of good and lawfull Money of Great Britain, with Interest for the same at and after the Rate of Five pounds for the Use of One hundred pounds by the Year on the Twelfth day of September next ensuing the date hereof without fraud or further Delay Then this Obligation to be void or else to remain in full force and Vertue.

Sealed and delivered
in the presence of us.
being first legally Stampt.

Alexr Peter

O Chapman

Jas Bedford

supply of cheap credit to the Dockyard workforce may have been seriously affected. With this Carpenter of the *Africa* at sea, the knock-on effects on the workforce could have been quite significant. Although this shipwright-cum-pawnbroker may not have been a popular figure, his services may have provided some relief. However, in spite of the hardship of being paid only four times a year, the wages for a shipwright were considered to be reasonable for the period. In contrast, private shipyards might pay higher wages but no regular employment was guaranteed.

WAR AND PEACE

Keeping control of the numbers of shipwrights and their servants proved difficult during the middle decades of the eighteenth century. The major problems arose from the need to keep ships in service in wartime and the need to recruit and maintain an adequately skilled workforce. Apprentices were granted to men as an inducement to increase numbers at Plymouth Dockyard. Due to the remote location of the yard, the local supply of skilled men was limited and was only resolved by importing shipwrights from the Thames area after December 1747. However, when peace came at the end of the War of Austrian Succession a year later, Plymouth was heavily oversubscribed. The number of apprentice shipwrights was almost treble the permissible ratio of boys to men. By 1751, the ratio had reduced but was still more than double the requisite number. All the Royal Dockyards expanded throughout the period, overstretching both financial and physical resources. At times of peace, not only were large numbers of sailors laid off as ships were decommissioned, but also large numbers of artificers. As the Navy shrank, the work – and the money supply – shrank with it. Dockyard Description Books were part of the measures taken to limit expense by selecting the less able workers for discharge. The artificers of higher quality would be maintained to preserve skills and to keep in good order the ships laid up in ordinary.[27]

In a further measure to limit the ratio of apprentices to shipwrights, a decision was taken by the Board of Admiralty to order the Navy Board to remove servants from fifth- and sixth-rate ships in ordinary. This meant removing apprentices from carpenters assigned to the smaller vessels that were laid up. Warrants to that effect were issued in November 1750. This no doubt caused problems for young boys in the middle of their apprenticeships. After only fourteen months' service, the apprentice of Alexander McCleod was discharged on these orders. McCleod had been carpenter of the *Margate*,

which was sold. He and his servant were then entered in to Portsmouth Dockyard. McCleod was appointed to the sloop *Jamaica*, his servant being discharged in accordance with the Admiralty orders. He had taken on the boy and bound him apprentice in full agreement with the officers of Portsmouth Dockyard before these orders were issued. The Navy Board must have issued a warrant to that effect.

In McCleod's petition of 24 December 1750, he complained that twenty-four pounds a year was insufficient to bring up a family with three boys. He may have taken a pay cut with the transfer to the sloop. With the additional loss of wages for his apprentice he was feeling the pinch. McCleod was not pleased that he was legally bound by his servant's indentures, the terms and conditions of which he could no longer fulfil. He would have to continue training the boy and feed him without any wages from the Navy to pay for it. As a warranted officer of a ship in ordinary, McCleod had been continued in employment when many of his comrades would have been discharged. As the country was now at peace, money had to be saved. He had probably kept his job because of his family circumstances. However, the Navy Board could not comply with his request; a laconic note on the back of the letter reminded McCleod of the Admiralty orders. The Navy Board did not allow the boy to be re-appointed.[28]

In 1768, a full five years after the conclusion of the Seven Years War, measures to reduce costs affected Carpenters of fourth-rate ships. On 1 July, the Navy Board received a letter from six co-signatory Carpenters in Chatham Dockyard. They petitioned the Navy Board that they were paid an allowance of seventeen shillings and sixpence per month for their servants. These men had the expense of providing tools, which their counterparts in other ships were not obliged to provide. This seems contrary to the received practice that all masters in all trades were supposed to keep their servants in tools. Why this should be so is not known. The Carpenters informed the Board that their servants were in the latter half of their apprenticeships and therefore were performing mens' work. They asked for their servants to be allowed able seamens' pay to compensate for their masters' out-of-pocket expenses in buying tools. The Board's decision is not known, but as there are no notes on the letter by any of the Board clerks one can assume the answer was in the negative.[29]

CHARACTER BEFORE ABILITY

Most of the surviving documents concerning apprentice shipwrights' behaviour are of a negative nature. This is not surprising when one realises from whom these letters and reports originated. Most of the reports are from the Dockyard Commissioners (the most senior officers in charge) justifying their actions in doling out punishments without

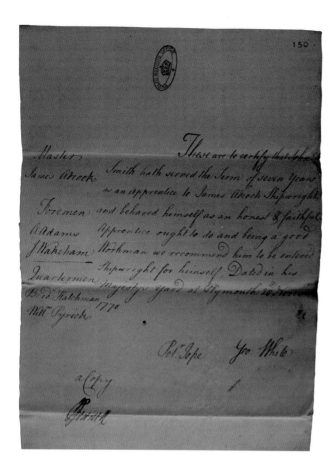

Figure 9. Certificate of John Smith, Plymouth Royal Dockyard. Dated 28 November 1770. National Archives, London: ADM106/1193/150.

obtaining prior permission. One of the most unusual cases involved a group of servants and an attempt to steal a boat for salvage money. According to Commissioner Richard Hughes' letter from Portsmouth Dockyard of 24 January 1750/1, shipwright Richard Shamman was being sued by three apprentice shipwrights. Hughes asked the Navy Board to pay Shamman's legal expenses. A secretary's annotation notes the Board agreement.[30] In John Shamman's letter, he and several others were rowing their boat which was handling badly. On beaching it, they discovered 'Several great Stones ty'd on to the lower Pintles of the Rother'.

Similar tampering occurred on two further occasions. Each time this happened, three apprentices in another boat made fun of Shamman and his crew, calling them 'old Double Bankers, Greyhounds, etc., and told us we were Clinkher'd and should be Clinker'd again at night'.[31] Shamman was far from being an old man: he was an able shipwright, aged thirty-one and with a good service record.[32] The boys eventually had their pay stopped, which would have caused financial loss to their masters. However, the boys served writs against Shamman to appear in court in Westminster. The Navy Board approved of the disciplinary action

taken and paid for Shamman's defence. The result of these actions is not known. The boys' masters were reprimanded and threatened with dismissal, along with their servants, if they did not intervene.[33]

Evidence of good behaviour can only be suggested at by the numbers of shipwrights who were entered in to the Dockyards after they had served their apprenticeships. On completion of his apprenticeship, a servant would be given his master's half of the indenture (providing the master had neither lost it nor sold it in the meantime). He would then ask at the Clerk of the Cheque's office for his certificate to be made out. The former servant would then take this to be signed by his officers. Figure 9 shows the certificate of John Smith of Plymouth Dockyard, issued 28 November 1770. This is a typical example of many such documents. It is interesting to note that this is qualitative and not quantitative. No mention of any shipwrights' abilities are mentioned, only how they behaved.

The certificate transcribes as follows:

> *These are to certify John Smith hath served the Term of seven years as an Apprentice to James Adcock Shipwright and behaved himself as an honest and faithful Apprentice ought to do and being a good Workman we recommend him to be entered Shipwright for himself; Dated in his Majesty's Yard at Plymouth 28th November 1770.*

This certificate bears the signatures of Smith's master, his foremen and quartermen, showing that Smith had worked in two different gangs during his time. In addition, he obtained two other witnesses to his behaviour on this document, a duplicate sent to the Navy Board, countersigned as such by the Commissioner. Smith could now be entered as a shipwright, collecting his own wages. Unfortunately, there is no evidence to indicate whether a warrant was issued to that effect.[34] The boy, now officially a man, could legally frequent taverns and theatres, play cards, marry and have children.

Whilst it is true that many shipwright apprentices were involved in several disturbances in the Royal Dockyards, the good behaviour seemed to outweigh the bad. However, the records that survive refute this when taken in isolation. The recorders were officers whose positions of authority were at stake. They had overall responsibility for the operation and organisation of the yards and had to justify their actions. These men could not only discipline the boys, but also the men to whom they were indentured. The most common offences were attempts to steal old lead or iron which could easily be concealed. The case of Richard Shamman and the attempted wrecking of a boat for salvage money is one of the more unusual cases.

Many people could take a strong drink every once in a while, but according to William Chandler's experiences, all three of his masters and their womenfolk could not. Poor anger management and personality clashes were the order of the day on many occasions. However, William preferred his first master when he was under the influence. When Richard Baker was drunk he was even-tempered; when he was sober he was fractious. In the confines of the forward cockpit of the *Sandwich*, where the Carpenter, Bosun and Gunner lived and worked, William found it hard to escape Baker's wrath and indignation.[35] Several times in the account of William's service in Portsmouth Dockyard he often described his life as harsh.

CONCLUSION

Biographical accounts of shipwrights and their apprentices are rare. The best example is this account of William Chandler, who served a total of twelve years in the Navy. Most of his account concerns how he lived as an apprentice shipwright in Portsmouth Dockyard. His living conditions were quite poor as he was passed from one bad master to another. What was most remarkable about William was how he kept his true identity secret throughout all his troubles. William Chandler was in fact Mary Lacy who ran away to sea disguised as a boy in 1759. Mary revealed her true sex in 1771, after she had served her apprenticeship. She may only have escaped suspicion by having several girlfriends; 'William' had a bit of a reputation! She resigned through ill health soon after she revealed her true identity. Mary successfully petitioned the Admiralty for a pension of twenty pounds a year for life. She apparently married Mr Slade, the Master Shipwright of Deptford Yard whom she had known in Portsmouth. Under the name of Mary Slade, she published her autobiography in 1773. She became a property developer and built a row of houses in Deptford High Street, many of which still survive.[36]

NOTES

[1] Stark, pp.125-167; Slade, pp.1-85. The author, born Mary Lacy, disguised herself as a man for a total of twelve years' naval service without being detected. William Chandler was her assumed name.

[2] Macleod, pp.285-287; Stephenson, pp.14-15.

[3] A carpenter in the language of the Navy Board meant a shipwright serving on board ship. Today we erroneously call them Ships' Carpenters to differentiate them from the other trade, known then as House Carpenters.

[4] Devon Record Office (hereafter D.R.O.): Item 4187M/E264: Indenture, Mr Alexander Peter & John Collings, 31 March 1768; 4187M/E265: Indenture, Mr Alexander Peter & Thomas Negus, 4 May 1771.

[5] D.R.O.: Item 4187M/E265 & E/266: Indentures, Mr Alexander Peter & Mr Line; Stephenson, pp. 33-34.

[6] Baugh, p.316; The National Archives, London: Navy Board In-Letters (hereafter, ADM106/item no./folio no.):

ADM106/1093/187.

[7] Stephenson, pp.11-20. Several volumes of Warrant Books survive for each dockyard. However, the sets are far from complete. Most indications of Navy Board instructions came from the annotations found on the original Navy Board In-Letters.

[8] McGovern, pp. 17-18 & 28. The original document is one of three Description Books prepared on the instructions of the Earl of Sandwich as a means of listing workmen by their ability. Men are listed as being 'well' or 'able', those men rated otherwise are not listed here but may have been recorded elsewhere for selection to be laid off. McGovern's work is an alphabetical transcription of the 1748 Description Book: ADM106/2976. Although catalogued as containing details for artificers at Deptford Yard only, it actually contains details for all the Dockyards and Roperies.

[9] D.R.O.: Items 4187M/E264 verso & E265 verso.

[10] Slade, pp.84-85.

[11] Slade, p.85.

[12] Slade, pp.85-86, 88, 101-102, & 105.

[13] Macleod, p.286; Knight, pp.179-180.

[14] Stephenson, p.17; The National Archives, London, ADM106/1079/456. This author's parentheses.

[15] Rodger, (2005), p.631.

[16] Anderson, (1924), p.59; Lavery, *passim*; Abell, pp.65-92.

[17] Slade, pp.89 & 107; Richardson, pp.266-267.

[18] Hattendorf, *et al*, pp.528-529. This reference is a transcription from ADM/B/153 Admiralty In-Letters, held at the National Maritime Museum, London.

[19] Richardson, pp.266-271.

[20] McGovern, p.95. There are fourteen Martins mentioned in this list, but no evidence to indicate if they were all related. Thomas Cox may have been discharged on his master's death or by the government cut-backs for which this list was prepared.

[21] ADM106/941/104.

[22] Stephenson, pp.32-33.

[23] Stephenson, pp.33-34; D.R.O.: 4187M/E266 & E267.

[24] Stephenson, pp.38-39; Richardson, p.269.

[25] Slade, pp.42 & 59.

[26] Slade, pp.122-135.

[27] Stephenson, pp.50-60; McGovern, pp.7-10.

[28] Stephenson, p.59; ADM106/1083/256.

[29] ADM106/1163/112.

[30] ADM106/1090/104.

[31] ADM10/1090/105. Rother is an old word for rudder. The boat would have been clinker-built. The boys are playing on words, implying that Shamman and his crew should be jailed for their bad rowing.

[32] McGovern, p.99. John Shamman was listed in 1748 as an able shipwright aged 29 with thirteen years' service.

[33] ADM106/1090/104 to /106 & /110; Stephenson, pp 27-29.

[34] ADM106/1193/150; Stephenson, p.22.

[35] Slade, pp.48-49.

[36] Guillery, pp.212-219.; Stark, pp.125-167.

NOTES ON SOURCES AND BIBLIOGRAPHY

Primary Sources in Manuscript

The National Archives, Kew, London, UK (formerly the Public Record Office)

Admiralty Papers: Navy Board In-Letters ADM106 series

Item No.	Signatories	Year
ADM106/941	M-O	1741
ADM106/1079	A-B	1750
ADM106/1083	I-O	1750
ADM106/1090	G-H	1751
ADM106/1093	P	1751
ADM106/1163	C	1768
ADM106/1193	S-Y	1770

The entire research used a total of 83 items dated between 1738 and 1770. Only those items containing folios used in this article are listed here.

National Maritime Museum, Greenwich, London, UK
Portsmouth Dockyard papers: Navy Board Warrant Books
POR/A/15 Warrants 23 March 1747 to 25 April 1749
POR/A/16 Warrants 27 April 1749 to 13 October 1752
POR/A/22 Warrants 16 October 1762 to 17 May 1765

Devon Record Office, Sowton, Exeter, UK
4187M Indentures of Alexander Peter, Carpenter, HMS *Mars*, 1768–1774
/E264 Apprentice Indenture of John Collings to Alexander Peter, 31 March 1768.
/E265 Apprentice Indenture of Thomas Negus to Alexander Peter, 4 May 1771.
/E266 Indenture of Alexander Peter to John Line, Esq., 12 March 1774.
/E267 Bond between Alexander Peter and John Line, Esq., 12 March 1774.
/E268 Letter of Alexander Peter to Mrs Line, undated.

Primary Sources in Print:

Richardson, S., *The Apprentice's Vade Mecum: or Young Man's Pocket-Companion*, London, 1726.

Slade, M., *The History of the Female Shipwright; to Whom the Government has granted a Superannuated Pension of Twenty Pounds per Annum, during her Life: Written by Herself*, London, 1773.

Lavery, B. (ed.), *Marine Architecture: or Directions for Carrying on a Ship*, New York, 1993.

McGovern, M.T. (ed.), *List of Workmen and Apprentices in His Majesty's Dockyards 1748: an alphabetical index transcribed from ADM106/2976 at the Public Record Office*, Southsea, 2002.

Secondary Sources:

Abell, Sir W., *The Shipwright's Trade*, Cambridge, 1948.

Anderson, R.C., 'Early Books on Shipbuilding and Rigging', *Mariner's Mirror*, Vol. 10 (1924), pp. 53-64.

Anderson, R. C., 'Eighteenth-Century Books on Shipbuilding, Rigging and Seamanship', *Mariner's Mirror*, Vol. 33 (1947), pp. 218-225.

Baugh, D.A., *British Naval Administration in the Age of Walpole*, Princeton, 1965.

Coats, A., 'Efficiency in Dockyard Administration 1660–1800: A Reassessment', *The Age of Sail: The International Annual of the Historic Sailing Ship*, Vol. 1 (London, 2002), pp. 116-132.

Haas, J. M., *A Management Odyssey: The Royal Dockyards, 1714–1914*, London, 1994.

Hattendorf, J.B., Knight, R.J.B., Pearsall, A.W.H., Rodger, N.A.M., Till, G., *British Naval Documents: 1204–1960*, Aldershot, 1993.

Guillery, P., 'The Further Adventures of Mary Lacy: "Seaman", Shipwright, Builder', *History Workshop Journal*, No. 49 (2000), pp. 212-219.

Knight, R.J.B., 'Sandwich, Middleton and Dockyard Appointments', *Mariner's Mirror*, Vol. 57 (1971), pp. 175-192.

Lane, J., *Apprenticeship in England 1600–1914*, London, 1996.

Macleod, N., 'The Shipwrights of the Royal Dockyards', *Mariner's Mirror*, Vol. 11 (1925), pp. 276-291.

Morriss, R., *The Royal Dockyards during the Revolutionary and Napoleonic Wars*, Leicester, 1983.

Morriss, R., *Naval Power and British Culture, 1760–1850*, Aldershot, 2004.

Richardson, H.E., 'Wages of Shipwrights in H.M. Dockyards', *Mariner's Mirror*, Vol. 33 (1947), pp. 265-274.

Rodger, N.A.M., *The Wooden World: An Anatomy of the Georgian Navy*, London, 1986.

Rodger, N.A.M., *The Command of the Ocean*, London, 2005.

Stark, S.J., *Female Tars: Women Aboard Ship in the Age of Sail*, London, 1998.

Stephenson, G.W.G., *Shipwright Apprentices in the Mid-Eighteenth Century*, unpublished MA Dissertation, University of Exeter 2006).

HMS *Bounty*

1:48 MODEL OF CAPTAIN BLIGH'S ARMED TRANSPORT

by John York

The history of the *Bounty* is well known. Films have been made, and books have been written, of her ill-fated voyage under Captain Bligh. Needless to say, I am not going into the historic facts, other than to say that the replica of the *Bounty*, built for the film *Mutiny of the Bounty* starring Mel Gibson as Fletcher Christian, was moored at the Australian National Maritime Museum for several years. It was privately owned at the time and made many daily cruises on the waters of Sydney Harbour. Sadly, it was recently sold and is now berthed in its new home, Hong Kong.

As a volunteer at the Maritime Museum, I demonstrate the art of model shipbuilding and found that having the ship moored at the Museum wharf of great help with regards the rigging requirements of the model. I was able to obtain a copy of the *Anatomy of the Ship* series on the *Bounty* by John McKay (Conway), which contained excellent plans, drawings and photographs.

THE MODEL

The model was built to a scale of 1:48 which made the overall length 920mm or approximately 3ft. I arrived at this scale by doubling the size of the plans 1.96 scale from the John McKay volume.

Above: Model showing close-up of stem head.

THE HULL

The frames were built up on a balsa wood mould and finished in the Admiralty style; that is, the frames below the waterline are exposed.

The finished size of the mould was arrived at by deducing the frames and plank dimensions for the mould on which to build the frames of the hull.

After the mould was sanded to shape slots were cut to receive the keel, but only part of the keel (the inner half); as well as the inner section of cutwater and sternpost.

After the above-mentioned work was carried out, stringer planks (one each side) were pinned into position to accept the

Below: Balsa wood mould or plug before shaping.

Below: Balsa wood mould now shaped. Also part keel and stringers marked to take frames.

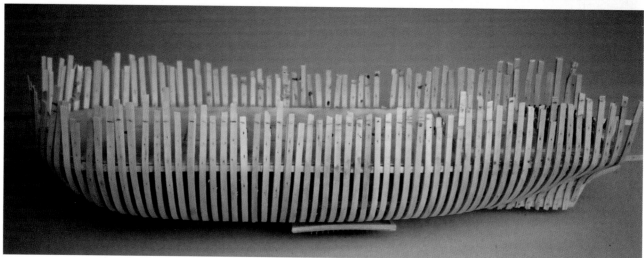

Above: Frames after taken from mould.

Below: Lower deck with potted breadfruit plants in place.

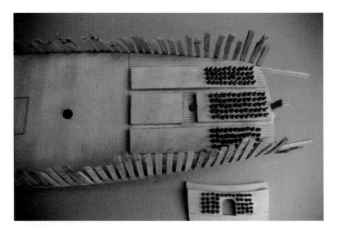

Below: Top deck ready for fitting.

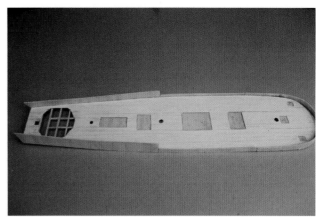

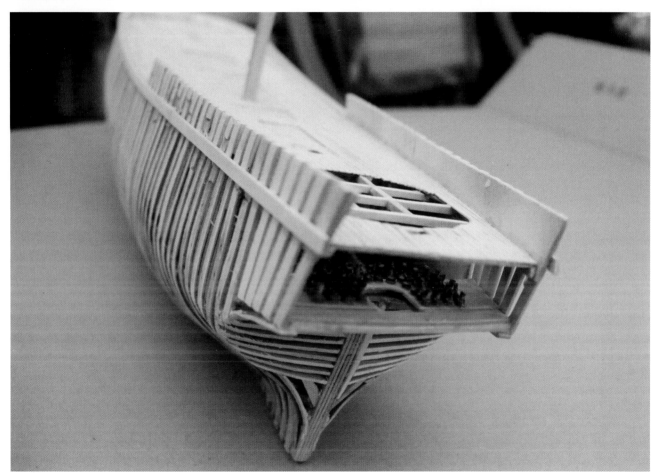

Above: Main deck now fitted showing cut on deck for viewing potted plants. Note the fashion pieces on stern in place.

lower deck later in the build. The two stringer planks are the only means to space and attach the frames to the upper part of the frame 'cage'.

In order to prevent the frames from adhering, the mould was covered with Glad Wrap, a thin layer of plastic film. This was wrapped around the mould prior to attaching the part keel, sternpost and cutwater, in addition to the two stringers.

I marked the positions on the keel and stringers, prior to

gluing the frames, to make sure the spacing would be correct when glued into place.

I made sure that the temporary pins in the stringers did not coincide with the frame positions as they have to be removed on completion when the frames are in place.

The frames are made up in two pieces of 1mm x 3mm lime wood planks or strips glued together and placed on the mould, keel and stringers. This must be done prior to the glue setting in

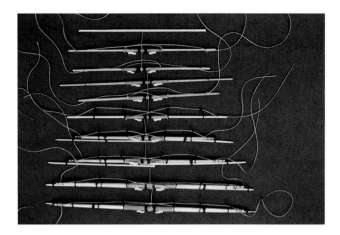

Above: The yards are made up ready for attachment to the masts. Note the copper wire used in parrels slightly deformed with side cutters, so as not to pull out.

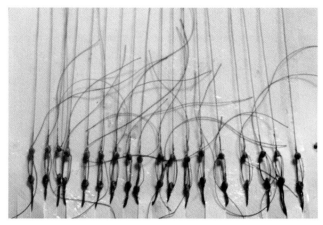

Above: Some of the shrouds and ratlines assembled ready to be placed on a tacky page from a photograph album to prevent tangling.

order to prevent them from flexing. It was helpful, I found, to soak the frame planks in hot water before fixing them into place, removing the excess water before doing so. It is also important to have the planks in close proximity to the mould before inserting the pins that hold them in place until the glue sets.

Most of the frames were continued right around the mould and glued to the half keel and stringer planks (the position for the lower deck). The bow frames towards the stern post, I handled as individual frame pieces, due to their different configuration. After the frames are in place and the glue has set, I lifted the frames, etc., from the mould.

No planking can be done until the lower deck and main deck are in place. The decks were cut from 2mm ply which also gives some rigidity prior to planking. To put this lower deck into place was quite a difficult job because of the tumblehome configuration of the hull frames, continuing to the top and, of course, the narrower opening.

Before this deck was fitted, I decided to put in place, in the after part of the ship, an area that was called the garden section. This area contained the potted breadfruit plants which were the main reason for the voyage. The plants were housed in this area because they needed light and also to be free of the salt spray. They were potted up in Tahiti and were to be transported to the Indies, but, as we know, they never reached their final destination. In fact, the area occupied by the plants was normally the quarters of the captain and the officers who were then moved accommodated amidships. The potted plants can be seen in the model through the opening in the top deck. With them in place, the deck was ready to be glued into position.

Putting this lower deck into the narrow space, and to bypass the now 'springy' frames, was quite a challenge. However, I lowered one side, then using two lengths of slippery card (from a photograph album), I was able to hold out the frames and slip the deck into place.

The next stage to be considered was the main deck. But before setting it in place, I made a stand in the form of a cradle to keep the hull build in a stable position. Openings were cut for the companionways and grills in addition to the cutaway section to display the breadfruit plants on the lower deck.

The deck was then planked with 2mm ply and a 2mm ply surround was glued to the internal part of the bulwark to attach and line up the frames. Some of the frames were held in place with crocodile clips while the glue was setting. Stringers were put in place for the main deck to sit on. The main deck, when added, was checked with a spirit level and then fitted in place.

Next, the hull was planked down to the waterline, starting from the bulwarks. After soaking the 5mm x 2mm planks in hot water, they were glued and temporarily held in place by pins; due to the fact that the cutwater had not yet been added I was able to carry the planning around the curve of the bow. When the planks were in place, I then added the cutwater, sternpost and the rest of the keel. Some filling between the gaps in the frames was carried out prior to this, before adding the additional part of the keel.

THE MASTS

Prior to stepping the masts, the three tops were made from wooden grating, the material cut to shape with appropriate size cutouts to surround the masts and made to accommodate the rigging. The edges of the tops are 1mm x 3mm, three walnut strips, laminated to the correct curves and 3mm x 2mm supports were put in place, as were the safety rails.

The crosstrees were made up from 2mm x 2mm and 3mm x 2mm walnut timber. Five mast caps were purchased and modified to suit.

I attached the yards to their appropriate positions with copper wire, holes being drilled in the yards and masts.

Above: Boats now completed with duck boards, frames, transoms and keels. Rowlock positions cut out.

Above: Showing deck layout forward.

Above: Mainmast detail.

A gap was left between the masts and the yards, and to create the illusion of parrels, a thin piece of leatherette was glued around the masts to resemble the collars. In addition, bands of black paint were applied to the side of the fixtures on the yards to replicate the iron work. Parrels are not in direct contact between the masts and yards, because to set sails, they have to clear the shrouds. The photograph on page 74 (top left) shows the complete set of yards, made mainly from bamboo cane.

A JIG FOR ATTACHING LANYARDS

This is a method I have developed recently after many years of struggling with the conventional method. It is quicker, easier and I think, more efficient.

After the shrouds are attached to the deadeyes, a jig can be made up quite easily from scrap timber to ease the task of fitting lanyard to pairs of deadeyes. A piece of plywood should have two holes drilled in it the diameter of the deadeyes being used, and spaced apart to suit the rigging of the model.

A centre slot is then cut to allow the pairs of deadeyes to be removed after the lanyards are in place. A couple of slots must also be cut to keep the shroud cordage in position. One deadeye could be attached to a part of the chainplate, doing so will not affect the procedure. The lanyard should now be threaded through the holes in the deadeyes. When this has been completed, the ends of the lanyard should be knotted together at the back to prevent it coming undone or slackening, thus upsetting the spacing of the deadeyes. These ends should not be trimmed off until immediately prior to attaching to the model.

If desired, the correct procedure can be carried on further by taking the remaining cordage and seizing to the top deadeye with a hitch. I suggest that, prior to attaching the cordage, put some glue on the ends to stiffen them. When dry, put an angle cut with scissors, or side cutters on the end. This will make threading the cord through the holes in the deadeyes much easier. It may sound a bit complicated, but in practice it is a quick and easy process.

After the shrouds are in place with deadeyes, a notched card is made initially for the mainmast shrouds. This will be used later for the foremast and the mizzen, cutting down the card to suit.

Before winding the ratline cordage on the card, spacers have to be added, just inward of the notches. This is to prevent glue from adhering to the card. Plenty of width should be left on the card in order to be able to turn it to the right position.

When ratlines are placed behind the shrouds they must be horizontal. Attaching the card with clips, the shrouds must be moved outwards slightly from the centre with pins, top and bottom. The reason will become clear later. Clips may not be necessary if the card is packed out.

All the crossover points have now to be glued together. The pointed end of a cocktail stick will be found very useful for applying the spots of glue. When the glue has dried, the ratlines can be cut from the card, taking out the pins and clips, and carefully removing the card.

The card will then be used for the mainmast port side, assuming that the starboard has just been completed. As the spacers are now on the wrong side of the card, they must be sliced off with a scalpel and put on the reverse side. The process can now be repeated for the other side. As spacers are now for the port side, the template will have to be used for the port side of the foremast first, cutting down the card if necessary.

The ratlines on the shrouds on the ship are attached to the front of the shrouds with eye splices and clove hitches, but the method outlined above is satisfactory for use on smaller model ships (and also looks the part). A small dab of paint

FIFE RAILS

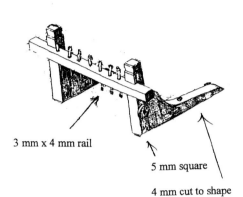

3 mm x 4 mm rail

5 mm square

4 mm cut to shape

PIN RAILS

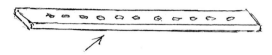

3 mm x 5 mm rail

cut and drilled to length

HORIZONTAL WINDLASS

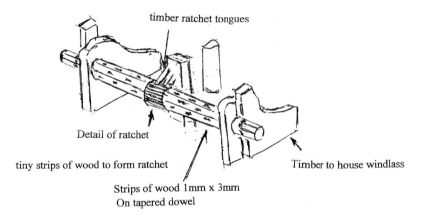

timber ratchet tongues

Detail of ratchet

tiny strips of wood to form ratchet

Strips of wood 1mm x 3mm
On tapered dowel

Timber to house windlass

BOATS

Boats were stowed on a pair of cradles, the
Lower, 23 foot launch, carvel built, sits in
The cradle

The 20 foot cutter, clinker built, sits above
The launch.

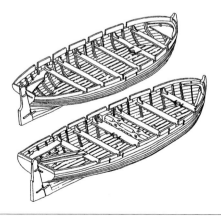

ANCHORS

Anchors are made up from bamboo cane (kebab sticks)

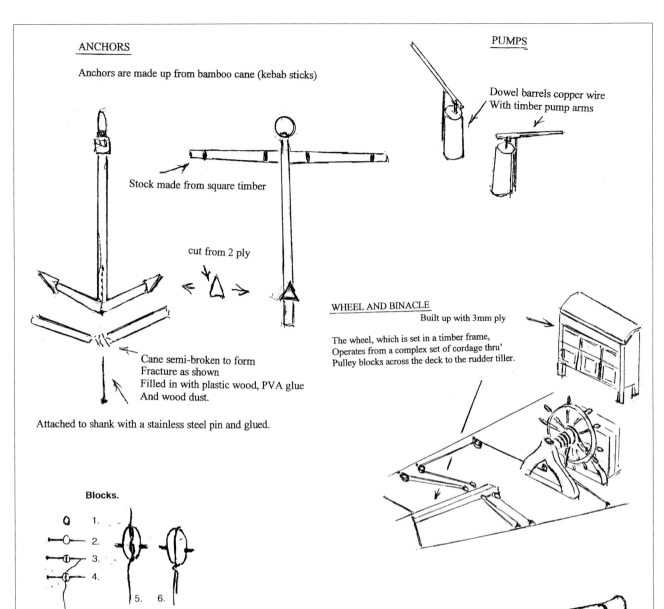

Stock made from square timber

cut from 2 ply

Cane semi-broken to form
Fracture as shown
Filled in with plastic wood, PVA glue
And wood dust

Attached to shank with a stainless steel pin and glued.

PUMPS

Dowel barrels copper wire
With timber pump arms

WHEEL AND BINACLE
Built up with 3mm ply

The wheel, which is set in a timber frame,
Operates from a complex set of cordage thru'
Pulley blocks across the deck to the rudder tiller.

Blocks.

1.
2.
3.
4.
5. 6.

1. Small ball of plastic wood pinched
   to shape.
2. Pin put through centre before it
   hardens.
3. Groove scored round block.
4. Cord tied on and secured with
   small touch of PVA glue.
5, 6. Enlarged sketch showing
   placement of knot, depending on
   purchases.

CONSTRUCTION OF GUN CARRIAGES AND CANNON BARRELS

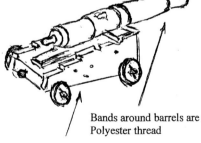

The cannon barrel is a piece of dowel shaped
And with holes drilled at each end. The rear
End, the pommelion, is a belaying pin glued
In the hole

Bands around barrels are
Polyester thread

Gun carriage 3mm ply

Carriage wheels are cast in a cut section of
A drinking straw. The casting medium is fine
Wood dust mixed with PVA glue.

The gun carriage wheels are glued in place to
The carriage. When dry, the axle holes are
Drilled to fix the axles

PARREL ASSEMBLY

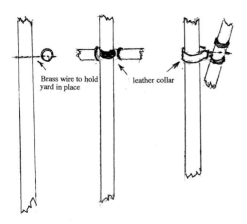

Brass wire to hold
yard in place

leather collar

Bearing in mind that these yards will
Not be raised or lowered on the model

POT PLANTS

Pieces of distressed cane
Are the plants (kebab sticks)

Small wooden washers are
The pots.

NOTE

Only part of the pots are shown
As most of the pots is in a recessed

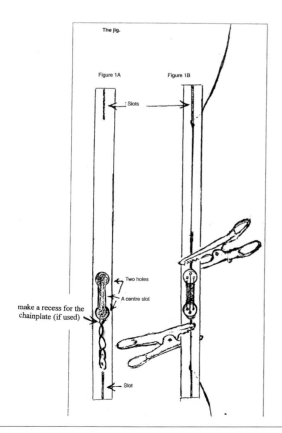

The jig.

Figure 1A   Figure 1B

: Slots

Two holes

A centre slot

make a recess for the
chainplate (if used)

Slot

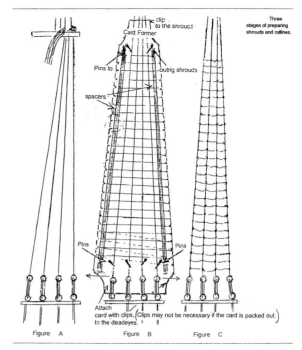

clip
to the shrouds

Card Former

Pins to

outrig shrouds

spacers

Three
stages of preparing
shrouds and ratlines.

Pins

Pins

Attach
card with clips. (Clips may not be necessary if the card is packed out.)
to the deadeyes.

Figure   A   Figure   B   Figure   C

Spacers are half-round kebab
Sticks..This is to prevent glue
From sticking to the card template.

HATCHES AND COMPANION WAYS

Companion way 'steps' are cut from
1mm x 3mm lime wood

Companion rails are made up from copper wire

CAPSTAN

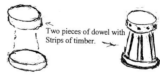

Two pieces of dowel with
Strips of timber.

Centre tapered dowel

CHAINPLATES

This section of copper wire squeezed with
Round nosed pliers to form a waist, then
Flattened, soldered and drilled to take
Simulated bolts

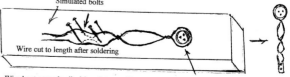

Wire cut to length after soldering

Wire bent around nails driven into an off cut
Piece of timber

Wire closed around deadeyes

mixed to the colour of the cordage was put on each crossover. The shrouds and ratlines above the mains are treated in the same manner, and with a new card template.

The finished effect will look just like a knot. The reason for the spacing out of the shrouds can be appreciated because there is some slack after taking out the pins (see Figure on preparing shrouds and ratlines on page 79).

By damping the now finished shroud (complete with ratlines) a slight sag can be produced in the ratlines by running a finger and thumb down the assembly, thereby imparting even more realism. Damping the cordage does not soften the glue (even though PVA has been used here), because the tiny spot of paint applied to each knot was oil-based, so they were waterproofed.

Incidentally, the shrouds around the mast are left glued into place, but leaving uncut tails on them, to be trimmed evenly. Then, if a shroud or shrouds come loose, by just wetting the PVA glue they can be pulled up tight again by these ends. Being trimmed evenly, it will be evident which cordage has slackened; it will be the shortest in the bunch.

If close contact between the shrouds and ratlines prior to being glued is not evident, place a pad of soft tissue paper at the back of a card template and mast, this will bulk it out. It cannot be emphasised too strongly that the ratlines must be in contact with the shrouds and spaced correctly prior to being glued. Only when the glue has dried should the wad of packing be removed.

RIGGING BLOCKS

Most of the blocks were made from plastic wood, a compound made of wood dust (Not sawdust) taken from the bag of a belt sander, and then mixed with PVA wood glue. As a matter of interest, I have tried commercial plastic wood and it does not mould or stay together.

THE BOATS

Moulds were made from balsa wood to form the plugs for the 23ft carvel-built launch and the 20ft cutter which was clinker built. The moulds were covered with kitchen Glad Wrap to prevent the planking from adhering. The planks were held in place with pins.

After removing the hulls from the moulds, keels and transoms were fitted, slots for the oars were cut and frames and thwarts and so on were added (planks used for building boats were 1mm x 3mm). Floor boards were cut to shape and lines were ruled to simulate planking. Frames were cut using 1mm x 2mm lime wood.

Rudder hinges made from brass strips were attached to the stern of each boat. Provision was made to the launch providing racks to allow alignment of the keel of the cutter to stay in place. Slings were attached to the boats and then attached to the pulley blocks.

RAILS AROUND BULWARKS

The rails were cut out oversize from 2mm ply and marked to the shape required. I then applied clear tape to each side of the shape to be cut to prevent the ply from chipping away while the cutting process was taking place.

When the cut outs were completed, the tape was removed from the underside and the rails were then glued in place. When the glue was set, the rails were sanded to the correct size and the remaining tape was removed from the top of the rail.

STERN DECORATIONS (FIGUREHEAD AND LANTERNS)

These were purchased, then modified for the stern and to suit the scale of the model. Using the decoration as a model, I recast them in Sculpey Modellers clay changing the shape to suit, before baking them in the oven, a process also used for the name plate.

CHAIN PLATES

These were made from copper wire and formed in a jig in the form of nails set in a piece of hardwood. The ends of the formed sections were flattened, then soldered and drilled to take simulated bolt heads when attached to the hull.

REFERENCES

McKay, John, *The Armed Transport Bounty*, *Anatomy of the Ship* Series (Revised Edition), Conway.

Cargo Liner *Benloyal*

A NOTABLE ADDITION TO THE BENLINE FLEET

by B. Baldwin

Among the many shipping companies that were formed, grew and flourished, during that period when Great Britain dominated the oceans of the world, not only with the Royal Navy but also with her merchant fleet, was a family business founded in 1839 by William and Alexander Thompson in the city of Edinburgh. Originally in the building industry they also operated ships through the adjacent port of Leith, bringing building materials from the Mediterranean to supply their sites in the city. This side of the business grew rapidly until they were not only handling cargo but also increasing numbers of passengers in well-appointed elegant vessels, frequently with clipper bows and beautifully panelled deckhouses, earning them the sobriquet 'The Leith Yachts'. In 1859 they made the first voyage to Singapore and China,

an area of the world which was to become increasingly important to them for the remainder of the nineteenth century and into the early years of the twentieth century. During this period, they established a reputation for a fast reliable service carrying cargo and passengers to an increasing number of ports in East Asia. It was not until 1919 that Ben Line Steamers Ltd was formed, a name that for the next fifty years was to be renowned for its service and reliability.

In the 1950s the perceived wisdom of most shipping companies operating cargo liners was that 16 knots was the most economical speed to operate a ship over long distances.

There were faster ships, but most charged premium rates for express service to the Far East. Ever conscious of their reputation and determined to stay at the forefront of the

Photograph 1. The finished model ready for its glass case.

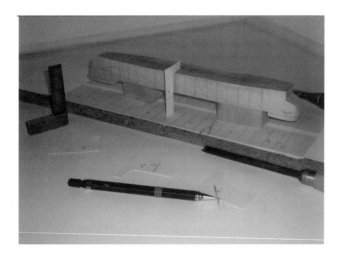

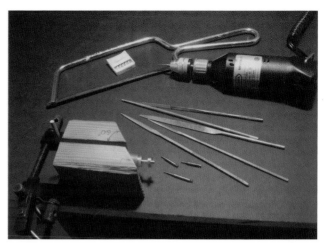

Photograph 2. Hull arrangement along with some of the card templates and tools used to produce an accurately carved hull.

Photograph 3. The propeller clamped between two wooden blocks with some of the tools used to shape the blades.

field, the company approached Charles Connell & Co. Ltd of Scotstoun Glasgow, a company who had built a number of ships for them in the past, to design and build a vessel capable of servicing their Far Eastern ports with an economical speed of 20 knots. The resultant ship, No. 489, was launched in 1959 to be named *Benloyal*, following a long held company tradition of naming their ships after Scottish mountains. Some 503ft between perpendiculars and 550ft overall with 72ft beam and 11,400gt, the slender hull had a long fine entry more akin to a destroyer than a cargo liner. With this hull form and propelled by two steam turbines driving a

single screw she was well able to achieve her designed service speed, but would she also achieve the required economy at that speed to be profitable? Many ship operators watched with some scepticism. She was to suffer the ignominy of shedding a propeller blade on her maiden voyage causing her to limp into her destination port where she found another *Ben* ship with a spare propeller. This was modified and fitted, enabling her to return at reduced speed to her home port for repairs. Despite this somewhat less than glorious debut she was soon back at sea proving herself and demonstrating that Connell knew their stuff when it came to

Photograph 4. The hull with hatches and the main deck house added.

building ships, and also causing the sceptics to lay down ships with a similar performance in order to remain competitive. During the 1960s and 1970s sea transport underwent dramatic changes, with the rapid expansion of containerisation. Ships like *Benloyal*, unsuitable for modernisation to carry containers, became more and more difficult to operate profitably, and in 1978 after a relatively short life of nineteen years this beautiful ship was sent to Korea to be scrapped.

HULL

I first became aware of *Benloyal* while leafing through a book of pictures painted by Robert Lloyd the well-known marine artist. Her sleek grey hull, with white superstructure topped by a yellow funnel made her immediately stand out from the rest of the ships depicted, beautifully painted as they all were. An enquiry to Glasgow University Archives, who hold the archives of Charles Connell & Co. Ltd brought forth a ⅛in = 1ft General Arrangement and Rigging drawings along with a ¼in = 1ft Hull Lines drawing. I do find this organisation a pleasure to deal with; they are most helpful and obliging. The ⅛in = 1ft hull sections were traced directly on to an A3 sheet of white paper, which was just large enough. Also on the sheet, two clear marks were made 12½in apart, 50ft at this scale. This was reduced 50 per cent using a photocopier to ⅛

in = 1ft, then again to ¹⁄₁₆ in = 1ft, and thereafter by small increments until the two marks were exactly 1in apart, thereby giving a scale of 50ft = 1in or 1:600, the scale I normally work in. The side elevation and deck plans were then

Photograph 6. Forecastle.

reduced to the same scale using pencil, compass, and normal drawing reduction techniques. An excellent coloured aerial photograph was obtained from FotoFlite of Ashford, Kent showing the ship under way.

With the reduced drawings to hand, a block of lime wood, cut to the outlines of the hull, was produced using card templates to check the accuracy of the hull shape as work proceeded on forming the plan, side elevation and shear. This in turn was marked with numbered station lines to correspond with the positions of the hull sections on the drawing, then secured to a building board similarly marked, the two sets of lines being aligned precisely. Photograph 2 shows the arrangement along with some of the card tem-

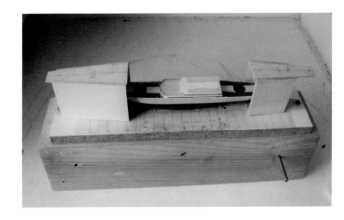

Photograph 7. Covers are used to protect work already completed.

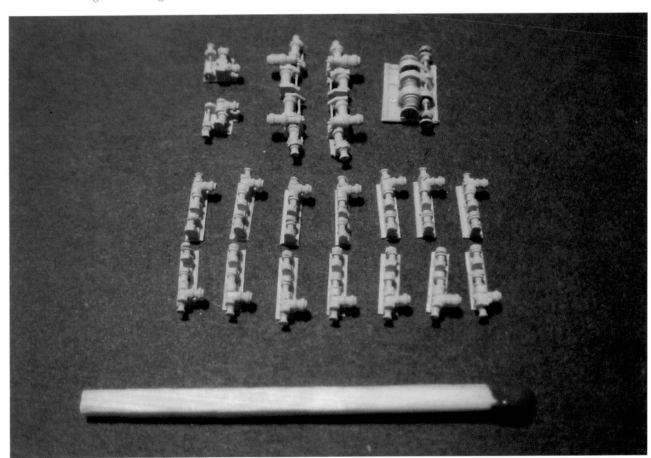

Photograph 8. The complex deck machinery.

plates and tools used to produce an accurately carved hull.

Bristol board, a very high quality card, 0.010in (0.25mm) thick was recessed into the hull block to form the flare of the bulwarks around the bow, continuing around the rest of the hull and poop deck where it projected 0.020in (0.5mm) above the top edge of the block forming a recess. Into this, the painted deck card would later be fitted. At this stage the anchor recesses were carved, and a hole for the propeller tail shaft drilled before the hull was given six coats of Humbrol matt white paint and, twenty-four hours after the last coat had been applied, sanded to a smooth finish. The surface of the hull was ready for painting, but this could not be carried

out until the bulwarks on the main deck had been fitted along with the propeller and the rudder. The former were cut from Bristol board complete with their clearing (wash) ports, pre-painted matt white and glued directly to the top of the aforementioned 0.020in projection around the hull.

Producing propellers for miniature models is never an easy task. The one fitted to *Benloyal* has four blades, is 0.40in (10mm) diameter, and making it from anything other than brass simply does not look right. The material used is ½in (12.5mm) diameter turning quality brass rod. A blank of the correct diameter and thickness is turned on to this, then clamped between two wooden blocks as is shown in Photograph 3. Saw cuts, parallel to the inclined face are made at 90-degree intervals around the blank. These are then opened out using the needle files, burrs, emery cloth, string impregnated with Brasso (metal polish) and a multitude of other devices to finish up with, hopefully, four polished, correctly spaced blades, identical in shape, profile, and pitch. It is a long but never tedious task. The rear cone is then turned to shape and the portion behind the blades reduced to the diameter of the propeller shaft. Once completed the component can be parted off and the shaft glued into the hole in the hull, the pre-painted rudder fitted and painting of the hull can proceed.

Paint colours for the hull were:

Bulwarks around the bow, the weather deck, and the area around the poop deck – white
Above the waterline – Humbrol 147 grey
Boot topping – Humbrol 105 green
Underwater – 3 parts Humbrol 186 mixed with 2 parts Humbrol 60

All coats were thinned using 30 per cent enamel thinners with several coats of each being laid on with a soft brush.

The dividing lines between the colours are kept sharp by using very thin masking tape. With painting complete, the pre-painted card decks on the forecastle, poop and main deck were cut to shape and fitted into the recesses described earlier. The unusual dull brown colour of the decks, which was produced by mixing a number of colours together, replicates the bituminous-based anti-corrosive dressing used by the company on the decks of many of their ships. I am often asked what size paintbrush I use to paint the ship's name and port of registration on to the hull. The answer is, I do not; each letter, around 0.040in (1mm) tall is formed using sometimes several pieces of painted wire laid on to a small area pre-coated with clear matt enamel paint.

With the addition of hatches and the main deck house the model had reached the stage shown in Photograph 4, allowing more detailed work to be carried out on both the forecastle and the poop deck (Photographs 5 and 6). This delicate work required protection during subsequent operations, provided by the covers shown in Photograph 7. An interesting challenge during the making of a model cargo liner such as this is the production of deck machinery, in this case twenty cargo winches of three different types plus the anchor windlass (Photograph 8). In the latter case, the cable wheels and brake drums were all turned from brass rod, integral with the shaft, then mounted on to the base with

Photograph 9. Showing midship area details.

appropriate bearing side-plates. The lay shaft for the warping drums is a length of 0.015in (0.4mm) diameter wire fitted between its own bearing plates with the drums stuck to the outside face. Cargo winches follow a similar sequence with the drive motors and gearboxes, also turned from brass,

glued at 90 degrees to the main shaft. As can be imagined, some of the parts are quite small, a warping drum for instance can be 0.030in (0.75mm) diameter and about the same in length, requiring special measures when parting off in order not to lose it. In an effort to avoid this, a short length

Photograph 11. The cargo cranes just abreast No. 5 hatch.

Photograph 12. The poop deck and after mast house; note the heavy lift derrick serving No. 5 hatch.

Photograph 13. A view of the forecastle showing the windlass and cable stoppers.

Photograph 14. This illustrates well the fine entry of the hull. Letters in the ship's name are 0.040in (1mm) high.

Photograph 15. View of stern showing the propeller and rudder.

of ⅛in diameter brass tube is pushed over the component and up to the parting tool to catch it as it drops off. But even this it not always effective, ending not infrequently in a fruitless search through swarf on the cross slide.

The centre island was quite straight forward. Decks were planked with holly, a technique I have described in a previous article (*Model Shipwright* 122), while the deck houses were cut from lime, the edges being faced with pre-painted Bristol board pierced with portholes or windows glazed from behind. Deckhouses of *Ben* ships were a little unusual. I mentioned in the introduction the beautiful panelling of the Leith Yachts; this tradition, of which the crews were extremely proud, was carried on even with the advent of steel deck houses. The crew applied repeated coats of varnish to the white paint, which eventually took on the appearance of light brown wood, whereupon the surface would be divided into panels using a dark brown paint; even the corners of the individual panels would carry a thistle emblem. This can be seen in Photograph 9. Mast houses, with masts, winches, handrails and rigging were completed before being fitted to the model. Note the two cargo cranes just abreast No. 5 hatch (Photograph 11). Work around the bridge and boat deck involving gravity davits, radar scanner, VHF aerial and many other very small

components was intricate and time consuming but very enjoyable. Finally, rigging of the masts and derricks was undertaken using 0.002in (0.0mm) tinned copper wire pre-painted with Humbrol 98.

When completed (around 700 hours over a period of 18 months) the model was mounted on two turned brass pillars and sealed inside a glass case of English chestnut finished with beeswax.

The model was awarded a gold medal and the Peter Jackson trophy at the 2008 exhibition of the Society of Model Shipwrights, a gold medal and the Prothero Thomas cup at the 2008 Model Engineering Exhibition at Ascot, and a Highly Commended at the 2009 Harrogate Model Engineering Exhibition.

REFERENCES.
Strachan, Michael, *The Ben Line* (ISBN 0 85955 187 3).

Lloyd, Robert, *The British Merchant Navy, Images and Experiences* (ISBN 1 901703 45 2).

Glasgow University Archives.

FotoFlite Ashford, Kent.

Miniature Handrails

AND DECK LADDERS

by B. Baldwin

HANDRAILS

The manufacture of handrails for miniature ship models to a scale of 1:600 (1in = 50ft) using fine wire, is not a new concept. It has been described previously both in *Model Ship-wright* and other publications. The method of winding wire, at the correct pitch, around a wooden frame in one direction to form the stanchions, then again at 90 degrees, to form the rails is simple and adequate for short lengths of rail in small quantities. However, this basic frame has its limitations when faced with the need to produce multiple lengths of rail, perhaps up to 10in (250mm) long as might be the case for the model of a passenger liner. It is difficult to maintain sufficient tension in the wire while winding on the stanchions, resulting in them laying at different heights and causing problems when applying adhesive to the stanchion/rail joint, where the two components must be in contact to achieve a capillary action for the adhesive. Even the smallest gap will result in an unsightly blob of glue.

To overcome these problems I have developed, over time, an adjustable frame capable of handling three lengths of rail up to 10in long with the stanchion wires held at uniform height and tension. This has resulted in an improvement in the appearance of the finished item and a considerable reduction in rejections. Photograph 1 shows the frame in its entirety; the two ends are firmly secured to one long side frame, the second side is joined to the ends by clamping screws through adjustable slots and can be forced away from the other side under the influence of the four long screws. A bridging block can be moved lengthwise, in steps of ½in (12mm), depending upon the length of rail required, while a second block, also adjustable, holds a length of dowel, just visible through the gap, enabling the frame to be held in a vice at a suitable angle whilst the work is carried out. Along each side are strips of wood, standing proud above the frame, carrying slots at the correct pitch for the stanchions; with steel pins 0.030in (0.75mm) diameter set at regular intervals down the edges. The fixed end is furnished with four 0.020in (0.5mm) diameter pins for each length of rail, two 0.080in (2mm) apart, the finished height of the rail, and two 0.10in

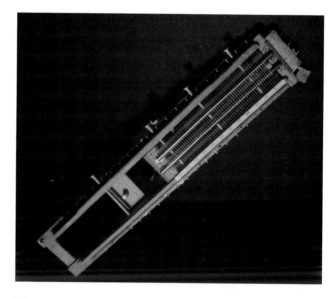

Photograph 1. Adjustable frame for handrails.

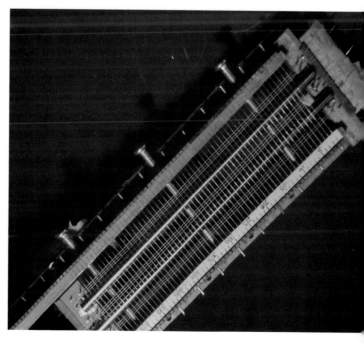

Photograph 2. Detail of the working area.

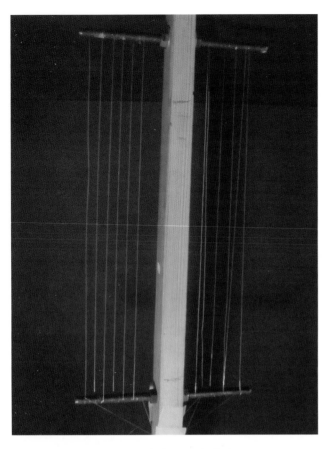

Photograph 3. Frame for painting handrail wire.

(2.5mm) apart. The adjustable bridging block is similarly equipped. One side also carries a graduated strip corresponding to the pitch of the stanchions. Between the end and the bridging block, run two precision steel rods each secured by adhesive. These are replaced each time the frame is set for a different length, Photograph 2 shows these features.

Stanchions are loaded on to the frame in the following manner. The clamps on the adjustable side frame are slackened, the tension screws backed off and the side moved in as far as possible before being re-clamped. A 4ft (1.3m) length of 0.005in (0.125mm) tinned copper wire is tied to a steel pin at the end of the side frame, the short free end being attached to the frame by superglue to prevent any slippage. The wire is then taken through the first slot, over the steel rods, which are slightly higher than the slots, and through the slot directly opposite, round an adjacent pin, back through the next slot, across the rods, through a slot, round a pin and so on until the required number of stanchions are in place. After the final stanchion, the free end of the wire is wound several times around an adjacent pin and secured to the frame with glue. At this stage, despite tension being kept on the wire during winding, the stanchions will not be even and taut. To achieve this, the clamps are slackened, the tension screws are wound in, forcing the side plates apart and tensioning the wires until they are evenly spaced, and being in contact with the steel rods, all at exactly the same height, before being re-clamped.

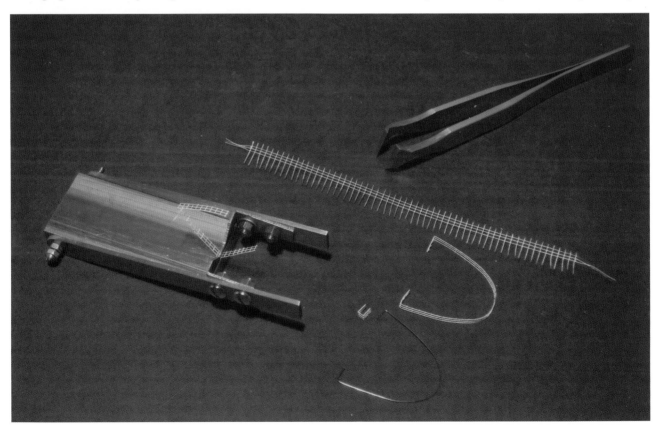

Photograph 4. Tools for forming handrails.

Photograph 5. Three axes manipulator.

Photograph 6. Manoeuvring a section of rail into position.

Photograph 7. The table saw.

Photograph 8. Jig for cutting treads.

Each stanchion can now be painted in the areas where the rails will cross it. I use white gloss enamel, which gives a better appearance than matt, but of course, the colour will depend upon the requirements of the model.

After a 24-hour period to allow the paint to dry thoroughly the rails can be laid on. These are made from 0.004in (0.1mm) diameter tinned copper wire pre-painted on a simple frame shown in Photograph 3. A number of lengths of wire, depending on the number of rails required, are cut from the frame; some ships have three, some four, most passenger liners have five, and joined together at one end. These are hooked over a pin in the end face of the bridging block and secured with a spot of glue. On the chamfered face of both the bridging and end block is a length of double-sided sticky tape. The first rail is taken round the outside of the guide pin, through the gap between the dimensioning pins, along the length of stanchions, between the end dimensioning pins, outside the guide pin, pulled tight, and pressed onto the sticky tape. It is then secured firmly by sticking a small piece of masking tape on top of it. If the prototype has a wooden top rail this first run can be made from 0.010in (0.25mm) wire painted brown. The bottom rail follows a similar mirror-image route. With both rails tight and well secured, it is wise to stick them to the first and last stanchion using superglue. This can be applied in minute quantities using the point of a needle. A bead of adhesive is dropped on

Photograph 9. Sequence of making the ladder.

to a flat surface, the point of the needle dipped into it and applied to the joint. If the two components are in contact the adhesive will, using capillary action, run between them forming an invisible joint. However, the adhesive will only remain workable for a few minutes. The intermediate rails can now be laid on and secured in a similar manner before completing the other two sets of rails on the frame. All the remaining joints can be glued using Humbrol clear enamel thinned with 25 per cent thinners. Each joint is touched in turn using a 4/0 brush, as the work progresses the graduated strip down the side is used to mark the point at which the brush needs replenishing, allowing the restart to be at the same point. All joints being complete, the assembly should be left for a least 24 hours to dry.

Having made the set(s) of handrails, the next sequence of operations is to cut them from the frame, divide them into the correct lengths, before forming them into shapes to fit around the various decks. The first is accomplished using the end cut wire snips shown in Photograph 4: each length is cut from the frame leaving a length of stanchion above and below the rails. These will later be trimmed flush with the top rail and around 0.010in (0.25mm) from the bottom rail using

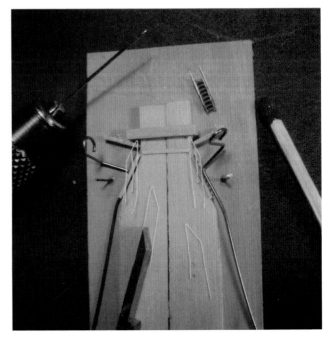

Photograph 10. Jig for mounting ladder handrails.

a sharp scalpel. Each individual length of rail, however, should have one or two stanchions left projecting above the top rail to facilitate handling while positioning it on the model. Straight lengths of railing are relatively easy to handle, just being cut to length and trimmed, the stanchion extension being gripped by tweezers before being moved into position on the model. Bends of 90 degrees are accomplished using a miniature press bender, the rail being correctly positioned above the groove in the brass block before the blade is gently lowered until the correct angle of the bend is achieved. Making a soft copper wire template first, then gently moulding the rail to suit, forms shapes that are more complex. A return bend, such as would be used around the top of a companionway can be formed using two 90-degree bends. Sections of rail can be manoeuvred into position on the model, using the three-axis manipulator shown in Photographs 5 and 6, before being secured using either superglue or clear enamel. The manipulator comprises two small machine tool slides bolted together at 90 degrees for the X and Y axes, with a standard scribing block affixed to the top supplying the Z axis. The latter mounts a brass block capable of gripping the tweezers.

Employing these techniques has greatly improved the appearance of handrails, reducing damage, and ultimately rejects, during forming and fitting.

DECK LADDERS

Another component required in the construction of a ship model is the deck ladder. On a cargo ship there may be around fifteen, but on a passenger liner there may be more than double this number. To manufacture identical units at a scale of 1:600, careful thought must be given to both materials and technique. A standard ladder would be a little over 3ft (1m) wide, with the treads pitched at 8in, and some 7in deep. Manually placing treads between the strings at this size with any degree of consistency is impossible; therefore, other methods had to be evolved. The technique is based on a small table saw, using a saw blade 1in (25.4mm) diameter x 0.020in (0.50mm) thick, with adjustable depth of cut, and incorporating a moving fence (Photograph 7). I am not sure if a similar device is available on the market as I made this one myself but any saw table with these facilities capable of running a 0.020in thick blade would suffice. Four pieces of Castello box, 1.125in x 0.312in x 0.025in (28.4mm x 8mm x 0.625mm) are cut, painted with thinned Humbrol clear matt enamel, and when dry painted the finished colour of the ladder. A fifth piece, the same dimensions, but 0.050in thick is placed against the angled face of the jig shown in Photograph 8. This face is at the same angle to the direction of motion, as the finished ladder will be to the deck. The four blanks, when dry, are then placed against this and held in place using a packing strip and a toolmaker's clamp. The depth of cut is set to 0.050in (1.25mm), and with the fence set and the saw running quite slowly, the first cut is made as close as possible to the right-hand side. When this cut is complete, the fence is advanced 0.030in (0.75mm) and a second cut made, the fence advanced and so on until nine cuts have been completed, this will produce eight treads. The fence is then advanced two pitches, and the procedure repeated. At the end of the second nine cuts the fence is again advanced two pitches and another nine cuts made. Twelve sets of tread have now been formed, four blanks with three sets on each. After removal from the jig, each blank is given another coat of matt enamel to stabilise the treads, which at this stage are very delicate, and when dry the 0.025in x 0.010in x 1.125in outer string is glued in place using dilute PVA. With the glue dry, the fence is set to cut the treads from the blank, using a 0.010in thick blade in the saw, leaving both strings of equal width. Photograph 9 illustrates the whole sequence. The sides of the strings and the treads can now be painted the correct colour using thinned paint. Having cut the ladders to length, they are ready to receive the 0.005in (1.125mm) diameter pre-painted wire handrails, which are formed, using finger pressure, around the steel former shown in Photograph 10. Also shown in this photograph is the jig used to mount the right- and left-hand rails on to ladders using super glue applied by the needle-point technique. Note how the ladder is held in the jig by spring wire clamps.

Much of the work described is very small and delicate requiring a bright light, steady hand, and a binocular magnifier of x3 magnification, or on occasions, a watchmaker's eye glass. However, I find it to be one of the most satisfying elements in the making of a miniature ship model.

27ft Naval Whaler

CLINKER BOAT CONSTRUCTION

by R. Burnham

I have outlined my interest in nineteenth-century naval pulling and sailing boats in previous articles on the construction of a 30ft Naval Gig (see *Model Shipwright* 134, 137 and 140). The 27ft whaler, Montague pattern model, is the second in a series of three. The third is planned to be the 32ft Cutter (lifetime permitting – the Gig took four years and the whaler two up until now). I served my apprenticeship on naval whalers in the 1950s so it is good to have another go, albeit in small scale.

The 27ft naval whaler is the longest serving wooden seaboat, dating from the latter half of the nineteenth century when they were basic whaleboats lightly rigged and without centre boards. Rear Admiral Victor Montague, Earl of Sandwich, was responsible for much of the modifications within the service leading to the design now known as the 'Montague rig whaler' which served the Royal Navy so well from approx 1916 until the 1960s. These were built under contract by dozens of small boatyards around the country, in two Marques the 27ft Type K and the 25ft Type L.

By the late 1930s they were built with an extra strake in the hull totalling fourteen planks per side, which rendered the use of portable washboards unnecessary. They were gradually phased out with the introduction of the so-called three-in-one, which had a Flat twin Enfield engine installed. They were not a success, too heavy to row or sail well. The stern used to sink badly under power, and if power was shut off too quickly, were prone to swamping with the stern wave catching up. The three-in-one boats were followed by the introduction of the Double diagonal motor whalers, which were better but still too heavy. These were the last boats to have provision for oars and sail. Various types of motor boats were then issued.

The expression 'sea boat' was used to denote the boat ready for launching at a moments notice. This was achieved with the mother vessel still underway although with much reduced speed. The whaler was fitted with 'Robinson's Disengaging Gear' comprising two tumbling hook blocks, so connected with a release line as to tumble simultaneously on the release of the line by the coxswains timing, thus dropping the boat into the water at the correct moment.

CONSTRUCTION

I build to a scale of ¾in = 1ft giving a length of 20¼in; this allows me to follow full-size building practice very closely.

I was very lucky to obtain sight of an original contractor's specification, which I had not seen since my apprenticeship, from a friend, who kindly allowed me to make a copy. This made things much easier as all dimensions, schedules and plans are given.

CENTRE WORK

I re-drew the plans to the ¾in scale. Body sections were transferred to thin plywood, forming moulds, allowing an extra distance of 4in beyond waterline 1 to allow planking when inverted. I also made up a keel/stem/stern post and deadwood/apron template to allow correct setting up. Normally whalers were built right way up, with the face of the keel 18in from the ground to allow working clearance.

The building board from the gig was reused, the centre line refreshed and the mould stations scribed on at the correct points. The moulds were then erected at right angles to the board, with the fore ones on the aft side of the station and the aft ones on the fore sides. This avoided the need to bevel the moulds. Notches were also cut out for the keel assembly.

THE KEEL ASSEMBLY

English lime was used to form the keel. The grain is very fine and looks much like the original American elm, swelling out amidships to allow for the centre board slot (which is not cut at this stage) with a chamfer taken off the top edges to form the garboard rebate. The stem and apron were formed from seasoned lime with correct curves, scarphed in position and located with bamboo pins.

The aprons were bearded off to almost the correct bevels, as was the stem and stern posts, which should be tapered off to ¹⁄₁₆th on the forward and aft faces.

The hog was formed from lime and bevelled to suit each station, scarphed into position on the keel and again pinned with bamboo. The keel was built up on the template and carefully glued flat. The whole assembly was fitted into position on the moulds and the stem and stern post screwed down to the base board by means of cleats to allow simple removal on hull completion. The edges of the moulds were waxed to prevent plank sticking. This completed the construction ready for planking.

PLANKING

The planking specification called for Wych Elm, 14 strakes per side, no strake being in more than two lengths. Well planed, both sides gauged to ³⁄₈in finished, edges showing fair lines inside and out, with the lands or lap to be ¾in.

Below: The completed model.

I used lime as the grain is so close to scale and it can be obtained in strips down to ¹⁄₃₂in thickness which corresponds in size very well when finally sanded.

Battens will be required to carry out the planking, say ¹⁄₁₆th x ¹⁄₁₈th planed fair and straight. As will clips, such as spring pegs shaped to suit, and rubber bands, such as the postman uses. The glue I use is CIS Velvo – which sets off in a few minutes and is slightly rubbery when cured.

First I divided up the centre mould to the required planks – 14 in number; this gives the widths at the centre section only at this stage. A Spiling plank is laid along the keel to obtain the correct shape of plank. This must be wrapped around to lay flat without forcing. This is just a piece of scrap timber or card long enough to extend full length; it needs to be wide enough to prevent edge bending. Wrap it around to lay flat, as close as possible to keel,

Above: Centre work.

clipped in place with clothes pegs or similar.

Mark off the keel line at each station with a pair of compasses. This gives you the shape required for the garboard. Mark in the station marks, end marks also, a sir mark on the keel and spiler to show correct location. Remove the spiler and run a batten around the marks and, if fair, pencil in. Cut to shape with a scalpel and offer up to the keel, hopefully only a little trimming will be required to get a good fit. Try on the other side which should match fairly closely.

Lay the spiler template onto the planking material, holding it in position with clips, and mark off the shape of the plank including the curved ends. Also add the station marks and sir mark. Lay off the planking width mark at the centre section, obtained from the mould mark. As the keel is tapered at each end the garboard will need to be wider at the ends than in the centre. Clip the batten along the garboard top edge allowing some extra width for fitting, initially straight through the centre mark, and pencil in. It is best to cut the plank from the main piece first, making it over wide; this is because the timber tends to spring away from the centre of the board, and will need remarking before actual plank cutting. Judgment will arrive with practice for this. In carvel work some edge setting can be carried out, but in clinker work the plank has to sit correctly without forcing, otherwise they will buckle away from the moulds losing the correct boat shape.

Reaffix the spiller and retransfer all the markings. Cut out to the lines.

Try the plank for fit and adjust as required, once a good fit is obtained, sight along the top edge of the plank, away from boat. The object is to get the top edge looking level and straight with the waterlines. Mark these points at each end and remove the plank. Lay flat and inspect. Clip the batten in position to the correct width at the centre, and to a fair curve to the marks at the ends. This is important as it forms the basis for planking the rest of the boat.

When happy with the shape, cut out the plank and plane the top edge fair to the batten line. Clip in position and check the shape, you should now have a straight top edge to the garboard plank viewed from the side away from the boat. If all is well, remove and mark a line along $\frac{1}{16}$th on the outside down from the top edge, this will show you where the next plank will come. Mark off the garboard for the other side at this stage with an allowance for fitting.

At this point small screws or hooks were fitted to the base of each station mould to take the rubber bands. I discovered clips do not work very well, tending to distort the spiling plank, the rubber helps to hold to the correct angle.

The garboard can now be fitted. Run a bead of glue along the hog and deadwood, and clip the plank in place using clips, rubber bands or whatever will hold the plank down tightly to the final position. Allow to cure.

Fit the other garboard in the same manner, ensuring the ends are at the same level as the other side before finally

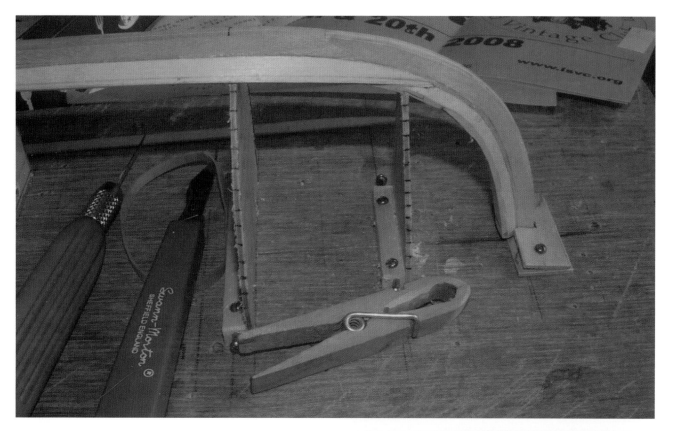

Above: Fore end garboard

fitting. When all cured and the clips removed, divide up for the planking widths at each station – remembering only 13 have now to be fitted. I mark with a needle point as a pencil is invariably too thick. Extend with a pencil down the side of the mould to make it easy to pick up as work proceeds.

Carry on planking in the same manner, spiling off a template first in each case. It is necessary to gently bevel off the outside top edge of the fitted plank to the $\frac{1}{16}$th mark; the amount to be removed is obtained by placing a straight edge touching the mould and top of the plank, and cleaning down until the straight edge touches the land mark, finally fair in between the moulds to match. When marking off from the template do not forget to add the land width on the top of the plank. Care must also to be taken to ensure that the edges are kept fair, adjusting as required with each succeeding plank until the sheer plank is reached. To fix, run a bead of glue along land and aprons. It also helps to insert brass pins into the land mark to give a guide when aligning the plank as they tend to slip around.

You will find that below the turn of the bilge the planks curve downwards, while at the bilge they are fairly straight. Above, they curve upwards towards the sheer line. It is good practice to cut the first plank below the sheer plank wider by the width of the rubber, so that the planking presents an even width to the eye.

The planks will require rebating in on the ends to obtain a flush fit at the hood ends. As we are using planks in one piece it

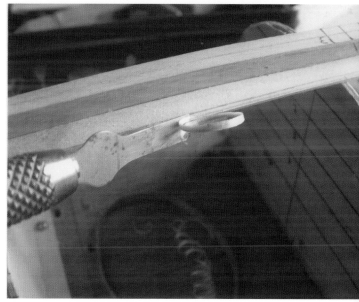

Above: Bevelling off lands.

is important care is taken to obtain a good fit at bow and stern.

When all is complete and cured the hull can be released, lifted off and placed into a shaped cradle support with stem and stern chocks to allow work to proceed on the interior. Spans should be placed along the sheer plank to restrain the hull from opening out. It will be found the bare hull is surprisingly firm. The sheer line must now be carefully planed in to the marks, ensuring nice and fair from all angles.

Next, the centre board slot should be cut out at the correct point, using drills to allow a coping saw blade to be inserted to cut the slot. Gently open out with a flat warding file to the full size 32thou (½in) in readiness for the centre board casing. This was built up off the boat with a template of the hog (which, of course, is slightly concave) using ³⁄₆₄in thick lime to form the sides, with spacers between to allow centre plate room, extending beyond the face down through the slot enough to come flush with the face of the keel. Cant pieces were fitted down each side onto the keel. (In actual practice these cant pieces or foundation pieces were of teak 4½in x 1½in thick, well fitted and bolted down with ³⁄₈in copper bolts clenched. These pieces were rebated on the sides to take the case side pieces, again of teak, 1in thick bedded and screwed with brass screws.) This was then glued down into position, ensuring that when standing vertical in the boat the height is just beneath the thwart level.

Below: Hull lifted off.

TIMBERING

Timbering is the next job. Using my Dremel with a rip saw blade they were cut from a piece of well-seasoned straight-grained apple. They were finished with a metal slitting blade and vernier fence, down to the final size of 55thou (⅝in) at the lower ends, 32thou (½in) at the tops, sided 55thou (⁷⁄₈in) at the lower ends, 47thou (¾in) at the upper ends, in full-size practice steamed and worked in one length from top of gunwale to top of gunwale, and where necessary are to be formed so as to take the gunmetal knees secured to the trunk. The timbers to receive them should be sided 63thou (1in) in the wake of these knees. Timbers should be spaced 7½in apart from centre to centre. They came off the saw with little requirement for further finishing other than slightly rounding off the top faces with a shaped metal scraper.

I use the sliding bridge to mark off for the timbers. I find this is the easiest way to do this particularly when the ends are reached in order to keep them parallel and because they require twisting to fit snug against the planking. I started

Above: Gunwales and risers completed.

fitting from the centre, fore and aft alternately; this allowed the glue to set before fitting the next one adjacent. The method of fitting is by supporting each timber with two fingers beneath each side of the keel, pushing down into the boat then over bending the tops into the boat. This allowed the centre to be placed firmly down on to the hog, then letting the tops spring out against the topsides.

I then clipped the tops in place whilst the timber settled into position. All this needs a certain amount of one-handed dexterity, but it can be done! I did not find it necessary to steam or soak either the timbers or planking, the apple wood is very pliable, only a certain amount of pre-bending and rubbing with the fingers being required.

Once each timber was safely bent in turn in this manner, it was removed and the back coated with a fine bead of glue, then quickly reinserted into position. The clamps were replaced, one tight and the other slack, and the top of the timber pushed down to bed in firmly all round the boat – pushing firmly down each side of the hog to make the timber follow the shape of the boat for as long as possible, before tightening the final clamp. Any surplus glue was cleaned off when part set (too soon and it smears). Once all completed and cured, we can move to the next stage.

GUNWALES

The next job is the fitting of the gunwales. First the timbers were cut back to just below the sheer line planking. The reason for this is that over time the planking would shrink, and if the timbers were not cut off, they would eventually push off the capping, which is only spiked in position. They were prepared from lime 65thou (1in) x 94thou (1½in) with a scratch bead formed along the lower edge then glued and pinned into position just above the sheer line running from the bow apron to the stern apron. Once cured the gaps between were filled with filling blocks. I then made up a batten from bow to stern, and marked on it the position of all thwarts, crutches, seat bearers, etc. This enabled the marking of the position of the swell blocks for the crutch plates. The blocks are 10in x 1½in x ¾in tapered 2in from each end, matching scratch beaded along lower edge and glued and pinned in position in way of the crutch plates, two to each thwart, although I have never seen them all used together. I would have thought the oars would be too short to be of much use, as a lot of leverage would be lost. They are usually single banked. Toe cleats were next fitted beneath the gun-

Above: Stem benches and skirtings fitted.

wales to support the end of the crutch pins. They were 6in long by ¾in thick, circular on front face, fitted to the land beneath the gunwale, glued and pinned in place.

The sheer plank and gunwale was next planed down to a fair line along the full length of the boat with the inside edge of gunwale slightly higher than the plank edge. It is now ready for the cappings to be fitted. Normally these would be steamed in position, but in the model a card template was made and a piece of lime marked out from this slightly wider, especially around the swell pieces than needed to allow for cleaning off. The cappings were formed in one piece of lime ½in thick by ³⁄₁₆in wide cut and fitted around the stem and stern posts then glued down in position, well clamped all along until cured. All surplus timber was then cleaned off until flush with the inside and outside of gunwale and swell pieces, the top being left until later.

Wedges were fitted beneath the timbers to form limber holes next to the hog, and the bow and stern breast hooks

were made and fitted from compass timber, glued and pinned in place to match the cappings. The risings were next, 1in x 1in lime fitted in two sections each side, the fore ones supporting the thwarts, the after ones set 2in lower running from beneath the aftermost thwart back to the apron. The upper edges to come horizontal with thwarts, front faces slightly rounded. To do this the backs must be bevelled off a small amount, then glued and pinned in position.

FLOOR BEARERS

The floor bearers were cut from lime 2½in x 1in. I found it easiest to fit the end bearers first. They were half cut over the timbers, ends bevelled to suit the shape of the boat at the correct level, then infilled with the remainder using a dentist's mirror and a straight edge to get all tops to the same level. The end bearers need to be slightly larger to allow a rebate for the retention of the grating. The mast steps were

Opposite: Stern sheets completed.

made from lime ⅛in thick and the same width as the hog well, snaped at the ends, scored over the timbers, glued and pinned in position. Badge chocks of 8in diameter (½in scale) were fitted over the lands each side of the bow below the rubber and glued into position.

As the majority of the inside work is now complete, the external work was put in hand. The rubbers were cut from lime fitted in one length of 1½in x 1⅜in, tapered towards the ends, top half well rounded, lower tapered off to nothing. Glued and pinned in position, they were then cleaned up and two coats of satin varnish applied.

The bilge rails were moulded 1¾in x 1in and fitted to the land which touches the ground when the boat is heeled over, the length of the rails is to be half that of the boat, the ends neatly tapered and rounded. Handholds 6in x ⅞in spaced 18in apart from centre to centre were cut in the faying side, well rounded off, glued and pinned in place. With all the fixtures now complete the first coats of paint were applied: inside, three well-thinned coats of Humbrol white. Outside, three well-thinned coats of grey, rubbed down between each coat, carefully cut in around the rubbers and finished with a coat of clear satin varnish.

Work now restarted on the interior. The skirting boards to bearers and bottom boards (3in x ⅜in and varnished before fitting) were next fitted and pinned in place. Then the gratings were made by making shaped card templates, gluing the grating parts to them as work proceeded. First the grating frame 2in x 1in halved together, then the bearers ⅟₁₆in x ⅟₁₆in half scored in from the back. Once cured the card was carefully cut off the face allowing the ledge scores to be cut in with the power saw. One pass is sufficient; if pulled back, the score is spoiled. Next the ledges were fitted

using the same material as the bearers half scored in place ⅟₃₂in and a dab of glue. Once cured the faces were cleaned off using a finely set sharp plane, until flush with the bearers, rubbed down with fine glass paper and varnished, then set aside until final completion.

The four gratings were ¾in batten and space. The upper bow sheet extends from the apron to the foremost thwart, with small lime fillets to support the ends. The lower one extends from fore bearer to aft bearer beneath thwart 2. In each case the width of these gratings at their fore and after ends is to be half the total width of the sheets at these positions and should extend the whole length of the sheets as one piece. The stern sheets grating extends from beneath the aft thwart pillar to the timber abaft the fore edge of the cross-bench. The sides were infilled with 1in side pieces pinned in position with fine brass pins.

The mizzen crosspiece is fitted next, 2in thick x 6½in in the centre tapered to 5½in at the ends, fitted upwards and to roundup in the centre ¾in, glued and pinned in position beneath the gunwales leaving a distance of 1in to the top of the capping. The front face is bevelled to take the backboard. A brass socket was turned up to take the mizzen mast. A sailing tiller was made with a plate brazed on the end to fix to crosspiece. A 2½in hole was bored through to allow the mast to sit in its step beneath, set to the correct angle 1:10.

The stern grating is made from ¾in batten and space rounded up to match the crosspiece and extending from the aft side of the backboard to the after breast hook. Cant pieces were fitted beneath the gunwales to carry the grating. Again a card template was cut to fit and a lime frame made-up to fit the gunwale and glued to the card. The ledges run athwart ships and were each made with the roundup in the

Below: Floor boards completed.

Below: Stretchers completed, also thwarts and knees.

Above: Overhead view showing shape of hull.
Above right: View looking forward.

centre and halved and glued into the frame pieces, with solid sections in way of the mast and ensign staff fitting. When cured the card was cut off to allow access to the face of grating. The batten spaces were marked out and cut in with a scalpel as the Dremel saw cannot be used. Then the battens were glued in position and cleaned off on completion, with a hole cut to allow clearance over the brass fitting and for the ensign staff with a neat round collar glued in place before being rubbed down and a coat of varnish applied.

Next the keelson was made up (6in wide and ⅝in thick in two pieces) and fitted around the centreboard casing butted at the halfway point, well fitted onto the timbers with each piece fastened down with brass D eyes and wood toggles. It extends from the aft end of the mast step to the first timber abaft the fore edge of the after grating frame. Where the two lengths of keelson meet at the centre board trunk they were made continuous by fitting a side piece 2in deep x 1¼in thick over the timbers down onto the hog glued in place, with mortises cut in to take the cradle battens of the floor boards.

STERN SHEETS

First, sufficient lime was cut to form the thwarts, and the stroke thwart fitted. This is because the stern bearers were screwed to the thwart by means of cant pieces for support at the fore ends. Two bearers of 2½in x 2in and spaced at 12in were made in lime and fitted across the boat with the fore edge 5ft from the after perpendicular. These were fitted underneath the rising cut in so that the top was flush with the

Right: This shows all the loose fittings.

Above: Towing bollard thwart.

top of the rising. Fore and aft bearers, set at 12in from the boat sides and curved to match, were then dovetailed into the cross bearers and extended to the after thwart cant pieces into which they were screwed. Further short bearers again dovetailed at their inner edge and halved up beneath the riser. The battens were glued and pinned into position. The outer and inner battens moulded ⅞in x 1⅛in curved and well fitted to the timbers at sides, with the inner ones 1⅛in x ⅞in with ½in spacers between slightly rounded on the tops and also across the stern.

Knee supports were fitted between the gunwale and cross-bench to support the backboard which is framed up with a centre panel. The upper edge is to round up 3in in elliptical form, the round commencing ½in above the upper edge of capping. The backboard is to incline aft 1 in 6.

BOTTOM BOARDS

Note that apart from the after one no further thwarts have been installed. This is because it would be very difficult to work in the bottom of the boat with them fitted.

There were five bottom boards, ⅜in thick, each side,

spaced at equal distances apart, extending from fore lower, to after sheets, and from the keelson along the bottom of the boat. They have air edges and were butted to the middle of the timber near the centre of each thwart. Each section is cradled together with two battens 2in by ⅜in. These need to be curved to suit boat bilge. Lower ends of the battens extend ½in under the keelson and into the side pieces mentioned previously. The battens were clenched together with copper nails, two to each batten, and then glued.

The lower edge of the lower bottom board is 1½in from the keelson and the boards about 4in wide amidships tapering to about 2⅝in forward and 3⅝in aft. Each section is secured with two brass buttons fitted on circular plates on the stretcher rail and bearing on brass plates on pieces fitted to the upper ends of battens. These brass turn buttons were made up on the lathe, and the button itself made from brass split pin arms filed to shape and located with fine brass pins in their correct positions.

STRETCHERS AND FITTINGS

The stretcher rails were in two varieties. The small type measured 1in x 3¾in and the large type 1in x 6in, with heel batten along the bottom edge, and 5in up from bottom to

Above: Bow view of completed hull.

retain feet in a seaway (the type fitted when I was an apprentice, so naturally these were the type fitted as being the best to use). The ends of them were cut into rails and galvanised steel cleats with the ends rounded down to suit.

STRETCHER CLEATS

Rails were fitted (³⁄₈in x 2in) extending from the after end of the lower fore grating to the fore end of the stern grating and fastened to the timbers with brass screws (glued and pinned). The lower edge is 1ft 2in below the upper surface of the thwarts and shows 0a fair line. In the model it is easier to spile off the shape and cut the timber to the curve found to show a fair line. Double cleats ½in x 2in were fitted to the stretcher rail and timbers.

To these were screwed horizontal galvanised angle cleats with matching holes to take galvanised pins to hold the rails in position at the desired setting. They were also fitted to the sides of the casing. Angles were fabricated from brass sheet and holes drilled, then pinned in position with brass pins. The locating pins were cut from brass wire. This completed the stretcher fittings.

Above: Showing centreboard case.

It was now time to make up and fit the six brass knees that support the centre board casing to the timbers. It was found easier and neater to braze two arms together rather than bending them, as a sharp corner could not be attained. They were formed out of brass split pins which have a rounding on the edge and which are perfect for this purpose. The arms need to be drilled to take tiny copper pins to hold them in position. They were 1in wide with the length of the upper arms 8½in and the lower arms 9½in. Two further knees will be fitted once the thwarts are in place.

THWARTS

These were formed 1in thick, with the exception of the midship thwart in wake of the strongback which was 1¼in and 7in broad, double kneed at each end, with shaped pads between knees, inner edge cut down to thwart, with drain hole cut through thwart to allow water to drain away. They were formed from lime, with scratch bead on each edge, pinned and glued in position. (Note: where items were fixed to painted areas, the paint was scraped away to allow a firm bedding for the glue). Thwarts should bed down onto the rising without the use of any filling pieces. At the same time as the strong back centre thwart was fitted the mahogany end pieces and cappings were also fitted to the centre board casings leaving a slot for the centre board handle to come

These pages: Views of the completed model.

through. The remaining brass knees were fitted horizontally in place from the centre board casing to the strong back thwart.

Once all the thwarts were fitted the knees were started, sided ⅞in with arms 12in long. Where possible I used compass grained timber to shape them. I made card templates for each as they are all different shapes. I temporarily fitted them in position and marked out the front shape so that they all matched together, with a nice fair sweep and round down to the thwart. They were all then glued and pinned in position, tops flush with the gunwale. Finally the pads were fitted in position between the knees and cleaned up flush with the tops, and then painted white to match a semicircle on the thwart.

RUDDER AND FITTINGS

The rudder was made up to the correct shape, 1in thick bearded down to ¾in on the back with cheeks ⅝in thick either side and the brass hangings fitted; the latter consisting

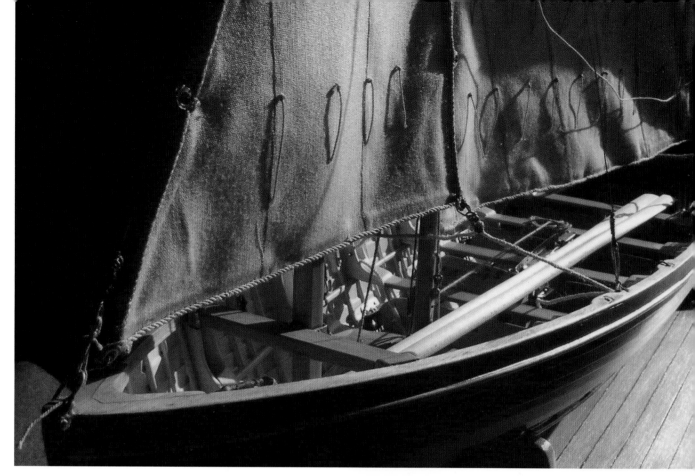

of a rod with a thin web at the top and a brass collar at the bottom fitted to the stern post. This allows the rudder to be lifted either partly to clear obstructions or to be removed completely for stowage. The rudder fittings comprise strips riveted to each side of the rudder to strengthen the blade at the bottom with a split collar to allow sliding down the rod, and a similar U bracket at the top. The cheeks were then riveted over the outside of these sandwiching in position. The head was cut down to provide bearing for the yoke which was made of wood. This was connected to the sailing tiller by means of wire strops adjusted with a bottle screw. The tiller itself was constructed on a T-shaped timber base and made solid with brass plates top and bottom riveted through and a clasp to fit around the mizzen mast bracket, secured with a drop-in pin.

SPARS

The main mast is 16ft 6in long x 3⅝in diameter and the mizzen 13ft 6in x 2½in diameter, and the main yard 15ft 3in x 2½in, mizzen boom 6ft 10in x 2in diameter. They were made up from straight grained lime, tapered and rounded. Mast bases were squared off to drop into the steps, with the correct angle of 1:10 it took some careful lining up. Carrying a lug sail the yard was tapered towards each end, starting at quarter point with holes cut in the ends to allow correct bending of the sails. Fittings were fabricated from brass and

the rigging made from my own rope, with standing rigging from twisted copper wire, painted with silver paint to represent galvanised wire.

TOWING BOLLARD

This item is peculiar to naval boats, and is portable. The bollard was made in lime 3½in x 3½in and is shipped into a collar on the after edge of the foremost thwart, with a pin to hold in position to prevent rising in use. The upper end is to pass through a galvanised steel clamp piece $1\frac{1}{2}$in x $\frac{5}{16}$in secured to a cross piece of oak (lime) $5\frac{1}{2}$in x $2\frac{1}{2}$in. The cross-piece must be well fitted between the gunwales and kept in position with small angle collars $1\frac{1}{4}$in x $1\frac{1}{4}$in fastened to the gunwales with copper bolts. One end is kept in position by a steel strip riveted across the collar top and the other end by a hinged strip, an eye plate and pin being fitted to secure the latter in place. The fittings were all brazed up in brass strip and painted silver on completion.

OARS

The five straight bladed oars (sweeps) were made up in ash, plus spare. Four were 17ft long, and one, the bow oar, 16ft. All were 3in diameter at the crutch, reduced were the hand grips, and tapered down towards the blade, with a web along the blade both sides. The blades, 6in wide, had copper strip tacked around the ends. No leathers were fitted. I made the oars in lime, using a template to mark them out, and then cut to shape on the Dremel saw, planing up finally with a fine plane.

BRASS WORK

The various brass fittings were then made up and fitted. The crutch plates were turned up on the lathe of size 0.20in x 0.10in x 0.016in thick from an old 13-amp earth plug and drilled in to take the crutch pin. The crutch pin was turned up on the lathe 0.34in long by 0.05in tapered down to 0.03in at the end leaving a small spigot on the top to assist when brazing. The crutch was formed from the brass split pins again, filed to shape, drilled at the centre to take the spigot. Finally it was brazed in position and cleaned up, with a small hole put in the bottom for the lanyard. The crutch plates were let into the correct position in the cappings and drilled down through the toe cleat for the crutches to fit.

The bow and stern ring plates were made up, fitted with the correctly shaped rings and secured with copper pins as were the lifting plates with long eyes to come up through the floor gratings with a neat brass plate fitted.

The centre plate was made up from brass and fitted in position with a brass bolt as pivot pin. Then the matching handle was riveted in place and the supporting cleats fixed on to the capping.

Belaying pins were made from brass panel pins. Naval ones are unusual in that they only protrude beneath the thwart, for safety in an open boat, but required care in belaying to ensure prompt removal if required. The mast clamp was made up and riveted in place, as were the gunmetal eye plates for standing rigging and main sheets. These were fixed in place on lime cleats fitted to the planking beneath the gunwales, and glued in position. Various cringles and shackles were made as required.

SAILS

The sails were made up by making individual templates to the correct measurements, with a round out on each side to give shape of a couple of inches. The material I usually use is cambric which comes in the correct colour, cream. This is cut up into scale cloth sizes of 24in wide with the warp or non-stretchy way along the length of each cloth. These should run parallel to the leach of each sail. The seams were overlapped by $\frac{3}{64}$in, thus making up a cloth big enough to make each sail plus hemming. At this scale stitching would look out of place, besides all the problems of puckering up, so they were fixed together with glue called fraystop.

The template was placed over the cloth and carefully marked out and cut with a scalpel, with the allowance for double turning added on. The glue is used to do the hemming presenting a very neat appearance when ironed. The corner patches were doubled and fixed in the same way. The final ironing sets the glue firmly and provides a waterproof bond.

A sufficient amount of rope to the correct size was made up on my machine using silver thread. This was then stitched around the port side of the sails, starting on the leach bottom, the ends being tapered as work proceeds. As I am left handed this works best for me. The stitching should lie in the lay of the rope and almost disappears, looking very neat especially if using the same colour. The cringles were made up on the lathe from brass rod, grooved for rope on the outside edge and chamfered on the faces. They can be made up with brass tube swaged out with small punches although I have not had much success with this method. They were sewn into position at the corners and reefing positions, turning the stitching in to look like rope around the edge of the cringles. Reefing points were inserted at the correct spacing and knotted either side to retain in place.

BASEBOARD

This was made up from $\frac{1}{2}$in ply with hard wood moulding to form a frame around the perimeter; bilge chocks were made up and screwed in position from beneath. Lime planking was then made up $\frac{3}{8}$in wide with photographic paper between each joint and fitted in position to represent planking. Finally a margin plank in hardwood was fixed to form a border and all were satin varnished.

Tautunu

THE ISLAND TOURING SHIP

by John Laing

THE SHIP

Tautunu was one of a pair of small ships built for the Gilbert and Ellice Islands Colony Marine Department in 1967 by United Engineers of Singapore. *Tautunu* and her sister *Temauri* were 84ft long with a beam of 20ft and a depth of 10ft. They were both measured at 116 tons gross. The T-boats, as they were called, were designed as government touring ships – taking government officials on periodic tours of the scattered islands of the colony, and also capable of carrying small amounts of cargo and inter-island passengers.

Unfortunately, the T-boats were not sea kindly and were capable, so it was said, of rolling on damp grass. Consequently they were extremely unpopular with the very officials they were meant to carry, and who avoided travelling on them whenever possible. As shipping of any kind was always in short supply in the Colony, the T-boats spent much of their working lives carrying supplies to the outer islands and bringing copra in to the central storage facilities at Tarawa for on-shipment to Europe. They also carried passengers between Tarawa and the outer islands and, sometimes, a very reluctant government official or two.

Below: Starboard bow view of the completed model.

Above: MV *Tautunu* moored in Funafuti Lagoon.

and hard pressed local government officials may have little or no time to deal with casual requests for obscure details about their local shipping.

I was fortunate with regard to information concerning *Tautunu* as I lived and worked in the Gilbert and Ellice Islands Colony for several years and was able to gather sufficient information on *Tautunu* and other local ships to make the building of detailed models possible. This material included photographs, written notes and copies of hull lines and parts of the ship's arrangement plans.

Using the above information, I was able to draw up a detailed set of plans for *Tautunu*, which were supplemented by my notes and photographs.

RESEARCH AND PLANS

Even in today's world of almost instant worldwide communication and information overload, information concerning ships operating in the remoter parts of the Pacific is difficult, and sometimes impossible, to obtain.

The only information concerning inter-island ships may be contained in government records of the islands where they operate; communication is often difficult; internet facilities sometimes almost non existent; surface mail uncertain,

THE MODEL

The model was built at a scale of 1:48, giving an overall length of 21in (53.3cm). The hull was constructed on the bread-and-butter principle, using eight vertical lifts of ⅝in (16mm) Australian Red Cedar. Vertical lifts were chosen in preference to the more usual horizontal lifts because of the underwater shape of the hull at the stern. The lifts were cut to the shape of the buttock lines and the internal waste material was cut out leaving plenty of room for fixing the lifts together. Once all the lifts were cut out they were glued and screwed together starting from the centre pair, and ensuring that the screws were well inside the hull line so that they would not get in the way during the subsequent carving

Below: Hull Lines plan.

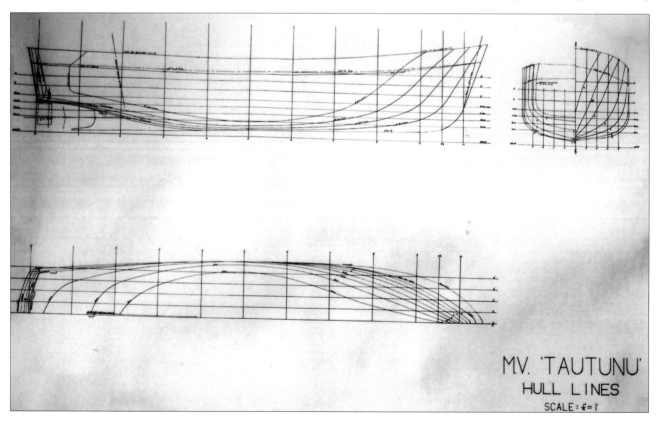

MV. 'TAUTUNU'
HULL LINES
SCALE: ¼=1'

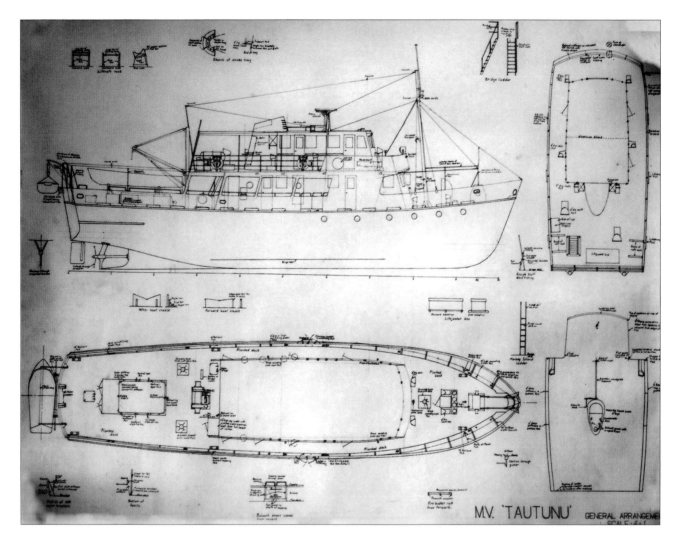

M.V. 'TAUTUNU' GENERAL ARRANGEME

Above: General Arrangement plan.

process. Screws were used in addition to glue to ensure that the hull structure remained stable in the long term.

When the glue was thoroughly cured the hull was carved to shape using various chisels and gouges, and finished with flat and half-round files and finally with sandpaper. The external shape of the hull was checked continuously by templates during the carving process to ensure the accuracy of the finished shape. The interior of the hull was left sawn without further finishing. With the external hull carving completed and the hull checked with battens to ensure there were no bumps or hollows, the remainder of the hull detail could be completed.

Deck beams and carlings of Australian Red Cedar were fitted so as to align with the various deck erections which would be fitted latter. The skeg, also of Cedar, was carved to fit the underside of the hull and was glued in place with epoxy resin. The bilge keels were cut to shape from aluminium sheet and their position on each side of the hull measured and marked. Narrow grooves were cut to accept their inner edge and they were fixed with epoxy resin. The flat plate rudder was made from aluminium sheet and fixed to the brass rudder post with epoxy resin.

The propeller shaft bracket was made up from a small piece of brass tubing and scrap brass sheet, which were silver-soldered together and fixed into previously prepared slots in the hull and the end of the skeg. The propeller shaft was of brass rod which protruded through the bracket sufficiently to allow the propeller to be fixed to it. The propeller was cut by hand from a piece of round brass rod of the correct diameter – the shape first being roughed out with a hacksaw and the final shape made with coarse and then fine files.

The porthole positions were marked on the hull, the centres cut out with a small drill, and then the holes enlarged with increasing sized drills until the correct size was reached. Gradually increasing the size in this helps to prevent the edges tearing out. The portholes were not completed at this time as I did not want to risk getting paint on the port glass. The small rubbing strips just above the boot topping at the stern were made up from scrap timber.

When the hull had reached this stage, it was given several thin coats of undercoat, rubbing down between each coat, and then several top coats, again rubbing down between

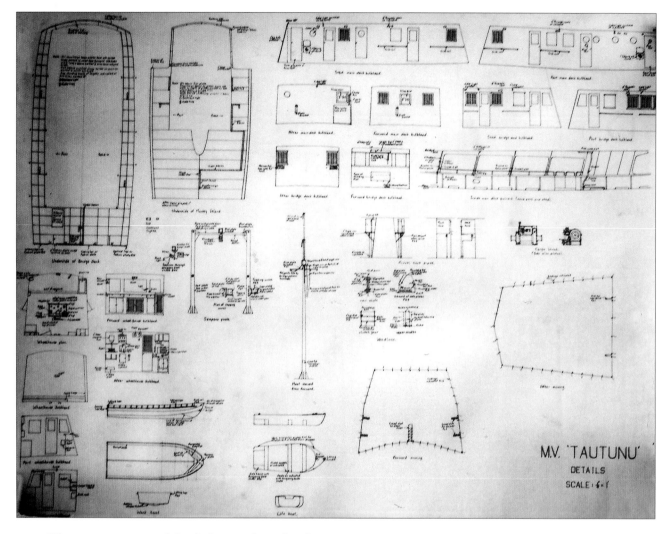

Above: Details plan.

coats. The waterways around the deck were also painted at this time.

With the hull painting complete, the final hull details were added – porthole glasses made from Perspex sheet and painted grey on the inside before fitting, draught marks cut from numbers produced in a plastic strip labeller and name lettering cut from sheet copper. The name and draught

Above: Details plan.

marks were made in this way to give them the raised effect that is visible on the ship.

With the hull complete the main deck planking was laid. The planks were cut from strips of timber veneer and one edge and one end of each plank was painted black to represent the caulking. Care must be taken always to lay the

Below: The hull under construction showing the vertical lifts of the bread-and-butter construction.

Below: Broadside view of the completed model.

painted edge and end of a plank to a bare edge to maintain the effect. A margin plank was first laid around the edge of the deck at the inboard edge of the waterway, and the planking laid to this, with the planks joggled into the margin plank at the bow. On completion, the planking was sanded and given several coats of polyurethane varnish to seal it.

The next job was the bulwarks. These were quite simple for most of the hull – 1mm ply cut to the shape of the sheer of the deck, but for the awkward curved section around the stem I cut and bent a section of aluminium sheet to fit after first having found the correct shape by trial and error with a piece of card. The bulwark stanchions were made from aluminium sheet, and the capping rail from a strip of scrap timber. As with the rest of the model, the bulwarks were painted when they were in place.

With the bulwarks in place, it was time to start on the deck fittings. The main deckhouse was a simple box construction made from 1mm ply. As the forward end was curved, the framing was made especially robust in this area to allow plenty of gluing surface. The windows, doors and portholes were cut out before the ply sheets were glued and dowelled to the frame. Doors were made from mahogany ply scored to represent the door construction with shaped brass wire handles, and the window curtains pieces of fine weave cloth glued behind the Perspex window panes. The engine room vents were made from aluminium sheet with the grilles coming from an old garden spray filter screen. The wooden grab rails were made from scrap timber rounded with a draw plate with end brackets filed up from brass sheet that had been drilled to accept the rails.

The remaining main deck fittings were now completed. The windlass frame was bent up from aluminium sheet with the shafts from brass wire and the gears salvaged from old clocks. The anchor chain was made from links hammered up to shape around a small pair of long-nose pliers. The anchors were made up from scrap aluminium fixed with brass pins and glued with epoxy resin. The many cowl ventilators were formed from copper shim in a multi-size doming block, the cowls being silver-soldered to brass tubing trunks and fitted into bases made up from scrap timber. The fire buckets were formed on the end of a scriber from copper shim and silver-soldered. The bucket rack was made up from scrap ply.

The cargo hatch on the after deck was made as a box from ply and detailed with wedge cleats, eyes and brackets from scrap brass with copper shim wedging bars and wedges cut from toothpicks. The hatch cover was finely woven japara silk.

The work boat, secured on chocks cut from scrap timber and brass, was stowed on the hatch. For a while it presented a bit of a puzzle, being of an open hard chine design. Finally I made it from aluminium strips formed over a wooden mould. The strips were pinned with brass wire and the whole fixed with epoxy resin. Once the basic hull was made, it was comparatively simple to detail the boat with a shaped aluminium floor, aluminium grab rails, painter and lifting slings.

Below: Starboard quarter view of the completed model.

Above: Completed model viewed from ahead.

Above: The completed model from astern.

The cargo winch was built up with shaped aluminium base rails, timber side frames and control box, and with the various drums and other details made from odd bits and pieces out of the scrap box. The davits for the lifeboat were bent from brass tubing, with the lugs for the fall blocks made from copper wire bent to shape and riveted over inside the tube. The ends of the tubes were sealed with epoxy which, when set, was filed to shape. The lifeboat was carved from solid timber with a timber keel fitted afterwards. The cover was cut from japara silk. Other small fittings on the main deck were assembled from scrap timber, aluminium and copper and fixed with epoxy glue.

The deck over the main deckhouse was cut from 1mm ply and its underside fitted with beams made from sheet aluminium. As the side stanchions and screen bulkheads were a complex shape, full-size card templates were made and trimmed until they were an exact fit for each side. The stanchions and screens were then cut from 1mm ply using the templates to get the correct shape. They were fixed to the sides with epoxy resin and clamped in place until the adhesive had time to cure fully. I was a little concerned at the time of building that the epoxy alone might not be sufficient to hold these structures, but there have been no problems with them at all.

The bridge deckhouse was complicated by the fact that I wanted to show the wheelhouse open with all its internal details. Luckily there was a chart table/equipment locker that stretched right across the fore end of the wheelhouse, so by building this on a solid core I had a good strong attachment point for the curved forward bulkhead. The wheelhouse shows all details including the steering console, radar, radios, lights, etc. The wheelhouse windows were of Perspex cut exactly to the size of the frames and fixed with a minute amount of epoxy adhesive. The louvres on the cabin windows were filed up from solid timber stock set into frames as it was thought that this would give a more even finish to the louvres than trying to make them from individual slats.

The funnel was constructed as one piece from solid timber with a rim of copper shim fitted around the top to make the recess in its after end. The louvres on the fore end of the funnel were cut from copper shim and fixed in place with epoxy adhesive. When completed, the funnel was cut in two at the level of the top of the deckhouse and the lower section glued to the deck and deckhouse bulkhead. Once the remainder of the bridge deck had been completed and the cabin top fitted, the upper portion of the funnel was positioned above and aligned with its lower section and glued in place.

With the lower section of the funnel in position the header tank with its many pipes could be made and fitted, together with the large wooden tray secured around the after end of the funnel. This tray had been made by a previous Master of the ship as he liked to entertain and wanted a handy spot for drinks, etc.

The railings were soldered up from copper wire and fitted before the cabin top. This called for the tops of the stanchions to be cut very accurately, but was easier than trying to fit the railings afterwards. The rail capping was made from small lengths of mahogany veneer which was glued to the tops of the rails. The lifebuoys were made from timber which was cut into pie slices and glued together so the grain ran more or less around the rims of the lifebuoys, making them stronger.

The containers for the inflatable liferafts were carved from solid timber, with the bands made from copper wire filed to a half round sectional shape and bent around the container. The cradle on which the liferaft container was stowed was made up from scrap copper sheet and soldered. The holding down straps were made from narrow strips of japara silk.

The cabin top was constructed in the same way as the bridge deck, with full framing on the underside. Large gutters were fitted along each side of the cabin top. These were made from aluminium sheet bent to shape and fixed with epoxy adhesive. The framing of the underside of the cabin top was a great help in positioning and fixing these gutters. The gutters drained into pipes which run down inside two of the rail stanchions on each side, and were used to supplement the ship's fresh water supply in this water starved area of the Pacific.

The radar mast was of brass tubing with the radar scanner built up from various small pieces of copper and brass from the scrap box. Construction of the radar scanner was helped by the fact that I had several photographs of the scanner taken from different angles. This was much clearer to me than working from a plan for such a complex piece of equipment.

The final jobs were to step and rig the masts and set up the awnings.

Above: The forecastle showing the various clock parts and other salvaged metal pieces used in the construction of the windlass.

Above: The starboard side of the superstructure. Various fittings mentioned in the text, such as the funnel tank pipes, lifebuoys, liferaft containers, and hospitality shelf on the funnel can be seen.

Above: The stern of the model showing the cargo derricks, work boat, lifeboat and cargo winch. The grey brackets inside the transom were for holding outboard motors under repair.

The mast was made from well-seasoned pine with a fine, straight grain. This timber was chosen to minimise any possible future warping. The mast was shaped to the correct taper in the square and then rounded by hand by cutting it so as to make it eight-sided first, and then rounding it with fine files and sandpaper. The crosstree was made from a length of brass rod. Rigging screws were made up from copper wire with fine brass tubing over it to form the body of the screw. The ship's brass bell was a lucky find of a correctly shaped piece of brass on the end of an old clock fitting in the scrap box.

The samson posts on the after deck were made from brass tubing as they had no taper. The open end was plugged with a small piece of timber and filed smooth. The cross piece and derricks were made from brass tubing. The topping winch fitted on the outboard side of each samson post was made up from interlocking pieces of aluminium sheet and fixed with epoxy adhesive. The working light on the samson post cross piece was made up in the same way. The large derrick blocks were made from copper shim cut and bent to shape over aluminium sheaves and through pinned.

The awning stanchions fore and aft were made from copper wire, soldered at the joints and fitted into holes in the bulwark capping. The after awnings were set up on wires rather than rods as this awning had to be taken down in order to work cargo. The after awning was rarely rigged on the ship, and was omitted on the model. The forward awning was more or less permanent on the ship and, for the model, was cut from japara silk. The awning seams were glued rather than sewn as it was thought that sewn seams would look out of scale.

The radio aerials were made from very fine copper wire taken from an old electrical coil with the insulators made from copper wire drilled to accept the ends of the aerials.

The completed model was supported on two plain wooden pillars on a varnished wooden stand made up from alternate strips of light and dark timber, and is displayed in a glass case.

Below: The stern of the model showing the propeller, propeller bracket and general hull detailing.

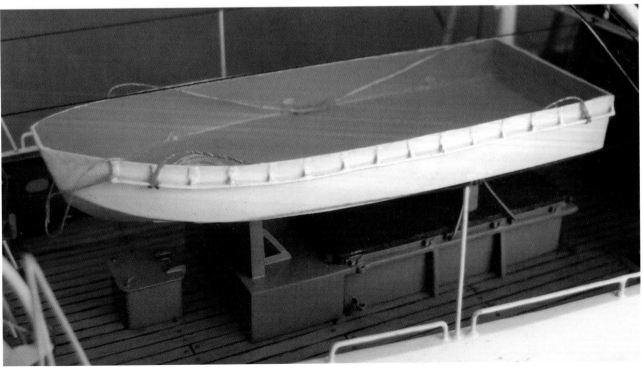

Above: The workboat on the cargo hatch. Note the battens and wedges securing the hatch cover.

Polar Opposites

NANSEN AND AMUNDSEN'S *FRAM* AND SCOTT'S *DISCOVERY*

by Rorke Bryan

The HMS *Challenger* expedition of 1872–76 and Adolf Nordenskiöld's journey through the Northeast Passage on *Vega* in 1887–89 triggered great interest in polar exploration throughout the international scientific community during the last decades of the nineteenth century and resulted in contracts for the first two ships specially designed for work in polar regions, the *Fram* and the *Discovery*. These brand new ships also represented a marked difference in design philosophy between Colin Archer of Larvik in Norway and William Smith, the Chief Constructor of the Admiralty in England.

Two of the key proponents of increased exploration were Fridtjof Nansen in Norway, and Sir John Murray in Edinburgh, the chief scientist on the *Challenger*. Nansen first visited the Arctic as a zoology student on the Arendal sealer

Viking in 1882. Shortly afterwards he was appointed curator in the Bergen Museum, and, a superb skier, started to plan an expedition to cross the Greenland ice cap. He was dropped off with five companions on the east coast of Greenland near Anmagssalik in July 1888 by the whaling barque *Jason* from Sandefjord. Nearly three months later, after successfully crossing the unknown ice cap, he and Otto Sverdrup walked into Godthåb on the west coast. He returned to Norway the following spring to an extraordinary national outburst of 'Nansenmania'; he was not only a national hero, but was recognized as the foremost polar travel expert. He immediately started to plan an expedition to drift across the Arctic Ocean in a ship frozen into the pack ice to test his theories about trans-polar ocean currents, for which he needed an

Below: Decampment of the *Fram* on the Nansen expedition, 1895. Hand-coloured lantern slide (Getty)

Above: *Fram* running downwind in the Roaring Forties during the Amundsen expedition to the South Pole. Although she was designed to carry two jibs and two fore staysails, Amundsen could only afford to replace two of the head sails lost in the fire at Horten. (Courtesy of Frammuseet, Oslo)

extremely strong ship which could safely withstand immense ice pressures. Having obtained 200,000Nkr (£10,311) from the Norwegian Government, Nansen approached Colin Archer in Larvik to design and build the ship, which eventually cost about 280,000Nkr (£14,435). Archer, already famous for innovative, extremely seaworthy pilot boats, was initially reluctant to undertake the project, but, intrigued by the challenge, he eventually agreed.

FRAM: A NEW CONCEPT IN ICE SHIP DESIGN

Recognizing the inverse relationship between ship length and strength, Archer initially planned a small ship, which conformed to Nansen's philosophy of polar travel by small, swiftly-moving teams. This contrasted starkly with the complex, over-manned Arctic expeditions of the Royal Navy, which ended so disastrously for Sir John Franklin and his men on board HMS *Erebus* and HMS *Terror*. Archer's design departed radically from traditional deep-bilged slab-sided Norwegian and Dundee barques like *Jason*, *Aurora* and *Terra Nova* which dominated the Arctic whaling/sealing trade. *Fram* was modeled on the small vessels working around Svalbard and Novaya Zemlya, whose rounded hulls were light enough to be lifted rather than crushed by ice floe pressure. Her hull would be extraordinarily strong, but combined with a shallow bilge and round, full lines to give no purchase for ice. She would be very broad to provide adequate cargo capacity and, recognizing the inherent weakness of the transom sterns of traditional whaling barques, she would be double-ended (see Figure 1).

The necessity to fit stores for a five-year voyage meant that *Fram* was bigger than Archer had hoped: length 128ft, beam 36ft and moulded depth 17¼ft of 402grt (307 net).[1] The hull was extremely strong; the keel was built of 14in square American elm, the stem of three massive oak timbers giving a fore and aft breadth of 4ft x 15in width, and the sternpost was double, of two 26in x 14in oak beams with strong counter timbers on each side (Figure 2). Between these were the rudder post and a well for lifting the propeller for protection in ice. The frames, doubled throughout to give an almost solid wall, made of oak grown to shape and seasoned for ten years at the Horten naval shipyard, were built up 10½in square courses riveted together, with butt ends connected by iron straps to prevent stretching (Figure 2).

Decks were 3–4in thick Norwegian pine on massive deck beams; main deck beams were American or German oak while poop and lower deck beams were pitch pine or yellow pine. Beams were attached to the frames by grown white pine knees with some reinforcing iron knees (450 of the more flexible wooden knees were used). The lower deck was raised over the engine room to provide space for the engine, and the poop deck was raised to provide headroom for cabin accommodation. Sixty-eight massive (7in x 10in) diagonal stays were fixed to the deck beams and sides by wooden knees for reinforcement against lateral pressure and the decks were also supported by stanchions.

Interior planking consisted of 4–6in thick pine, while there were two exterior layers of oak planking, the inner 3in thick and the outer 4in thick. Outside was greenheart ice sheathing from the keelson to 18in below the shear strake, 3in thick at the keel, increasing to 6in at and above the water-line. A composite of coal tar, pitch and saw dust was boiled and poured between the interior and exterior planking for insulation. Apart from the massive bracing, the hull was a solid wall, 28–32in thick. The bow and the stern were pro-tected for 6ft along the hull by an iron casing of plates or closely spaced iron bars and heavy U-shaped iron frames gave additional protection to the rudder.

Fram was designed as a three-masted schooner for easy handling by a small crew (Figure 3) with an 87ft foremast, 109ft mainmast and a mizzen 86½ft above the waterline.

Masts were Oregon pine and standing rigging was steel wire, with fine spun hemp running rigging worked by a windlass and steam-powered winch. In addition to fore-and-aft sails, gaff topsails were set on the main and mizzen masts, two square sails on a 46ft snow mast forward of the foremast, a flying jib, a jib and two fore staysails, and two main topmast staysails. These gave a total sail area of 6472 sq.ft, less than on many other polar ships, but she was not a bad sailer and could often reach 9 knots, and be sailed with only two crew on watch. The 220hp triple expansion engine built by Akers Mekaniske Verkstad, Christiania, could be run with one, two or three cylinders, giving a speed of 6 knots[2] with 2.6 tons of coal per day. With bunker capacity of 300 tons she had a range of almost 17,000 miles.

Accommodation was under the poop deck, with four large single-berth cabins around the galley, berth space in the large (182 sq.ft) saloon and two four-berth crew cabins abaft the saloon beside the rudder housing (Figure 2). Great care was taken with insulation to prevent condensation; metal bolts were covered with felt, then the walls, floors and ceilings were lined with three layers of light paneling separated by cork shavings, reindeer wool and felt. The doubled doors were insulated with reindeer wool and had 15in high sills. Heating was by an oil-fired stove and electric light was pro-vided by a windmill-driven dynamo, and natural light by a triple-glazed skylight. The navigating bridge was abaft the mainmast, above a deck house containing the chart room and a study. The hinged funnel abaft the deck house could be retracted when the ship was under sail. Each of two large

Figure 1. Sheerlines of *Fram*. (After C. Archer, 1898)

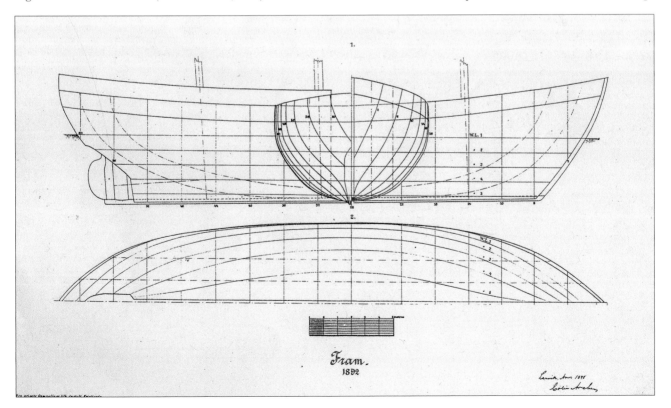

Figure 2. Plan, interior arrangements and structure of *Fram*. (After C. Archer, 1898)

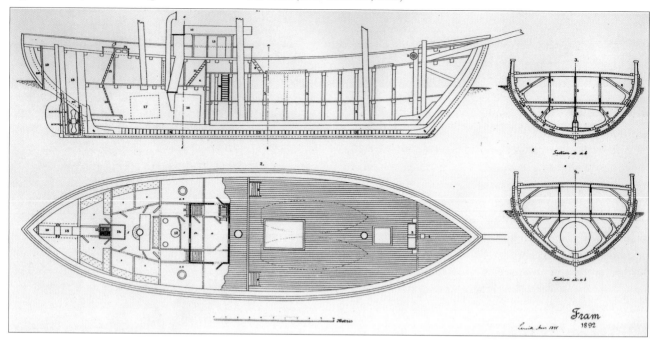

Figure 3. Sail and rig plan of *Fram* as originally drawn by Colin Archer. (After C. Archer, 1898)

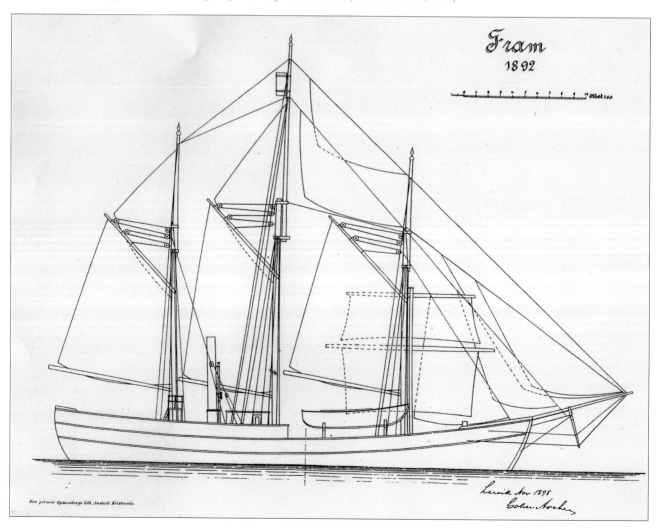

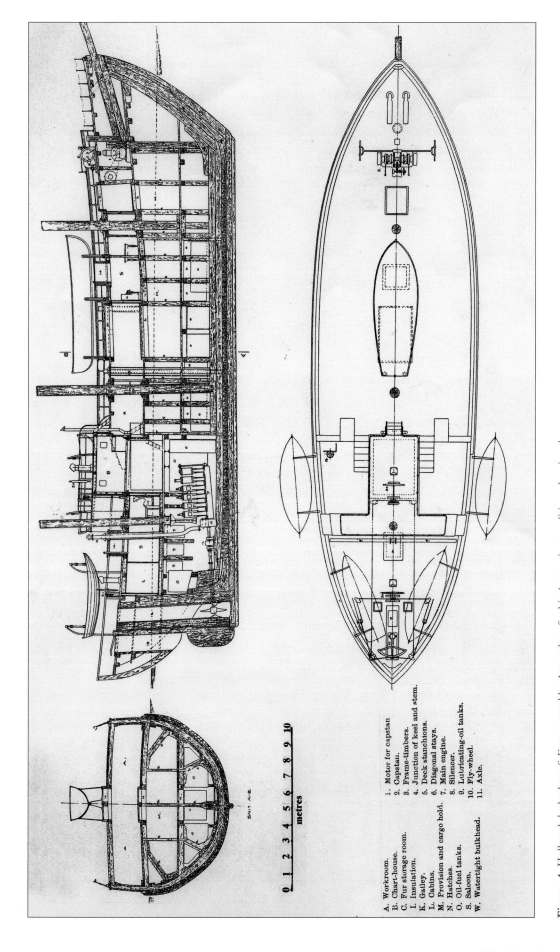

A. Workroom.
B. Chart-house.
C. Fur storage room.
I. Insulation.
K. Galley.
L. Cabins.
M. Provision and cargo hold.
N. Hatches.
O. Oil-fuel tanks.
S. Saloon.
W. Watertight bulkhead.

1. Motor for capstan
2. Capstan.
3. Frame-timbers.
4. Junction of keel and stem.
5. Deck stanchions.
6. Diagonal stays.
7. Main engine.
8. Silencer.
9. Lubricating-oil tanks,
10. Fly-wheel.
11. Axle.

0 1 2 3 4 5 6 7 8 9 10
metres

Figure 4. Hull and deck plan of *Fram* as used by Amundsen for his Antarctic expedition, showing the spar deck added for Sverdrup's 1898–1902 Arctic expedition. (After C. Blom, 1912)

(28ft long) half-decked boats could fit the entire crew, and there were four 20ft light sealing boats, a small Norwegian pram and a 20ft motor pinnace designed by Archer.

Nansen's celebrated voyage on *Fram* has been described in his book *Farthest North*,[3] in many papers and articles and in Huntford's fine biography.[4] *Fram* sailed part way across the Northeast Passage becoming frozen-in near New Siberian Island in late September 1893. She then drifted back westwards in the ice to northern Svalbard, before returning to Tromsø in August 1896. Nansen and Johansen left the ship on 14 March 1895 at 84°4′N in attempt to sledge to the North Pole and reached 86°14′N before turning back to Franz Josef Land where they wintered. In June 1896 they arrived at Frederick Jackson's expedition camp at Cape Flora and shipped to Norway on the supply ship *Windward*.

Few flaws were found with *Fram* during the expedition. As expected from her hull design, she rolled ferociously, and, heavily-laden, she was very wet, shipping seas continually over her low foredeck. According to Archer, she leaked slightly when launched at Larvik and this increased a bit by the end of the voyage due to shrinkage of the caulking, but even then required only 30 minutes of pumping per day. The engine and boiler gave trouble with leaking steam pipes and injectors which had to be repaired and there were some problems with the bilge pump. Several changes were made before Otto Sverdrup took her on a four-year expedition to the Canadian Arctic from 1898 to 1902 during which he attempted to circumnavigate Greenland and explored the Canadian Arctic islands. A spar deck was added, 7 ½ ft above the old foredeck, providing space for a cabin surrounded by several state rooms and a large workroom. The old chart house, forward of the funnel was removed and replaced by a large water tank; the foremast was raised and stepped to the lower deck, and a 10in x 12in false keel was attached below the original keel (Figure 4).[5] The new spar deck can be seen by comparing the two models shown on these pages. This

Below: Model of *Fram* showing the ship as originally launched in 1893. (Author's photo, Frammuseet, Oslo)

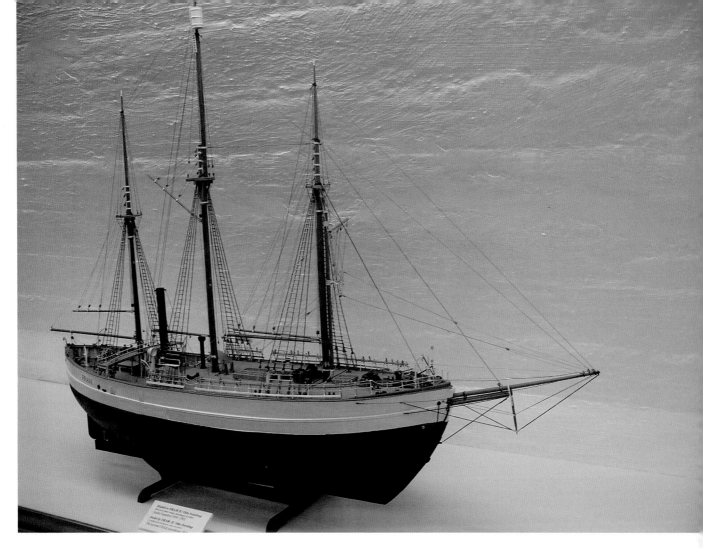

Above: Model of *Fram* showing the ship as modified by addition of a spar deck forward of the bridge for Otto Sverdrup's 1898–1902 expedition to the Canadian Arctic. (Author's photo, Frammuseet, Oslo)

greatly reduced *Fram*'s tendency to ship water over the bows and increased her freeboard by over 3ft.

AMUNDSEN'S *FRAM*

In 1909 Roald Amundsen started to plan an expedition to reach the North Pole. Amundsen was on the first expedition to winter in the Antarctic on Adrien de Gerlache's ship *Belgica* and later was the first person to complete the Northwest Passage on *Gjøa* during a three-year voyage. Like most explorers he was chronically short of money and had actually been bankrupt during the *Gjøa* venture. He certainly did not have the funds to buy or build a ship so *Fram* was vital to his plans. She was owned by the Norwegian State, but Nansen's support was key and was also pivotal in persuading the Norwegian parliament to grant 75,000Nkr (£3,866) to Amundsen to renovate *Fram*. After Sverdrup's expedition, *Fram* had been laid up at Horten as a naval ammunition magazine. She was well preserved but much of her equipment including sails, stored in a nearby warehouse, was destroyed by fire in 1905 and had

to be replaced. The hull was basically intact but the cork, reindeer hair, felt and linoleum insulation had rotted, and the interior pine paneling also had to be restored.

The most significant modification to *Fram* was replacement of the triple-expansion steam engine by a four-cylinder 180hp directly reversible diesel motor built in Stockholm (Figure 4) which took considerably less space, required little maintenance and was much more economical and efficient for ice navigation. Ninety tons of diesel oil were bunkered in several tanks providing a range of approximately 95 days or 11,500 miles. The only disadvantage was that the engine was relatively high-revving (at 250rpm) and could only be fitted with a small (6ft diameter) propeller sufficient only for 4.5 knots. The retractable funnel was replaced by an exhaust pipe to a large valve on the bridge. Modifications to the rigging included a new mizzenmast, moved slightly further aft, an upper foresail yard which turned her into a topsail schooner, increasing the overall sail area to 6,644 square feet, and standing gaffs on all three masts (see artwork on page 118). A protective zinc-plated skin, installed in 1903, was removed as Amundsen felt that this would be torn by the ice, and a heavier 1.01-ton port anchor was installed. To counter *Fram*'s weather helm tendency, the heaviest stores were placed in the stern and the extreme afterpeak was filled with cement and iron. Finally, a spar deck awning was rigged to shade the expedition's huskies.

Amundsen obtained government support by stressing that his expedition would be a scientific one and not simply a race to the North Pole. However, in the same week in September 1909 Frederick Cook and Robert Peary each claimed to have reached the North Pole. Both claims are now believed to be fraudulent, but Amundsen's plans were transformed. He could now only raise funds for his Arctic expedition if he could demonstrate another major exploratory triumph. He decided that this must be the South Pole. Realizing that this would probably not be accepted by the Norwegian Government or by Nansen, he kept all preparations secret, except from his brother and *Fram*'s commander, Thorvald Nielsen. To maintain secrecy he completed all preparations in Norway; apart from a brief visit to Madeira, *Fram* would travel directly to the Ross Sea, Antarctica, where he would establish his base at the Bay of Whales.

Fram was totally different from ships previously used for polar exploration, and Amundsen also disagreed completely with Scott and Shackleton's reliance on ponies for key transport. After his experience with the Inuit in Arctic Canada, Amundsen placed his faith entirely on dogs. Ninety-seven Greenland huskies were loaded at Christiansand on 9 August 1910 covering almost all the free space on deck, including the bridge, then Fram weighed anchor immediately (just before the bailiffs arrived!). Even the crew were not informed of the real destination until they reached Madeira on 5 September. In Funchal, as the anchor was being raised, Amundsen told them that they would be making a detour via the South Pole to the Arctic! He offered to release anyone who wished and promised to double the pay of those who remained; all accepted. Apologetic letters were posted by his brother, to Nansen and King Haakon VII as soon as *Fram* had sailed and a telegram was sent to Captain Robert Scott, then on his way south on his ill-fated expedition to the South Pole, to inform him that he now had a competitor.

Fram was delayed by calms near the Equator, but once into the westerlies she performed well, logging one day's run of 201 miles, an average of 7.25 knots. Amundsen was pleased: 'The ship was no racer, nor was she an absolute log', though he complained about her maneuverability in traffic, saying that she was 'extraordinarily slow and awkward in turning'. He was delighted with her seaworthiness in conditions so different from those for which she was designed: 'a vessel it would be difficult to match for seaworthiness.' The new spar deck transformed her into a very dry ship that needed only two freeing ports compared with the twelve large freeing ports required to drain *Discovery*'s deck. Nielsen later wrote that he could walk dry-shod on the deck in his carpet slippers in a Southern Ocean gale. Amundsen's main concern on the voyage south was the huskies' condition, but there were few problems as they were allowed to roam free over the deck (although muzzled) after Madeira. Several were lost overboard south of the Cape of Good Hope, but the birth of pups more than compensated so that they actually had 116 dogs on arrival in Antarctica.

Amundsen entered the Ross Sea well to the east, between the 175th and 180th meridian, to reduce delays in the pack ice. They entered the pack on 2 January 1911 at 66°30′S, 176°E and were through in four days, anchoring in the Bay of Whales on 14 January. Amundsen immediately set out on skis to find a base site and was immensely relieved to find that at this location the ice cliff was only 6 metres high. Within a few hours a suitable site for the hut, Framheim, was found, 2½km from the ship. There were also abundant seals at the ice edge to provide fresh meat for men and dogs. The dogs were quickly moved on land to start hauling supplies and hut materials. The hut was ready by 28 January and most of the stores were ashore by 4 February. By 16 February a food depot had been set up at 80°S and *Fram* had left for the winter. Several more depots were laid to 82°S and 60 tons of seal meat was collected to feed the dogs before the middle of April when the nine men settled down for the winter.

Amundsen was determined to start for the South Pole as early as possible and on 8 September they set out. Initial progress was good but the temperatures soon dropped to −700°C and they had to rush back to Framheim suffering from severe frostbite. On 19 October five men with four sledges set off again towards the Pole, covering the 99 miles to the 80°S depot in four days. Continuing southwards compact surfaces often allowed them to be towed on skis by the sledges as they averaged 23 miles per day. By 10 November they could see the Transantarctic Mountains and on 17 November they forced their way onto the Axel Heiberg Glacier. The dogs were outstanding, on one occasion climbing 5,000 feet over 17 miles with fully loaded sledges to reach the top of the glacier by 20 November at nearly 11,000 feet. The final trek across the Polar Plateau started on 4 December at 87°S. Traveling was now easier, but the weather was overcast raising concerns about the accuracy of their dead reckoning navigation. However, a sun sight on 7 December matched the dead reckoning of 88°16′ precisely. The same day they passed Shackleton's furthest south from 1909 and reached the South Pole a week later. The journey of 780 miles from Framheim had taken 57 days.

They celebrated with cigars, meticulously surveying their location, then, leaving messages for Scott, set out for Framheim on 18 December. With light loaded sledges, they made rapid progress, descending onto the Ross Ice Barrier on 6 January. Visibility was poor but they easily located their well-marked depots and on 25 January they dropped down the last slope to Framheim, only 39 days from the Pole, for an average daily journey of 20 miles. *Fram* had returned to the Bay of Whales on 8 January and loading started almost immediately, and two days after the polar party returned, they were ready to leave. Some heavy pack ice was encountered but they were able to work through quite quickly between 180° and 175°W. Then they met almost constant headwinds for weeks; while *Fram* was immensely seaworthy, even in a hurricane she remained dry and sound causing Nielsen to call her 'the best sea-boat in the world',[6] beating close-hauled was not her strong point. Amundsen also noted that *Fram* 'light, as she was now, surpassed herself in rolling.'

In Hobart, Amundsen sent telegrams announcing the success at the Pole. *Fram* stayed in Hobart for two weeks while the propeller was repaired, the engine cleaned and the topsail yard spliced. Despite keeping the topsail furled because of the fragile state of the yard, she sailed splendidly passing Cape Horn and reaching Buenos Aires on 25 April. Amundsen sailed separately to South America on SS *Remuera*, traveling incognito as Engelbrecht Gravning, complete with false beard and dark glasses.[7] He remained in South America to work on a book for which his brother Leon had negotiated a fee of 111,000Nkr (£5,722), eventually returning to Norway in July 1912. *Fram* remained in Buenos Aires for two years, deteriorating with rot and worm damage, before returning to Oslo in July 1914.

Amundsen was widely honoured but his triumph was quickly overshadowed by the Scott tragedy. He revived his plan for the Arctic drift with a new ship, *Maud*, in 1918. However, *Maud* never got north of 76°51′N and by 1923 only managed to repeat Adolf Nordenskiöld's 1878–9 voyage through the Northeast Passage with Amundsen again bankrupt. He turned to aircraft and after several failed attempts in fixed-wing planes, he flew over the North Pole with Umberto Nobile in the airship *Norge* in May 1926. Two years later, while attempting to rescue survivors of Nobile's 'Italia' expedition, his plane disappeared without trace over the Barents Sea.

Fram lay neglected at Horten until 1929, when she was brought to Sandefjord for repairs, then to Trondheim for exhibition, before returning to Horten in 1930. Eventually funds were raised to draw her up on land across the harbour from Oslo in March 1935 and a museum around her opened in 1936.

DISCOVERY: LAST PRODUCT OF A GREAT SHIP-BUILDING TRADITION

The British National Antarctic Expedition of 1901–04 resulted directly from the 1895 International Geographical Congress, which identified the exploration of Antarctica as a key international scientific challenge. It became a reality because of the persistence of Sir Clements Markham, then President of the Royal Geographical Society. In his youth Markham took part in one of the Royal Navy expeditions to the Canadian Arctic, where he became obsessed with polar travel and the methods used by the Royal Navy. In the intervening years he became very influential and remarkably talented in political intrigue. Like many of his activities, the National Antarctic Expedition had been mired in controversy since its inception, due to tension between the scientific objectives of the Royal Society and Markham's thirst for the glory of reaching the South Pole. The tortuous path to the eventual departure of the expedition has been recounted by Markham[8] and Holland[9] and in more objective accounts by Savours,[10] Yelverton,[11] and Skelton and Wilson.[12] Markham's machinations led to the resignation of the highly-respected scientist Sir John Murray, while other obstacles included a huge 33-person Expedition Committee dominated by old Arctic hands from the Royal Navy. Markham also feuded with the scientific director appointed by the Royal Society, Professor J. W. Gregory, who resigned because of Markham's intransigent insistence that the scientific programme must be controlled by a naval commanding officer. The ambitious goals eventually agreed were geographic exploration of the Ross Sea sector of Antarctica, a magnetic survey of regions south of 40°S and meteorological, oceanographic, biological and geological research.

The expedition budget, originally set at £150,000, was another major obstacle. The Admiralty declined financial assistance, but seconded several officers including the overall commander, Markham's protégé, Robert Falcon Scott. The expedition was sponsored by the Royal Society and the Royal Geographical Society, but they had raised a mere £14,000 in the first year. Only a timely donation of £25,000 from Llewellyn Longstaff, a paint manufacturer, allowed Markham to order a ship. The British Government eventually matched all contributions so that by August 1900 a budget of £93,000 was available.

Markham has often been criticized for wasting money on a brand new ship when the expedition could have been served as well by an old whaler or sealer, but the exact sequence of decisions about the ship is unclear. Apparently Markham did consider purchasing an old whaler, but decided that those available were unsuitable because the planned magnetic research required a ship free of iron or steel.[13] The Expedition Committee, strongly influenced by the naval officers of Arctic vintage, had hoped to use the old HMS *Discovery* built as the whaler *Bloodhound* in 1872 by Alexander Stephen's shipyard in Dundee and used by the Nares Arctic expedition in 1875–6. However, the Admiralty decided that she was too frail for serious polar work and advised the Committee to commission a new ship from Colin

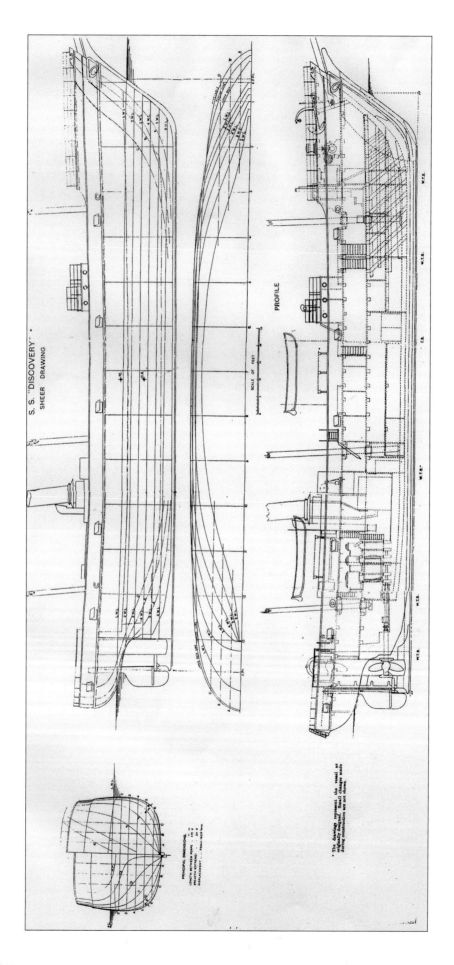

S. S. "DISCOVERY" ·
SHEER DRAWING

PROFILE

SCALE OF FEET

PRINCIPAL DIMENSIONS.
LENGTH BETWEEN PEPPS.   172 0
BREADTH (EXTREME)   34 0
DISPLACEMENT ... About 1620 tons.

* The drawings represent the vessel as
originally designed. Small changes made
during construction are not shown.

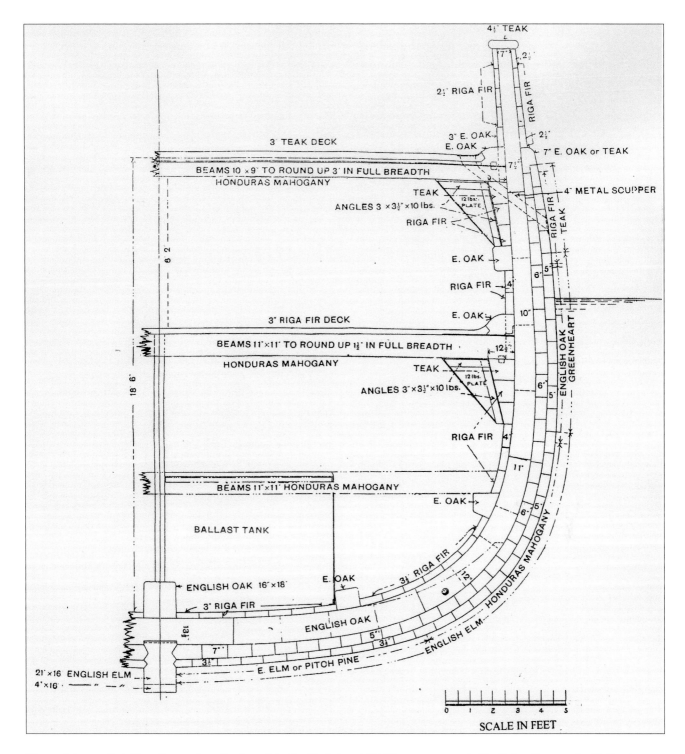

Figure 5 (opposite). Sheerlines and profile plan of the Smith-designed SY *Discovery* commanded by Robert Scott on the National Antarctic Expedition, 1901–04. (After W. E. Smith, 1905, Transactions of the Royal Institute of Naval Architects)

Figure 6 (above). Midships cross-section of *Discovery* providing details of hull construction. (After W. E. Smith, 1905, Transactions of the Royal Institute of Naval Architects)

Archer in Larvik. However, the pressure of national prestige was too great and it was decided that the ship should be designed and built in Britain. W. E. Smith, Chief Constructor at the Admiralty[14] was chosen for design and in December 1899 the new ship was ordered from Dundee Shipbuilders yard, who underbid Vickers for the contract by £30,663. After design alterations the eventual price was £34,050 plus £10,322 for the engines.

Discovery, the first ship to be built for research and exploration in Britain since Halley's *Paramore*, provided an exceptional opportunity to design an ideal polar ship and to choose between two distinct philosophies of ship design: a traditional 'slab-sided' whaler/sealer hull or the innovative 'saucer-shaped' hull of Colin Archer. Unfortunately, the result was much less than ideal, perhaps reflecting too much interference from Executive Committee members. Some innovations were incorporated, but the new ship was essentially a conservative, conventional whaler like those built for many years in Dundee or Norway. These were strongly built to resist ice, with flared bows for ice-breaking, but the main emphasis was on passage-making capability during ocean voyages to whaling grounds. Smith did incorporate some of Archer's ideas in *Discovery*, but rejected a saucer-shaped midsection because of his concern about sea-keeping capacity in the Southern Ocean.[15] Even so, though *Discovery* was seaworthy, she still rolled abominably, reaching arcs of 74° in the South Atlantic, 94° in the Southern Ocean,[16] and arcs of 100° several times per minute during her later Arctic career.[17] Smith considered, but rejected, bilge keels as he felt that they would impede work in ice,[18] but detachable bilge keels were eventually installed during a refit in 1925.[19]

Discovery's lines and dimensions (Figure 5) closely followed Nares' old *Discovery*, but she was 10ft longer to allow a substantial captain's cabin without significantly reducing her coal capacity. With a registered tonnage of 485 and overall length of 172ft, beam of 34ft and 16ft draught,[20] she was larger than previous Antarctic ships except HMS *Challenger*. She was robust with 11in thick oak frames, 10in apart, 4in thick inner planking of Riga fir, and double outer planking: a 6in thick inner layer of pitch pine, Honduras mahogany or oak, and an outer layer of 5in elm below the waterline and pitch pine above, to give a total thickness of 25in. Outside was sheathing of greenheart aft and iron bark[21] forward of the fo'csle break. The massive side structure was reinforced by three tiers of transverse beams of Honduras mahogany and seven 3in thick watertight Riga fir bulkheads. The lower tier beams were particularly strong: 11in square, 3ft apart, but these had to be omitted for about 40ft in the engine room, the weakest part of the hull. The keel was English elm, with pieces connected by horizontal scarphs, each extending over two frames. Apart from the very strong scantlings, Smith included several unusual features. The bow was protected by steel plates for more than 3ft behind the stem and a long overhanging counter with a rounded stern gave some ice protection to the rudder and the propeller. This rather ungainly stern (see photograph opposite), strongly criticized by old whalers in Dundee, produced awkward stern lines (Figure 5) and reduced her speed, particularly in light winds, but did keep the deck drier in the heavy Southern Ocean seas.

Accommodation was designed for over-wintering. Seven officers' cabins with large cabins for the captain and navigating officer surrounded a large central wardroom (273 sq.ft) with petty officers' cabins and the crew's mess directly forward of the wardroom. There were no portholes, both wardroom and crew mess being lit by skylights and double-glazed deck lights. Artificial lighting was primarily by paraffin and acetylene, though experimental electric lighting was also set up with a small steam dynamo and a windmill. The dynamo worked well, but the windmill collapsed during one of the first blizzards of the winter. Small phosphor bronze stoves in the wardroom and the mess were only marginally adequate. There was a 161½ sq.ft magnetic observatory, just aft of the foremast, and two laboratories for oceanographic research and storage of dredging gear. *Discovery* was equipped with two 23ft whale boats and a 14ft skiff aft, a 16ft jolly boat and a 23ft cutter amidships.

Discovery was a fully rigged sailing ship, but was fitted with a more powerful engine than the whalers and sealers which had previously worked in Antarctica. The triple-expansion engine, manufactured by Gourlay Bros. of Dundee, worked with two 10ft 3in cylindrical boilers at a pressure of 150 lb per in^2 and were designed to produce 450ihp at 90rpm (they actually gave 570ihp during sea trials).[22] These would provide speeds up to 8 knots with a coal consumption of 9 tons per day.[23] *Discovery* actually reached 8.8 knots on her sea trials.[24] Bunker storage for 240 tons of coal and zinc-coated steel freshwater ballast tanks for stability were provided though the tanks were ultimately found to be unnecessary. On the outward voyage they were filled with coal; 335 tons were crammed aboard when *Discovery* left New Zealand.

The rigging was one of *Discovery*'s major flaws. Like most sealers and whalers, she was barque-rigged (Figure 7) but her masts were unusually short for a ship of her size: mainmast 100ft 11in, foremast 98ft 1in and mizzen 86ft 8in, all from the waterline. Smith thought that taller masts with longer running gear would be difficult to handle when sheathed in ice. The yards were disproportionately long, with main and fore yards of 60ft giving an overall sail area of 8705 sq.ft, only marginally greater than on the old *Discovery*. Scott found her a sluggish sailer in light winds, which he attributed to the short masts, and noted that she was a very stiff ship and 'could have carried a much larger sail area with advantage. As it was the mainsail and jib were the only sails we took off

Above: Views of *Discovery* moored along the Thames Embankment above Blackfriars Bridge, London, showing the ungainly cruiser stern which drew such criticism from old Dundee whalers.

for a gale, and I think that rarely, if ever, have top-gallant sails been carried through weather such as ours'.[25] According to Smith, she was a very good sailer in strong winds, occasionally reaching 11 knots under sail alone, and once made 233 miles in 24 hours, with a quartering gale.[26] However, after crossing the Bay of Biscay, Scott said that 'it soon became evident that the *Discovery* did not possess a turn of speed under any conditions'.[27] The masts were also too far aft making the ship difficult to steer. Considerable weather helm was necessary to maintain course, which acted as a brake when running with yards square, and *Discovery* could only beat at 87° to the wind compared with 70° for most commercial vessels.[28] Her poor sailing performance, caused by the rig and the hull design, significantly delayed the journey south and required much more steaming (and coal) than expected.

Discovery was registered as a yacht to avoid Board of Trade regulations on loading, but was given permission to fly the White Ensign.[29] She left Cowes on 6 August 1901 (see the artwork on page 132) with forty-nine men. By Madeira, other problems become apparent. Off Lisbon, two parrels (supporting the yards) on the main and foremasts broke in a light (Force 3) wind and what was referred to by Scott as 'the Dundee leak' re-appeared. This had been discovered before departure, but shortly after leaving Madeira, there was 2 feet of water in the hold. No floor had been installed so many stores were destroyed. The leak continued throughout the voyage, requiring repeated visits to the slipway, and, in fact, plagued *Discovery* throughout her career. The main cause was shrinkage of the unseasoned timber used in her construction because the ship was built in Dundee where properly seasoned timber was not available (in Norway Archer had substantial supplies).[30] Satisfactory seasoning of oak requires some ten years, so this could not be easily solved (there were

other problems with the wood used, as the specifications shown in Figure 6 were not closely followed; for example, teak specified for the deck was replaced by Riga fir). The leak was very difficult to find at sea because of the double planking, but when the coal tar coating was scraped off on a slip in New Zealand additional problems appeared. Several bolts were defective, nails were loose and some large holes bored in the lower hull (presumably by mistake) had been filled with wood shavings and cemented over. There were also small wormholes in the greenheart sheathing which allowed water to seep between the planks. These were not caused by marine borers but are frequently found in greenheart and the affected wood should have been rejected in the shipyard. The Dundee builders actually recommended the ironwood sheathing more customary on whalers but the Expedition Committee preferred greenheart because of its 'give and slipperiness'.[31] Although greenheart was often used for ice vessels, it is difficult to work, is very subject to shrinkage on drying, and does not hold nails well. The eventual compromise was to use greenheart to the break of the fo'csle and ironwood (or ironbark) at the bow, where steel plates were nailed.

Because of repairs at Madeira, the leakage and restowing of stores and the slow passage down the Atlantic, Cape Town was not reached until 3 October. Despite the leak, the broken parrels, trouble with the engine bearings, the excessive rolling (which on one occasion resulted in swamping of the magnetic observatory), and her poor sailing performance, Scott claimed to be satisfied with *Discovery*, describing her as 'the finest vessel which was ever built for exploring purposes'.[32] However, because of the delays, much of the planned oceanographic programme and a visit to Melbourne had to be abandoned. *Discovery* did visit Macquarie Island, before reaching Lyttelton, New Zealand, on 30 November.

Figure 7. Mast and rigging diagram for *Discovery*. (After W. E. Smith, 1905, *Transactions of the Royal Institute of Naval Architects*)

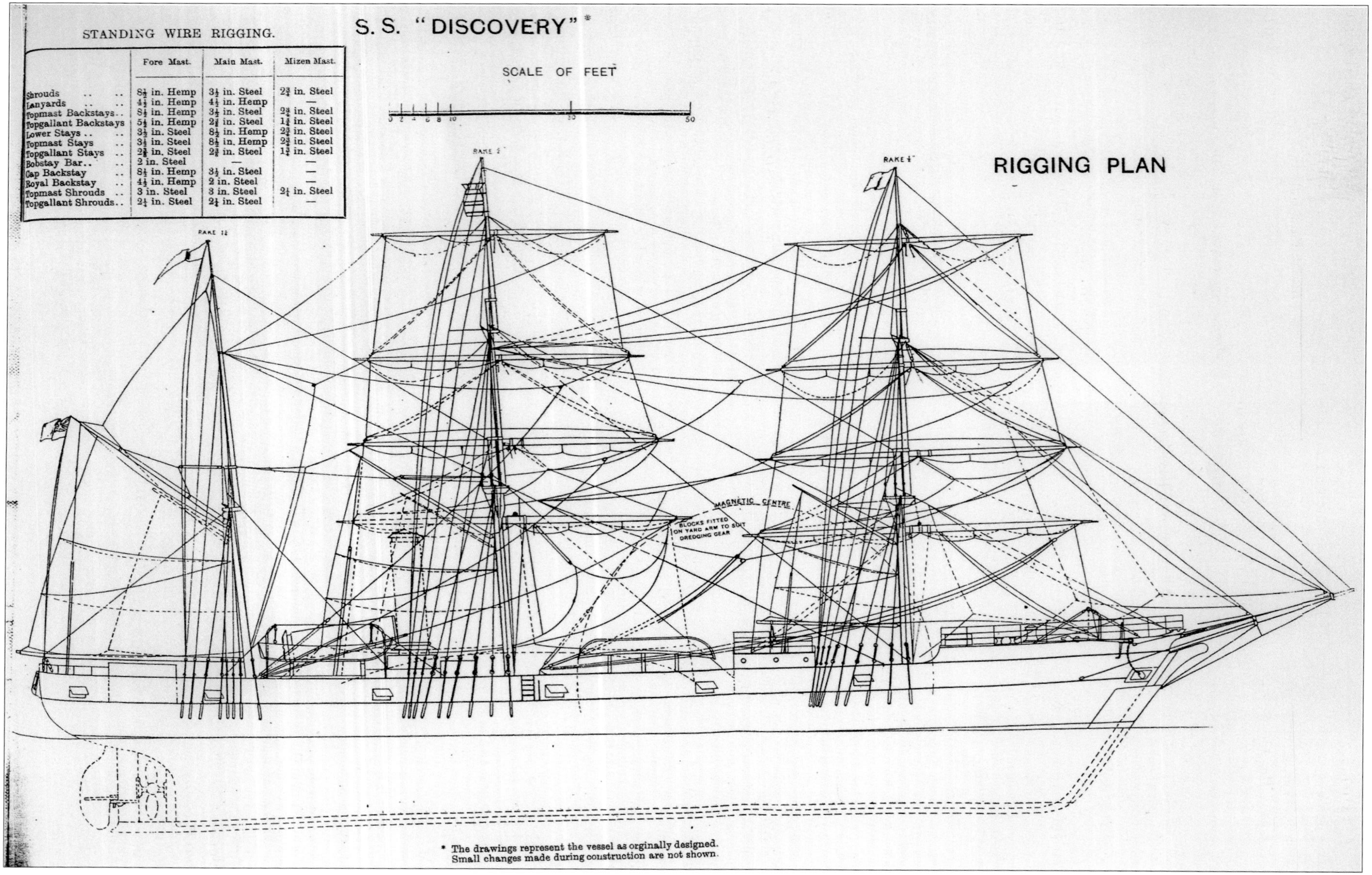

RIGGING PLAN

S. S. "DISCOVERY" *

SCALE OF FEET

STANDING WIRE RIGGING.

	Fore Mast.	Main Mast.	Mizen Mast.
Shrouds	8½ in. Hemp	3½ in. Steel	2¾ in. Steel
Lanyards	4½ in. Hemp	4 in. Hemp	2¾ in. Steel
Topmast Backstays	4½ in. Hemp	3½ in. Steel	2¾ in. Steel
Topgallant Backstays	5½ in. Hemp	2½ in. Steel	1½ in. Steel
Fore Stays	3½ in. Steel	8½ in. Hemp	2¾ in. Steel
Topmast Stays	3½ in. Steel	3½ in. Hemp	2¾ in. Steel
Topgallant Stays	2½ in. Steel	2½ in. Steel	1¾ in. Steel
Bobstay Bar..	2 in. Steel	—	—
Cap Backstay	8½ in. Hemp	3½ in. Steel	—
Royal Backstay	4½ in. Hemp	2 in. Steel	—
Topmast Shrouds..	3 in. Steel	3 in. Steel	2¾ in. Steel
Topgallant Shrouds..	2¾ in. Steel	2¾ in. Steel	—

MAGNETIC CENTRE

BLOCKS FITTED BUT
ON YARD ARM TO
DEGAUSSING GEAR

* The drawings represent the vessel as originally designed.
Small changes made during construction are not shown.

At Lyttelton *Discovery* was slipped twice in attempt to cure the leak. When she sailed on 21 December, she had a heavy deck cargo including forty-five sheep and twenty-three sledge dogs and 'the Plimsoll line had sunk so deep it was forgotten'.[33] Scott was worried that the deck cargo would be lost in the Southern Ocean, but they had unusually calm weather. *Discovery* docked briefly at Port Chalmers where two volunteers from HMS *Ringarooma*, Jesse Handsley and Tom Crean joined, and 45 tons of coal were added to the deck cargo.[34]

Discovery crossed the Antarctic Circle on 3 January 1902 entering pack ice which required firing up the second boiler. To conserve coal, steaming was generally confined to one boiler, which, in calm open water would use 3½ to 4 tons of coal a day for a speed of up to 5 knots, compared with 6 tons a day for 7 knots with both boilers fired.[35] On 8 January they reached Borchgrevink's old base at Cape Adare, then steamed south, dredging and sounding along the Victoria Land coast, forcing through light pack ice into McMurdo Sound on 12 January. Several days later, steaming along the Ross Ice Barrier, *Discovery* reached her farthest south of 78°36′S, near the eastern end of the Barrier where new land, named King Edward VII Land, was discovered.

With new sea ice forming, *Discovery* then turned back to moor for the winter off Ross Island in McMurdo Sound, where a long promontory provided protection from ice pressure. A small hut was built on shore, but the plan was to spend the winter on the ship and a snowbank was built around her to provide wind protection. Although specially designed for winter accommodation, the ship was not comfortable because of poor insulation. The mess was fine but the wardroom and cabins were very cold as the sides and decks were uninsulated. Ice progressively accumulated, 'several people have had to literally chip out their mattresses'[36] and Scott himself had to sit with his feet in a box of hay. Despite the attention given to insulation on *Fram* and their Arctic experience, no members of the Expedition Committee seem to have thought about the problem. Though lighting with patent lamps and acetylene lamps was good, condensation was a continuing problem and the phosphor bronze stoves designed to use anthracite burnt out quickly with steam coal.

Apart from the discomfort of the ship and temperatures which dropped to −50°C, the main problem encountered during the winter was scurvy due to the reliance on canned food. This was largely solved on the ship by adding fresh seal to the diet, but it appeared again during sledge trips in the following summer because the seal meat was boiled excessively before departure. The main sledge trip, due south, combined dog sledging and man-hauling, as Robert Scott, Ernest Shackleton and Edward Wilson forced their way across the Ross Ice Barrier to 82°16′S. None of them knew anything about driving dogs who failed badly on the return journey because of a completely inadequate diet of dried codfish. By mid-January all three men showed symptoms of scurvy and Shackleton's condition deteriorated particularly quickly until he was unable to haul the sledge. As Scott and Wilson's health also declined, survival became very tenuous; when they reached the ship on 6 February all three had advanced scurvy and were immediately bed-ridden.

While *Discovery* was ice-bound in McMurdo Sound, Markham was trying to raise funds for a relief ship in the belief that 'the force of public opinion would eventually compel the Government to provide a second ship to act as a tender to the first'.[37] He was wrong and the Government refused additional funding but he managed to raise £3,880 from public subscription and the New Zealand Government, enough to buy an old Norwegian whaling barque. The 297 ton *Morgensen*, built at Tonsberg in 1872, was renamed *Morning* and William Colbeck, veteran of Borchgrevink's *Southern Cross* expedition was appointed as commander. *Morning* had only a 31-year old 84hp engine and the best daily passage she could manage on the voyage south was 170 miles.[38] Despite her pathetic engine, she penetrated the pack ice quickly and was in sight of *Discovery* by 23 January before being stopped by 10 miles of fast ice. Over the next few weeks stores and 20 tons of coal were hauled across to *Discovery*. Colbeck wanted to break *Discovery* out, but Scott was confident that the ice would clear, so *Morning* left for New Zealand. Scott was wrong, the ice did not clear, and *Discovery* and her crew were stuck for another winter in McMurdo Sound.

The plight of the ice-trapped expedition now caused some commotion in London. Markham immediately started lobbying for funds for a second relief ship, but the Government finally lost patience and demanded that the Societies turn over responsibility for arranging relief ships to the Admiralty. *Morning* was purchased from the Societies and another Stephen-designed whaling barque, *Terra Nova*, was purchased from Bowring Brothers in St. John's, Newfoundland. *Terra Nova* joined *Morning* in Hobart and the two ships reached the ice edge in McMurdo Sound on 5 January 1904.

New Admiralty orders to Scott stipulated that if *Discovery* could not be freed within six weeks, she was to be abandoned and expedition members transferred to the relief ships. It took more than a month of sawing and blasting through the 8ft thick ice, but at last, on 14 February *Discovery* floated free. She was almost immediately driven aground in a Force 10 gale, listing heavily with waves breaking over the stern 'the beams and the decks buckled upwards...thick glass deadlights were cracked across...with the heavier blows one could see the whole ship temporarily distorted'.[39] Clearly she could not stand this for long, but after nine hours she suddenly slipped off the shoal into deeper water. Amazingly, the only serious damage was to her false keel and rudder. The spare rudder, which was only half as large, seri-

Above: SY *Discovery* passing the Royal Yacht on departure from Cowes, 6 August 1901. (By kind permission of the Governors of Dulwich College)

ously affected her sailing ability on the way back to New Zealand: '...our small rudder...had so little effect on the ship that we could only keep our course by constantly trimming our sails....The *Discovery* is an impossible sailer and now that we have had to fall back on the spare rudder we can scarcely get on without steam'.[40]

Only 80 tons of coal were left to reach New Zealand, far too little for adequate ballast, so *Discovery* rolled abominably, burying herself in the waves, 'the upper deck has been awash and water has been pouring down through the skylights and chimneys'.[41] By the time she met the other ships at Auckland Islands, only 10 tons of coal were left, but with their help all three were able to reach Lyttelton on 1 April. By comparison, the remainder of her voyage to reach Portsmouth on 10 September was uneventful.

Scott was ambivalent about *Discovery*. His praise for her as 'the finest vessel ever built for exploring purposes' seemed tailored to official sponsors and rings hollow beside his frequent criticism of her sailing qualities. Her lethargic sailing could not be offset by her engine because of her very limited coal capacity and resulting delays and her excessive rolling destroyed the oceanographic programme. These problems, together with leakage, poor ventilation and poor insulation show that she was certainly not an ideal exploration ship, though perhaps not an 'incubus' as described by A.G.E.

Jones.[42] The flaws were partly due to design and partly to construction, exacerbated by the lack of suitable timber in Dundee, but probably the most telling criticism was that she was far too expensive, costing five times as much as de Gerlache's *Belgica* and Borchgrevink's *Southern Cross* together. She achieved nothing that was not later surpassed by the much older and much cheaper *Terra Nova*, used by Scott on his final 1910–13 expedition.

Despite her flaws, Markham had hoped that *Discovery* would be maintained as an exploration vessel, but the Societies were soon forced to sell her for £10,000 (less than 20 per cent of her cost five years earlier) to the Hudson Bay Company. She was used in the Canadian Arctic and as a supply ship during the First World War and then was laid up until 1925, when she returned to Antarctica for use by the Discovery Investigations for whaling management activities in the Southern Ocean. Funding for the Discovery Investigations came from revenue collected from whalers operating in the Falkland Island Dependencies; between 1921 and 1933 £1.62 million in revenue was collected of which £668,000 was spent on the Investigations.[43] *Discovery* was purchased from the Hudson Bay Company for £5,000 and comprehensively re-fitted at Vospers in Portsmouth for £114,000. The masts, yards and rigging were all replaced, and the taller main and fore masts were moved forward (by 8ft and 4ft respectively), following Scott's recommendations for improving sailing performance.[44] The topgallant was divided for easier handling and the sail area was increased by 20 per cent. The hull was replanked inside and out, a new

Above: Model of *Discovery* in her winter quarters off Hut Point, Ross Island, McMurdo Sound. (Author's photo, Praesidio Museum, Ushuaia, Argentina)

deck and deckhouses were fitted, biological and chemical laboratories were built and extensive oceanographic research equipment was installed.[45]

The first Discovery Investigation under scientific director Stanley Kemp left Dartmouth in September 1925 sailing via Cape Town to South Georgia where biologists carried out research on whales, before continuing to the Falkland Islands then back to Cape Town by June 1926. Kemp was thoroughly dissatisfied with *Discovery*: 'Square rigged vessels of the Antarctic type are quite unsuitable for the work we are engaged on and the *Discovery*....is worse than any other vessel of her class. Her sailing qualities are inferior, her speed less, her coal consumption greater and her bunker capacity little more than half'.[46] Virtually no work was possible on the last stretch of the voyage from Bouvetøya to Cape Town. Kemp insisted that a new ship was essential for the whale research programme, which led to construction of the first true British oceanographic vessel, the RRS *Discovery II*, launched in 1929. In the meantime, in Cape Town, *Discovery* was at last fitted with the bilge keels rejected by William Smith in 1900, and her topgallant yards were sent down to reduce windage before a second voyage to South Georgia and the Antarctic Peninsula.

Despite her unsuitability for oceanographic research, *Discovery*'s Antarctic career was not yet quite finished. By the 1920s, the modern Antarctic whaling industry, which

started at South Georgia in 1905, had resulted in serious territorial competition, and there was particular concern in Australia about Norwegian intentions in East Antarctica. The British Australian New Zealand Research Expedition (BANZARE) of 1928–30, led by Sir Douglas Mawson, was framed as a scientific expedition, but the main objective was to hurriedly plant the Union Jack over the largest possible area of East Antarctica,[47] particularly in the largely unexplored sector from 95°E to 20°W. After tortuous negotiations, the British Government eventually leased *Discovery* for 'the exceptionally low rate of £8,000 per annum'.[48] The very experienced ice-captain, John King Davis, veteran of expeditions with Shackleton on *Nimrod* and Mawson on *Aurora* was appointed captain.

During the 55-day voyage from London to Cape Town, Davis became quite disenchanted with the ship which he compared very unfavourably with *Aurora*, being smaller, less powerful, with less coal capacity[49] and much more expensive. He felt that 'she has been ruined from a sailor's point of view by laymen putting in all sorts of arrangements....like bilge keels',[50] and agreed entirely with Kemp: 'a more unsuitable ship for oceanographical work than *Discovery*

Above: Bow view of *Discovery* at her berth along the Thames Embankment. (Conway)

could not have been built'.[51] He was most unimpressed with her sailing ability though she carried more sail than *Aurora*. In Cape Town he had the heavy main yards and the topgallants removed to make her easier for his inexperienced (in sailing ships) crew to handle. Overcrowded with twenty-six crew and twelve scientists, *Discovery* sailed from Cape Town on 19 October 1928 and entered pack ice off East Antarctica on 12 December at 65°18′S, 80°12′E. Mawson and Davis were at loggerheads from the start, squabbling over the sounding programme, and what Mawson regarded as Davis's excessive caution about bringing *Discovery* into ice. Davis was justifiably nervous about getting *Discovery* stuck in heavy ice with very limited coal stocks and was not impressed with 'that bloody rubbishing business of raising the flag ashore'.[52] It was not until 13 January that they finally managed to land and proclaim British sovereignty on the tiny Proclamation Island at 65°50′S, 53°37′E. By 26 January, with only 120 tons of coal left, Davis insisted on

heading north to dock in Adelaide on 31 March.

The first BANZARE voyage was not very successful and convinced Davis to end his distinguished Antarctic career. Mawson managed to raise £6,000 from a private supporter for a second voyage, with Davis's first mate, K.N. Mackenzie as captain. Crowded, overloaded, with an aircraft and forty people on board, and drawing 17 feet, *Discovery* left Hobart in November 1930. The sounding programme started well, but Mawson complained about *Discovery*'s incessant rolling and flooded decks. Arrangements had been made to take on coal from the new Norwegian whale factory ship *Sir James Clark Ross II*. Bunkering in rough seas was tricky but a tethered whale carcass acted as a buffer between the ships and 100 tons of coal were loaded.[53] Then they started a long, hazardous journey along the coast of East Antarctica from Oates Land to Enderby Land. MacKenzie soon felt the strain of navigating through heavy gales in unexplored and uncharted ice-strewn waters, particularly on New Year's Eve when he had been on deck for eighty hours, as huge ice floes, taller than the masts were hurled against the ship by hurricane winds. Wherever possible landings were made and territory claimed, but sometimes it was only possible to throw a copper cylinder containing a proclamation onto shore. After a last proclamation on 18 February at 67°47′S, 66°53′E, *Discovery* headed north to reach Hobart on 19 March. The second BANZARE voyage was much more successful, covering some 12,500 miles, charting more than 3,000 miles of the East Antarctic coast and cementing Australian claims to the sector, which was declared as Australian Antarctic Territory in 1936.

Discovery's Antarctic career ended when she arrived in London on 1 August 1931. From 1932–6 she was laid up in London, and she was turned over to the Boy Scouts Association as training ship for Sea Scouts. Moored along the Thames Embankment above Blackfriars Bridge she was managed by the Scouts until 1954, before serving as a drill ship for the Royal Navy Volunteer Reserve until 1979. She was then handed over to the Maritime Trust and was restored over the next seven years before being moved on a floating dock ship to a permanent location at Discovery Point, Dundee.

NOTES

[1] Archer, C., 'The Fram', pp.1-16 in *The Norwegian Polar Expedition, 1893–96*, Christiania, 1898.

[2] In an emergency in the Kara Sea during her first voyage *Fram* actually managed 8 knots under steam.

[3] Nansen, F., *Farthest North: Being the Record of Exploration of the "Fram", 1893–96 and of a Fifteen Month Sledge Journey by Dr. Nansen and Lieutenant Johannsen*, Christiania, 1897.

[4] Huntford, R., Nansen, *The Explorer as a Hero*, Duckworth, London, 1997.

[5] Blom, C., 'The "Fram"', Appendix 1 in Amundsen, R., (tr. A.G. Chater), *The South Pole: An Account of the Norwegian Antarctic Expedition in the "Fram", 1910–1912*, John Murray, London, 1912.

[6] Nilsen, T., 'The voyage of the "Fram"', in *ibid*.

[7] Bonham-Larsen, T., (tr. I. Christopherson), *Roald Amundsen*, Sutton Publishing Ltd, Stroud, 2006.

[8] Markham, Sir C.M., *Lands of Silence*, Cambridge University Press, Cambridge, 1921.

[9] Markham, Sir C. (ed. C. Holland), *Antarctic Obsession*, Erskine Books, Bluntisham.

[10] Savours, A., *The Voyages of Discovery: The Illustrated History of Scott's Ship*, Virgin Books, London, 1994.

[11] Yelverton, D.E., *Antarctica Unveiled: Scott's First Expedition and the Quest for the Unknown Continent*, University Press of Colorado, Boulder, 2000.

[12] Skelton, J.V., and Wilson, D.M., *Discovery Illustrated*, Reardon Publishing, Cheltenham, 2001.

[13] This requirement was soon relaxed to an absence of iron or steel within 30 feet of the magnetic observatory, and eventually to minor measures such as hemp rather than wire shrouds.

[14] Smith had a rather chequered career. He designed the Royal Yacht *Victoria and Albert*, which turned out to be so dangerously under-ballasted that it nearly capsized on launching. He was subsequently fired during the First World War on the direct instructions of Winston Churchill, then First Lord of the Admiralty.

[15] Smith, W.E., 'The design of the Antarctic exploration vessel *Discovery*', *Transactions of the Institute of Naval Architects*, 47 (1), 1905, pp.1-42 + folding plans.

[16] Royal Geographical Society Antarctic Archives 12/1/13;11.28.1901, cited by Yelverton, (2000) *op cit*.

[17] Jones, A.G.E., 'The steam yacht Discovery', *The Mariners' Mirror*, 66 (4), 1980, pp.68-70.

[18] Smith, (1905), *op cit*.

[19] Savours, (1994), *op cit*.

[20] Smith, (1905), *op cit*.

[21] This has been variously referred to as iron bark or ironwood which covers a range of different Australian eucalyptus species used in construction of whalers and sealers.

[22] Skelton and Wilson, (2001), *op cit*.

[23] Savours, (1994), *op cit*.

[24] R.W. Skelton, cited by Skelton and Wilson, (2001), *op cit*.

[25] Scott, R.F., *The Voyage of Discovery*, MacMillan, London, 1905.

[26] Smith, (1905), *op cit*.

[27] Scott, (1905), *op cit*.

[28] Yelverton, (2000), *op cit*.

[29] Jones, (1980), *op cit*.

[30] Yelverton, (2000), *op cit*.

[31] Jones, (1980), *op cit*.

[32] Scott, (1905), *op cit*.

[33] Bernacchi, L., *The Saga of the Discovery*, London, 1938.

[34] Church, I., *Last Port to Antarctica: Dunedin and Port Chalmers: 100 Years of Polar Service*, Otago Heritage Books, Dunedin, 1997.

[35] Scott, (1905), *op cit*.

[36] *Ibid*.

[37] Mill, H.R., *The Record of the Royal Geographical Society, 1830–1930*, (London, 1930).

[38] Jones, A.G.E., 'Captain William Colbeck', *Fram*, 1(1), 1977–1985.

[39] Scott, (1905), *op cit*.

[40] *Ibid*, letter to Scott-Gregory, cited by Yelverton, (2000), *op cit*.

[41] Scott, (1905), *op cit*.

[42] Jones, (1980), *op cit*.

[43] Hart, I.B., *Whaling in the Falkland Island, 1904–1931: A History of Bay-based Whaling in Antarctica*, Pequena, Newtown St. Margaret's, 2006.

[44] Hardy, A., *Great Waters*, Collins, London, 1967.

[45] *Ibid*.

[46] Correspondence between Dr Stanley Kemp and Dr Calman of

Above: *Discovery* in August 2007 alongside at Discovery Point, Dundee, where she is open to the public. Behind her is Dundee Heritage Trust's interpretation centre which has exhibits relating to both the ship and polar exploration. (Paul Brown)

the British Museum, cited by Savours, (1992), *op cit.*

[47] Price, A.G., *The winning of Australian Antarctica: Mawson's B.A.N.Z.A.R.E. voyages, 1929–31, based on the Mawson papers*, Angus and Robertson, Sydney, 1962.

[48] Government documents cited by Savours, (1992), *op cit.*

[49] *Discovery*'s coal capacity was contentious; Davis set this at 300 tons and estimated 6–7 tons/day steaming at 5 knots, giving a maximum range of about 11,000km, but coal consumption would be much higher working in ice. Mawson believed that she could carry 450 tons of coal. In fact she could carry just over 400 tons with 60 tons on deck and 20 tons loose on each side of the engine room. Crossley, L. (ed.), *Trial by Ice: The Antarctic Diaries of John King Davis*, Bluntisham Books, Erskine Press, Bluntisham, 1997.

[50] Letter to Mawson cited by Crossley, *ibid.*

[51] Letter to Antarctic Committee cited by Crossley, *ibid.*

[52] Jacka, F., and Jacka, E. (eds.), *Mawson's Antarctic Diaries*, Allen and Unwin, Sydney, 1988.

[53] *Ibid.*

Motor Tug *Nangee*

AN INTERESTING WORKING MODEL

by Tom Gorman

During late October I was asked by a friend if I could build a model of *Nangee* for his wife using a Mobile Marine Models complete kit as the basis and enhancing it as required. As my next commercial commission was not due to start before the end of April 2010 and I had a few months in hand, I agreed. The outfit was duly collected, unpacked, and all the parts supplied examined. Many modellers seem to start work on a model without first making themselves aware of the instructions or plans, but I much prefer to spend some time at least becoming fully familiar with the general arrangement drawings. In this particular case, as with all of Mobile Marine

Models semi kits, there is no instruction manual. There is an envelope of printed templates and some notes, but the model tug builder has to prepare and work from the drawings and his own experience and with help, where required, from Bryan Ward and his staff. It saves a great deal of heartache and time if the drive units are laid out over the plans of the ship to full scale size. By so doing it is possible to envisage where access will be needed and where it is most easily available, from the drawings.

PROPELLERS AND RUDDER

I invariably start my model building by locating propeller shaft(s) and rudder(s) followed by couplings and motor(s) all

Below: Finished model afloat.

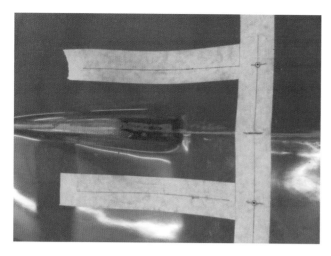

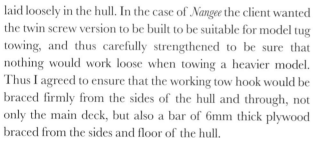

Above: Underside of hull showing marking for steerable Kort nozzles location.

Above: Close-up of perimeter timber fixing.

laid loosely in the hull. In the case of *Nangee* the client wanted the twin screw version to be built to be suitable for model tug towing, and thus carefully strengthened to be sure that nothing would work loose when towing a heavier model. Thus I agreed to ensure that the working tow hook would be braced firmly from the sides of the hull and through, not only the main deck, but also a bar of 6mm thick plywood braced from the sides and floor of the hull.

Locating and fitting twin steerable Kort nozzles with their carefully manufactured 4-blade propellers and shafts is a task that requires patience and care. The propellers, obtained from The Prop Shop, are a close fit inside the nozzles and must revolve without touching the nozzles at all of the turning positions. To centre the shafts I first marked the location of the Kort nozzles and then made a disc of 3mm thick plywood to fit neatly inside each nozzle, the ply being drilled centrally to accept the end of each prop shaft in turn. Each nozzle was adjusted and fitted to the hull through the mountings supplied and, in turn, each shaft was fed through a suitable slot cut in the fibreglass hull. The slot, using the shaft fitted into the ply disc in the nozzle, was adjusted until it was truly lined up. A shaft support, made from a short piece of brass tube and a small plate of brass silver soldered together, was made to suit each shaft. Each one was slotted over the shaft and its location marked on the hull and a slot was cut through the hull to accept each support. Each shaft with support and with its propeller was then fitted in place and very carefully aligned so that each nozzle could move without fouling its propeller. When all was true each piece was tacked in place with a blob of thick superglue, and finally fixed using easy sand filler with hardener. This is very easily described but not quite so easily done.

MOTORS

When the shafts and nozzles were secure, I turned to the fitting of the motors and couplings. Here, at the client's request, I used universal double couplings of the nylon and brass pattern to allow the large motors to be set at a slight angle from the shafts. The motors, in their supplied cradles were mounted on a timber base that was secured to the hull with easy sand filler after tacking with superglue. The timber base was suitably painted before being installed. Finally the battery (12-volt 7-amp/hour) was placed ahead of the motor base and the model was place in the test tank (domestic bath) and checked for deadweight. It took 4 pounds of lead to bring the model down almost to the waterline; most of this was at the extreme stern to compensate for the weight of the battery located well forward in the hull. All of this indicated that battery, motors and couplings would be accessible through the opening that would be covered by the super-structure. The steering servo and linkage to the steerable nozzles would be accessed through a large hatch in the main deck, visible in the photographs. The steering servo was, in fact, mounted in a piece of ply secured across the hull just above the position where the shafts entered the hull and with the servo centrally fixed.

HULL AND DECKS

The drive units were then removed from the hull, the hull was washed thoroughly with warm water and detergent to remove any trace of the release agent used when making the hull. Masking tape was placed over the locations of all the deck relief ports to prevent drills from wandering and any damage to the gelcoat of the hull as the ports were opened out. This was accomplished using a 1.5mm bit in a low voltage drill to drill a series of holes round the perimeter of each port, the holes were connected using a sharp scalpel and the edges of each hole were lightly filed to a smooth finish. At

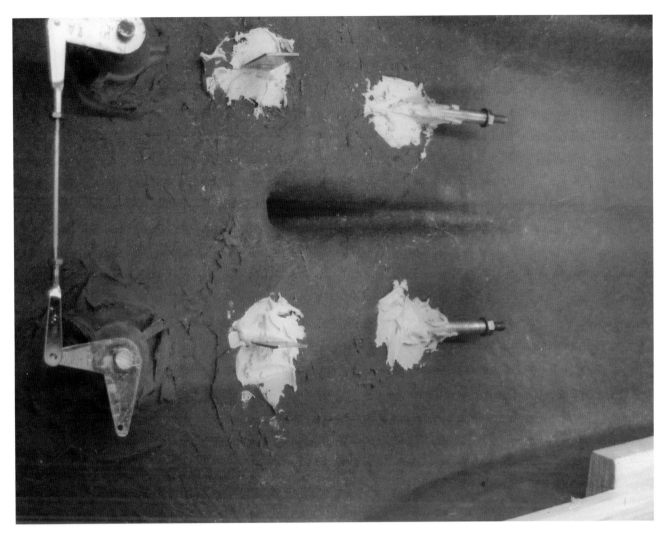

Above: Detail of propeller shaft and Kort nozzle fixings inside hull.

Above: After deck in place at stern, opening of access hatch suitably trimmed.

Above: Forward deck in place on hull, coamings for superstructure still to be fitted.

Above: Mounting with servo, note lead weights fixed beneath servo tray.

Above: Further view to show motor mountings and servo coupled to steering system.

Above: Stern area showing bulwark supports and deck plating.

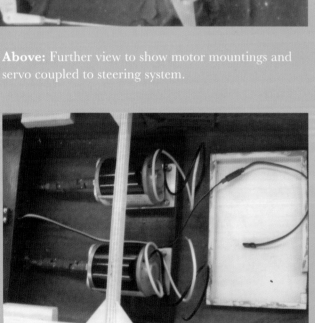

Above: Twin motors, drive couplings and battery tray fitting into hull.

Above: Working tow hook installed just forward of stern hatch.

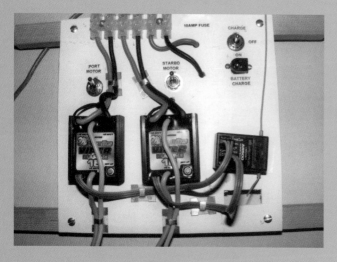

Above: Radio tray detail.

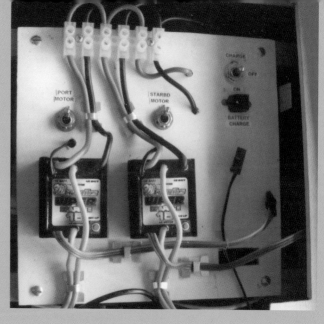

Above: Radio tray in place in forward hatchway above battery.

Above: Towing winch forward of tow hook with bollard between.

Above: Further detail of tow hook also showing capstan on port side.

Above: Overview of superstructure under construction.

Below: Superstructure.

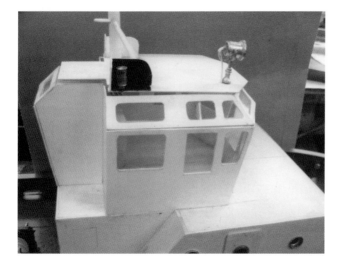

Below: Stern of model to show name and port of registry.

six locations round the bulwarks of the hull were marks indicating positions of the Panama guides for ropes when mooring, and these were drilled out and finished with a round file to accept the cast white metal fittings supplied with the kit. A larger oval port was to be fitted at the centre of the bow and the location for this was also opened out. These units were not fitted at this stage but the holes were prepared.

Next I marked off and fitted the necessary plywood strip supports round the perimeter of the main deck and round the bow deck area. Such supports were made from 10mm wide strips of 3mm thick ply glued just below the level of the relief ports by a depth enough just to allow the decks to lie flush with the bottom edge of each port. This strip was tacked in place using thick superglue. After this had set a second identical strip of 3mm plywood was glued over the first using PVA to increase the total thickness of the beams. A variety of spring clips and clothes pegs were used to hold all in place until glues cured. Easy sand filler was used to rein-

Below: Overhead view of superstructure.

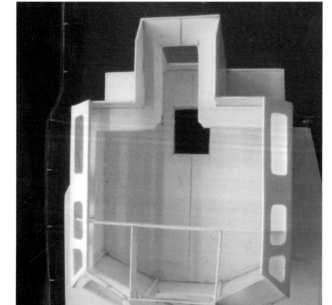

Below: Main mast with Christmas tree of lights.

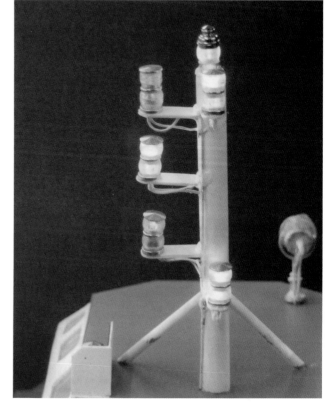

Above and below: Superstructure in place on hull.

force the ply strips. Using the template supplied in the kit the main stern deck was traced on to card – cereal packet card – by means of carbon paper, and the card pattern was cut to allow the aft deck to be assessed and marked before any attempt was made to cut the deck from fine plywood.

Once the stern deck was cut, and here I deviated from the kit by using 1.5mm plywood instead of the recommended 3mm ply, it was tried in place and glued down using PVA. The reason for using 1.5mm plywood was that I wanted to plate this deck with 1mm styrene sheet, first to simulate the steel of the real deck and secondly to permit easy fitting of small styrene parts such as bulwark supports. To support the deck transversely a number of beams were made from 6mm thick plywood and secured across the hull, carefully measured to ensure that the plate of 6mm plywood to carry the working tow hook was accurately located and other deck support beams did not foul the large deck hatch opening. In the same manner the fore deck was copied from the template drawings, cut out of 1.5mm plywood and glued in place.

To gain a fine finish to the inside of the bulwarks they were lightly sanded and were sheeted with 0.5mm styrene sheet glued in place with contact cement. Allowing this work to become secure overnight the main and bow decks were next

plated with 1mm thick styrene cut mostly into plates 100mm x 60mm and fitted working from the centre of the deck out to the bulwarks; each plate at the deck edges being cut to fit to the styrene of the bulwarks. For those who have not attempted to plate a timber deck in this way, the procedure is fairly easy. If two or three coats of liquid poly are applied to the timber deck (each coat being allowed to dry before applying the next of course), the timber will have a plastic coating and small plates of styrene can be attached using liquid poly. Ensure that the plastic coating of the timber is quite dry before fitting the plates with fresh liquid poly otherwise there may be a tendency for the styrene sheet to wrinkle.

The next task was to cut the bulwark supports, using the templates from the kit as a guide, but using 1mm thick styrene. Each support is attached in the appropriate location using liquid poly and an artist's fine soft brush. At this time I decided to paint the hull before proceeding further. Using the requested colour scheme, I proceeded to paint the hull. The relief ports were first covered internally with masking tape to prevent any spray coating the decks and the whole hull was given three coats of grey primer from the Halford range. This was allowed to dry for a couple of days before it was checked and lightly sanded. The waterline was marked with a soft pencil clamped to a large square and with the hull set truly level on a flat surface. Using Tamiya masking tape the upper hull was masked to the line and the lower hull was given four coats of red oxide primer, also from the Halfords range, and when this was dry the lower hull was masked to the line to allow the upper hull to be sprayed bright blue; three coats were required for good coverage. The hull was then set aside for a weekend in the airing cupboard to permit the warm conditions to fully cure the paint.

DECK FITTINGS

While waiting for the hull to cure a start was made upon some of the deck fittings. The main winch and the winch/windlass units came as small kits in separate bags with small detail sheets to aid construction. I assembled and painted the winch unit. The winch/windlass was then assembled. When both had been completed suitable 'rope' supplied in the kit was wound on to the rope drums and suitably finished. They were set aside to be installed at a later time. The hydraulic crane was also supplied as a small kit and was assembled although painting was left to a later time as work on the main model was again done.

Contrary to accepted practice for a Mobile Marine Models tug, I decided to build the entire superstructure from styrene sheet. Plywood coamings were made and fitted round the access hatch over which the superstructure was to fit and the template pack allowed me to make card templates from which to mark off and cut the styrene sheet. The vertical walls of the lower part of the deck house were made from 1.5mm thick styrene and the upper section was made from 1mm thick sheet. Locations for portlights and windows were marked and cut from each individual sheet as necessary, and transparent styrene was cut and glued to the window openings using liquid poly, taking care to avoid any of the liquid from touching the clear glazing. Although the task of building up the deckhouse required a degree of patience and care, the parts cut to the templates fitted extremely well.

The assembly was left unpainted until further work could be done. The small mast, shown on the general arrangement drawing was too small to allow wires feeding the total of eight lamps to rest inside, so it was replaced with a styrene tube from the Evergreen range of 6mm bore and very slightly taller than that shown on the drawing. Platforms to carry the lamps were made from small strips of styrene and tiny holes were drilled in the tube beneath each platform to allow the wires to be fed into the tube. I had decided to use grain of wheat lamps rated at 12 volts within the small but very neat lamps available from Mobile Marine models, and

Above and opposite: Views of the finished model.

to extend the life of such lamps by feeding them from a pack of NiHr batteries rated at 9.6 volts. The lamps were bright enough at this voltage to satisfy the client. To replace a blown lamp this small on this model would need almost a complete new deckhouse so the lower voltage was deemed wise. The photographs illustrate the completed mast. In addition to the eight lamps on the mast, starboard and port lights and a searchlight were fitted and four floodlights were also installed and illuminated, a total of 30 wires all partly concealed in the superstructure. A sturdy platform was also installed in the deckhouse to carry the 9.6-volt battery pack. To permit the battery pack to be re-charged it is connected to the wiring loom through a small socket matching the Futaba plug of the pack; the battery pack, incidentally, matching a Futaba transmitter pack.

The bulwark rails were next made using templates traced from the bulwarks themselves and these, after painting, were glued with superglue to the tops of the bulwarks and the supports. The main deck hatch was made from a layer of 1.5mm ply cut larger than the opening by 10mm all round and a layer of 3mm ply cut to fit the opening was glued to the 1.5mm sheet with the grain running in opposite directions to prevent the plywood from twisting or curving. The underside of this hatch was painted to render it watertight but the upper was fitted with 10mm wide strips of 0.8mm plywood all round the sides and across the centre. Individual planks of 0.08 x 6mm wide plywood were then used to plank the rest of the deck, and a black lining pen was used to blacken the edge of each plank before it was glued in place with PVA, and the whole surface was lightly sanded and varnished on completion. Finally the 10mm wide strips were painted blue of a shade slightly darker than the hull, using artist's acrylic medium.

To control the motors and rudder a panel was made up. It was arranged to provide a charging socket, necessary to allow the main 12-volt drive battery to be charged without removing it from the model. Removing the battery is not impossible but difficult. A centre off two way switch was installed to direct current from the battery to the main drive system or to the charging socket. A 10-amp fuse was also fitted into the wiring loom between the battery and the panel. On the panel the current from the battery is directed to the twin electronic speed control units of Mtronics manufacture, they too provide independent control of each motor. It had been decided to use a Spectrum 2.4g radio system and the tiny receiver was also mounted upon the control panel. The lighting system is completely separate from the main drive system, and is contained completely in the detachable deckhouse. Testing of the control panel proved all to work correctly as expected.

At this point work on the model was down to detailing and paint finishing. The funnels provided in the kit were primed with grey before being masked off and painted; from the top black, red and blue in bands. The initials S and O in white formed a logo on the red band of each funnel and were applied using white Letraset, my stock slowly diminishing as such lettering is no longer made. The depth marks, name and Port of Registry were applied using BECC lettering and the hull was sprayed with satin varnish to seal the lettering and provide a final finish. Bollards, swan neck vents, searchlight (illuminated), radar scanner, master compass and many other small fittings all supplied in the kit were fitted after each had been painted the appropriate colour. The anchors were secured into their recesses in the hull and suitable stud link anchor cable was fitted from deck over the gypsies and to the cable locker.

I am often surprised and pleased at the rapid help I receive from the suppliers who provide the small parts needed to finish a model. I needed flat bar stanchions to complete the guard rails for this model and, as I prefer to solder such rails in sections and ensure that the top rail is bigger in diameter than the intermediate rails, I contacted James Lane only to find his range of etched fittings does not extend to larger than a scale of 1:48. He did, however, provide some flat bar material so that I could make up my own units. These were quite quickly produced in a small jig made to suit and each stanchion was soldered into the groove of a 10BA bolt that could easily be glued into a suitable hole drilled, where required, in the decks. They made up into acceptable and fairly substantial guard rails and were painted white before being installed.

Finally the model was floated in the test basin and then taken to the pond at Goole for sea trials. Such trials were successful and the model proved to have a bollard pull of some 6½ pounds. The new lady owner expressed her delight with the model saying that she looked forward to trials when towing a larger model.

ADDENDUM

Nangee kit – Mobile Marine Models, tel: +44 (0)1522 730731.

E.S.C's – Mtronics, Westbourne Model Centre, tel: +44 (0)1202 763480.

Small fittings, hinges etc. – Model Dockyard, tel: +44 (0)1872 261755.

Grain of wheat bulbs, cable, switches etc. – Squires, tel: +44 (0)1243 842424.

Spray paints – Halfords

The Painting of Ships 1750-1850

AUTHENTIC PAINT COLOURS OF NAVAL VESSELS

by Jonathon Kinghorn

The frequently asked question, 'what colour were the yellow stripes on HMS *Victory*?' is not as easy to respond to as might be thought. The quick answer is that they were painted with ochre, a muddy yellow derived from a natural ore. But although little containers of 'yellow ochre' paint are readily available to modellers off the shelf can they really reproduce what the paint applied to Nelson's flagship, in say 1803, really looked like? This article is not about scale effect and rendering colour or sheen accurately on models. It is about historic paints and how they were applied, and it is more concerned with naval vessels than merchant ships, for which records are even scantier.

Paint was applied to ships principally as protection for their timbers and incidentally for decoration. Historic paint bears little resemblance to the stuff available today and used straight from the can. It was made up on the day it was needed by mixing powdered mineral pigments with a binder and with thinners to make it easier to apply – usually linseed oil and turpentine respectively. White lead was often added to improve opacity. While strong and bright colours were available they were very expensive, and were used sparingly and then only on the most special vessels. Ordinary ships received the cheapest paints, hence the colours of these were much duller than expected today and the finish generally flatter. In service paint faded or darkened on exposure to light, and it weathered – although ironically historic linseed oil paints with lead as a colour base were much more durable than modern acrylic paints for exterior use.

Besides inadequate records, it is impossible to be certain of the exact colours seen on historic ships because the shades produced varied due to several factors, chief among which was the quality and proportion of the materials used at the time the paint was mixed. Different batches used on the same ship at the same time could vary appreciably! Contemporary models suggest colour schemes, but cannot be relied upon to be an accurate record of how vessels appeared because of the conventions used by model-makers, and the very different paints and the often enhanced decoration applied to miniature vessels. While some artists were sticklers for getting

Above: Transitional style: a single narrow band of yellow and a narrow yellow strake grace the side of HMS *Sans Pareil*, seen here shortening sail, *c.*1800–02. (National Maritime Museum, PU6039)

the details right in their paintings, others were not, so paintings and the engravings made of them have to be used with caution as sources. It falls to the modeller to come to a decision based upon his research and ultimately any personal taste. For all of these reasons, and more, no modeller today can expect to get historic colours 100 per cent right, but some understanding of historic paint on ships will lead to choices which will be closer to the likely reality.

Royal Navy dockyards generally issued just four colours of paint: black, white, yellow, and red. Merchant ships used the same colours for the same reasons, affordability and durability. Black employed probably the oldest pigment known to man, lamp black (soot), which made a stable paint with a bluish undertone. White was made with white lead (lead carbonate), a toxic pigment manufactured since ancient times. It produced an off-white rather than the brilliant hue expected today, and it darkened noticeably on exposure to light. It also tended to yellow or brown on contact with

atmospheric sulfur. The basic colour was a warm white like that of earthenware mugs today, but William Mowl advised that on older ships it 'was the colour which one associates with tobacco stains.' The pigment was supplied in kegs as a thick viscous paste which could be used for waterproofing and even as a marine glue. White paint was highly impractical for bulwarks and fittings on all but the most prestigious vessels (those most likely to receive constant maintenance) for 'every grain of dust, and every touch of a dirty finger, will leave a mark upon it.'

Red was an extremely durable colour made from red lead (lead tetroxide), but it produced a paint more brick red than scarlet. It had good hiding power and was often used for interiors and deck fittings of warships; probably not, as so often believed, because it would mask the sight of blood in battle, but simply because it was extremely practical and cheap. (Officers' quarters, which became part of the gundeck in action, were generally whitewashed).

Yellow was made from ochre, which is essentially rust-stained clay. Used raw, ochre produces muddy earth tones from cream to brown. The pigment makes a quick-drying paint with good hiding power and excellent permanence. But, as supplied by the naval dockyards this yellow was 'so very dark a colour that it makes the ship look very dirty and dismal'. Steele advised captains to dig into their pockets to 'pay the painters for additional white to be mixed with the yellow'.

The standard dockyard colours could of course be combined; yellow and white give shades of buff, which one contemporary evidently described as 'baby puke yellow'. Other, more expensive pigments could be introduced – if the captain dug into his own pocket – to create yet more shades. The popular stone colour was made by adding a little Sienna and Umber to a mix of white and yellow. Vermillion gave an attractive but expensive colour that did not wear gracefully. An affordable blue was widely available from the 1750s in the form of Prussian blue. This man-made pigment, first created in Berlin in 1704, provided an intense deep blue colour. But with no good yellow pigments available until much later greens were still difficult and expensive to create. While green was a popular and practical choice for the upper deck and boats by the early nineteenth century it was still not available from the Royal Navy's dockyards.

As today, preparation was a vital first step when painting a ship. Dirt, pitch, tar, and loose paint were scraped off and holes and tears would be filled with putty. Knots were primed with red lead, and then the paintwork would be washed down or rubbed with a rag and a little turpentine to remove

Above: The familiar Nelson style bands of ochre seen on the preserved ship HMS *Victory*. (Conway)

any remaining dirt and grease. Usually three coats of primer would be applied, tinted to suit the planned top coat, with chalk for white, or a slate-coloured mixture of black and white for green for example. The expensive pigments would be employed only on the final coat. Oil-based paints dry through chemical reaction as contact with the air causes the oils to oxidize and to crosslink. It would take several days to paint a ship, and the weather had to co-operate and be neither wet nor too hot or the finish would be marred.

There were few, if any, regulations governing the style in which a ship should be painted, and such decisions were usually left to the captain, who might be swayed either by accepted conventions, current fashion, or personal whim. The classic mid-late eighteenth-century style for British warships was for the sides of the ship to be 'payed bright' with rosin (distillate of turpentine) and the wales to be picked out in black. Prussian blue might be applied to the upperworks and stern, with some detail perhaps picked out in yellow. Inboard would be painted red. The larger and more prestigious a vessel, the more likely she was to carry elaborate decoration, but increasingly this was painted rather than carved. Figureheads were painted white by the naval dockyards, but might have their details picked out later with colour. Gilding was used less and less.

By the 1780s wales were still black but it was becoming fashionable in European navies to paint hulls red or yellow rather than pay them, and to paint them black above a certain line of wales and below the main wale, thus forming a broad band of colour along their black sides. One of these bands might cover more than one line of guns and by the 1790s they often ran roughshod over the wales to roughly follow the lines of the gunports. In this case battens or lengths of cord would be temporarily tacked on to the hull as guides for the painters.

The extraordinary variety possible within this fashion is illustrated by the record of the French and British ships at the Battle of the Nile kept by Colonel Fawkes, a witness to the engagement. He lists ships with plain red and yellow sides of various shades and ships with yellow sides with a black strake between the upper and lower rows of gunports; red sides with a black strake between the upper and lower gunports; yellow sides with two narrow black strakes between the upper and lower rows of gunports; red sides with a small yellow stripe; red sides with a black strake between the upper and lower rows of gunports; light yellow sides with a black strake between the upper and lower decks; and a broad light yellow side, with small black strakes on a line with the muzzles of the guns and two between the upper and lower decks. In addition he noted that HMS *Theseus* had her hammock cloths

Above: White bands project forward on to the stem on a model of the French ship *Valmy*, made in the shipyard at Brest, France 1838–42 in the Museum National de la Marine, Paris, France.

Above: Late style: HMS *Victoria* is seen here with white bands projected forwards on to the stem in this 1859 painting by William Frederick Mitchell. (National Maritime Museum, PU6217).

painted yellow, with black 'ports' to make her look like a three-decker.

Within the Royal Navy at least style seems to have settled down and writing in 1804 Steele noted:

> Various modes are pursued in painting ship's sides; but the following appears the most general and approved. A yellow streak, from the ribbands of the channels forward and aft, cutting a line through the ports; another streak on the moulding above it. The broad yellow from the lower part of the upper deck port holes to the lower part of the quarter gallery; the lower part of the yellow to be painted in a straight line; the upper part with a small sheer, carried entirely forward to the cut water. Frigates are generally painted with a bright yellow side, and black upper works; the yellow about two inches above the upper part of the ports, and carried down to the line of the lower part of the quarter gallery.

In 1803, before Nelson raised his flag in her, HMS *Victory* completed her major refit and was painted in this manner with three bands of yellow roughly following the gundecks. By the time of Trafalgar her gunports had been painted black to create the now familiar chequerboard pattern. Nelson came to favour this style of painting and

required all ships under his command to adopt it, largely to make it difficult for the enemy to identify their opponents. The so-called 'Nelson fashion' was widely imitated, especially after Trafalgar. But it was never stipulated by the Royal Navy, or ubiquitous within it, although it did come close to establishing a uniform style. Later in the Napoleonic Wars bands of white became popular and in 1817 one of the Royal Navy's few regulations governing the painting of ships required that all lines along hulls should henceforth be white and should project forwards and wrap around the stem.

Paint technology was transformed in the mid-nineteenth century through a series of discoveries including emulsions and the first synthetic pigments. By 1880 these new paints were readily available in tins, in a wide range of colours, ready to use. But the black-and-white chequerboard style of painting ships remained the norm to the end of the sailing navy, and was widely seen on merchant ships, sail and steam, for many years.

REFERENCES

Fordyce, Alexander D., *Outline of Naval Routine*, London, 1837, pp.51-53.

Mowl, William, *Building a Working Model Warship: HMS Warrior 1860*, Naval Institute Press, 1997.

Paul, L., 'British Ships Painting at Aboukir', *The Mariner's Mirror*, vol. IV, (1914), pp.266-74.

Reynolds, Hezekiah, *Directions for House and Ship Painting* (A facsimile reprint of the 1812 edition with a new introduction by Richard M. Candee), American Antiquarian Society, Worcester, Massachusetts, 1978.

Ronnberg, Erik A.R., 'Paint and Colours for American Merchant Vessels, 1800–1920: Their Study and Interpretation for Modelmaking', *Nautical Research Journal*, Vol. 36, No.4, December 1991.

Steele, D., *Observations and instructions for the use of the commissioned, the junior and other officers of the Royal Navy, on all the material Points of Professional Duty. Including also, forms of general and particular orders for the better government and discipline of His Majesty's Ships: Together with a variety of new and useful tables; among which are, General Tables for Watching Ship's Companies in all Rates; — For shewing the Stations of the different Officers at Quarters; — For the General Appropriation of Men at Quarters, in Ships of every Class; — For Furling Sails; — Mooring and Unmooring; — Making and Shortening Sail; — Tacking Ship, &c. &c. With an Appendix; being a complete set of forms for watch, station, and quarter bills for ships of war. By a Captain in the Royal Navy*, London, 1804.

HMS *Warrior*

A MONITOR FOR THE HERITAGE LOTTERY FUND

by Wyn Davies

I have often been asked what it is like to be one of the few specialist monitors for the Heritage Lottery Fund. Well, it is certainly interesting, quite varied and often educational as I hope this article will demonstrate.

My personal background covers some forty years in engineering, initially in the aircraft industry, then in the marine world. During this time I managed to accumulate three degrees, a couple of diplomas and, more importantly, a useful stock of 'hands on' experience.

I was perhaps lucky; both branches of engineering encouraged learning to operate the machines we were to design and build. With the College of Aeronautics at Cranfield came free flying lessons, and with the Royal Corps of Naval Constructors came several months at sea serving with the Royal Navy.

Equally valuable were the numerous opportunities the marine industry in particular gave for foreign travel. Nearly always directly related to business I was exposed to different maritime cultures and many different ways of doing things, some of which may have rubbed off!

Possibly as a result of all this I was accepted as a monitor by the relatively newly formed Heritage Lottery Fund in 1999. As I recall the formalities then were few, the day rate was acceptable to my then employers (ten years later it has only recently been increased) and our bid was acceptable to the HLF. Shortly afterwards two tasks landed on my desk.

One of these tasks was a major project to replace the timber decking on the weather deck of HMS *Warrior*. Now owned by the Warrior Preservation Trust, after lying for

Above: *Warrior* at Milford Haven before restoration.

Above: *Warrior*'s upper deck while at Milford Haven.

Above: The famous ship had been used as a hulk.

many years at Pembroke Dock as a hulk, she had been rescued and taken to Hartlepool for restoration in 1979. This had followed as closely as possible the original design as, in true Admiralty fashion, many of the original drawings had survived. The original decking had been of Pitch Pine laid directly on the iron deck. A native of North America, Pitch Pine was favoured for this sort of application as its high resin content acted as a preservative. Pitch Pine is not easily found today in the sizes needed for shipbuilding, and the restoration team in Hartlepool had been pleased to find an adequate supply from the flooring of an old mill which could be cut and planed to the right size for *Warrior*.

One of the more influential features of *Warrior*'s design, as it turned out, was the fact that her weather deck had no camber. There was some sheer, but this lack of camber meant that the deck's drainage relied in large part on the roll of the ship. Unfortunately her mooring at Portsmouth Historic Dockyard did not allow her to roll and this had resulted in any water that arrived on her deck tending to stay there.

Whether there were hidden defects in the timber, whether the resin had finally lost its usefulness or the bedding material had disintegrated is not certain, but the result was that water soaked through the timber and lay on the iron deck. In effect the lower half of a plank was permanently wet and eventually rot set in.

On discovering the rot the ship's staff realised the planking had to be replaced, this time with an eye to the lower levels of maintenance to which a preserved ship is limited. It was decided to replace the pine with a hard wood that would last longer. From a purely shipbuilding point of view teak is probably the best wood to use, and the best comes from Burma, with a well-founded reputation for durability.

The team put together a costed proposal on this basis and made an application to the HLF for support to what was roughly a £1 million project, and this is the point at which the monitor first appears on the scene.

Although the main job of a monitor is literally that, monitoring the progress and expenditure of a project and adding value whenever possible, it had become usual for a monitor to review the application documents, particularly the technical and financial proposals, to ensure they were sound before an HLF case officer would consider a grant. (It should be noted that HLF procedures have changed somewhat since the introduction of their Strategic Plan 3 in 2008.)

Provided the assessment did not find any hidden black holes in the finances, and it is surprising how many times this does happen, then the next step would be for the HLF to weigh this application against others they had received that quarter and against the available budget, and with luck the applicant would receive funding. HMS *Warrior* was granted an award in December 2000 and set out to select a contractor and buy the timber.

The timber to be supplied was best Burmese Teak, quarter sawn, blemish free, in lengths as long as possible; but not shorter than 13ft. Unfortunately, modern forestry operations seem to revolve around the ubiquitous container, so the traditional 36 to 44ft lengths are no longer obtainable. Overall the project would absorb some £400,000 of teak and was planned to last around four years.

As luck would have it, shortly before work started I was attending a Maritime Heritage Conference in Wilmington, North Carolina. Wilmington is home to the preserved battleship USS *North Carolina* and a visit to her was part of the conference proceedings. The first thing that met the eye on stepping on to her upper deck was the brand new wood deck being finished off with sanders and pitch. The new deck was composed of some Indonesian hardwood, but I am sure Captain Dave Scheu will not mind me revealing that I had guessed right and that it was best quality Burmese Teak that had been gifted to the ship some years earlier. By the time they had raised the money to lay it down it was no longer politically acceptable to mention Burma in public. It served as a useful and timely reminder of some of the problems with laying a new deck.

Returning to *Warrior*, the next step in the proceedings as far as the monitor is concerned is meeting the client's team. The *Warrior* was somewhat different to other preserved ships in that she had a well-defined management structure developed over the years since her restoration. It is not uncommon with newly established rescue projects to find a group of enthusiasts with a common cause but little or no management or organisational skills.

Normal procedure over the next four years would be for the project to be visited by the monitor at roughly monthly intervals, to coincide with the financial reporting and draw down requirements of HLF. The visit was aimed at ensuring the work had been carried out as claimed and that the draw down application was mathematically correct. This involved a large amount of paperwork as the contractor's invoice usually came with several bills for materials attached.

In this case the monthly visits also involved my sitting in on the project management meetings, by invitation of the team. During the early meetings the logic for using teak was formalised and we were introduced by the supplier, Timbmet

Ltd of Oxford, to the forestry management routines of Burma. These had been put in place by the British Raj some 180 years ago and were still being used. Unfortunately for Burma, their political isolation meant that they could not get any international recognisable certification, but for the purposes of this project the forestry management scheme was deemed acceptable.

The exact design of the new deck was also decided during these early meetings. In view of the problems outlined above it was felt that the replacement should be, in effect, a 'Chinese deck'. In other words, an air gap was to be left under the planking to allow the wood to be ventilated and to keep it above any pools of water. In addition a good screeding was to be laid to smooth out the iron deck and protect it from corrosion.

With these decisions made and a contractor in place – the Maritime Workshop from Gosport – work started on removing the old wood. It had been hoped to re-use some of the timber as souvenirs, but in the event it proved too rotten for this. Work then started on the first third of the upper deck. This split had been decided upon to allow the Trust to continue to take bookings for weddings and corporate functions whilst the work was in hand, an important contribution to the Trust's income.

Above: USS *North Carolina*. Sanded deck is in foreground.

Above: *North Carolina*'s deck being prepared for re-caulking.

Above left: Bow cleared. This view shows the rows of bolts left that had to be removed and the easily splintered remains of the original planks. (Warrior Preservation Trust)
Above right: Timber being inspected plank by plank after delivery to the Oxford works.

Work was hampered initially by some very unseasonal weather. After losing a few loose covers to the high winds it was found that a polytunnel, purchased from the local garden centre, made the best protection for the workers and the bare deck and work then progressed well.

In parallel with the work at the ship, the arrival of the first part consignment of timber entailed a journey up to Oxford to inspect it. Every plank was inspected on both sides for flaws and overall for straightness. If my memory serves me we found no flaws and most if not all of the few slightly warped planks found a use around the margins or in some of the deck furniture that was rebuilt later.

The visits continued until all the timber had been delivered and inspected. To ensure enough seasoned planks were available when required some batches were kiln dried, but whenever possible it was allowed to season naturally. The site chosen by the company's founder was perfect for this. It was on the up slope of a scarp where on most days the prevailing wind blew straight through the yard; fine in July, but a bit cold in December.

Once the deck had been stripped of its rotten planking it was cleaned, the old bolts removed and the surface prepared for the screeding. Strips of timber were then laid across the ship to support the new deck planks. As the lengths of the planks were much shorter than would have been laid originally, it was decided to scarph the timber so that there was one length of planking from one end to the other. If required a false joint could be introduced to replicate a joint at 44ft or so, although this was deemed unnecessary in the end. In another change from the original it was decided to use polysulphide sealant to pay the planking edges. This required a different shape to the plank's cross section and a strip of timber inserted as the base for caulking between the planks on to which the polysulphide was poured. This arrangement

had the advantage that the caulking material could be machine sanded to a final finish with the planks.

As far as the monitor was concerned I suspect that this project was a rather straightforward introduction to the role, involving few serious problems, no disagreements and no over spend. It certainly did not prepare me for some of the eccentricities that I was to run into on other jobs.

ACKNOWLEDGEMENTS
The author would like to acknowledge the support received from the crew and staff of HMS *Warrior* 1860 during his time as monitor, in particular Captain David Newberry RN and Commander Ron Broom RN, and their successors, Commander Ken Jones RN and Lieutenant Commander Tony Ford RN.

All photographs are from the author's collection with the exception of that top left on this page. The author apologises for any others that may have been published to the Heritage Lottery Fund and have come unacknowledged into his possession during the project.

ABOUT WYN DAVIES
Wyn Davies is a Senior Consultant with Frazer-Nash Consultancy Limited, specialising mainly in the maritime heritage sector and modern naval auxiliaries. He has worked on over twenty different heritage craft either as a consultant to the owners or as an advisor to the Heritage Lottery Fund and has had eleven papers published on various preservation topics.

Wyn started his naval architecture career in 1972 when he joined the Royal Corps of Naval Constructors, having previ-

Top: First plank down. This view clearly shows the smooth screeding and the cross timbers on which the plank rests, keeping it off the iron deck.

Above: The final plank was laid during a formal ceremony by HRH Princess Alexandra on 4 February, 2004.

Above: The finished result.

ously spent seven years in the aircraft industry. For the last 25 years he has worked for commercial consultancies.

BIBLIOGRAPHY

Suggested further reading:
The Forestry Manual of the British Empire,
http://www.archive.org/stream/schlichsmanualof00schl/s
chlichsmanualof00schl_djvu.txt
Brown, D. K., *Warrior to Dreadnought, Warship Development 1860-1905*, Chatham Publishing, 1997.
Steam, Steel and Shellfire: The Steam Warship 1815-1905, Conway's *History of the Ship* series, Conway, 1992.

Useful websites:
Heritage Lottery Fund:
http://www.hlf.org.uk/Pages/Home.aspx
National Historic Ships:
http://www.nationalhistoricships.org.uk/
HMS *Warrior* 1860: http://www.hmswarrior.org/
USS *North Carolina*:
http://www.battleshipnc.com/page1.php

Three Fishing Boat Models

DEVELOPMENTS IN DESIGN

by William Macintosh

SULAIR II
Scale: ½in = 1ft
Length: 46ft

This model has been built as the first in a series showing the changes in the inshore fishing boats that I had lived and worked amongst from when I was old enough to get to the harbour (boat daft was my mother's name for it). *Sulair* repre-sents a type of boat used for the seine net fishing in the 1940s and 1950s from the many small harbours in Scotland. This type was often the ex-ring net boats that had been built by yards such as Noble of Girvan. They were good-looking craft with very eye-pleasing lines, but often they proved to be underpowered and lacked the draft for towing the nets as the demand came for higher/bigger nets, and more ropes were being used.

Above: Starboard view of *Sulair II*.

Above: Sutherland 4-gear winch, Beccles coiler, and seine ropes port and starboard.

All the fishing boat models I have built so far have been examples of the differing types that were used from the 1940s onward. I would really like to build a named boat, but detailed plans for boats of the era are hard to come by, most having been dumped or burnt when the yards closed. I would not even try to build one of those that I worked on way back; forty to fifty years is a long time ago.

Sulair II was built using Harold Underhill's hull plan for a west coast herring ring net boat. The plan was altered a bit with the forefoot being squared off and the quarters made a bit fuller and turned in at the rail. There were no plans for the wheelhouse, winch coilers and the rest of the topside fittings. These were constructed from memory and some photographs.

The hull was made up of 5mm good quality ply, in the centre board and slotted frame method. There are 26 frames altogether, midships every second one is set in from deck level the after two being set in as cant frames to get the rounded stern. The planking is of 5mm x 2mm strips, and the deck planks are 4mm and joggled into the margin board. All the planking on the model was cut from Venetian blind strips. The masts are turned out of 15mm square beading.

The Sutherland winch and Beccles coilers were based on details from photoraphs and memory (there is a good photograph of a Beccles coiler in the SN website), the V-pulleys and tension wheels (painted red) seen on the outer ends of the coilers are made up from snap/poppet studs, the winch drum and guide-on pulleys are turned out of an old ash broom handle, really good for turning out small parts. The rigging screws (turnbuckles) on the rigging are made of single-strand copper wire cable, the outer cover being cut to the size of the centre piece then eyes made on the ends of two short bits of wire. I superglued one end, then adjusted the size of the other so that I could pull the rigging tight while gluing it. The anchor is carved out of a piece of ebony. Fuel points, bilge pump and ice scuttles are fitted on deck.

The wheelhouse is made up with an inner skin of beech veneer, the panelling being laid on, with strips of pine in the centres and mahogany strips used for the outer bands, the whole thing then being sanded down to a smooth finish. The mahogany windows were then added and glazed from the inside. The interior of the wheelhouse is equipped with wheel, clock, barometer, compass, Gardner engine controls,

Above: Port side of winch. Note rollers for guiding ropes on to winch drums.

Above: Deck layout of small 1950s seine netter.

straps for windows, Mk 5 Decca navigator, Kelvin Hughes paper sounder, single sideband radio, and seat locker and deck grating. The navigation lights are made from scrap brass bits painted the appropriate colours.

Below the waterline the model is fitted with anodes on the rudder and after hull with the transducer for the sounder fitted farther forward.

The propeller and some of the small double blocks plus the lettering for the name, numbers and so on, are about the

Above: Starboard quarter view showing seine net laid on ready to shoot, fish pounds beside wheelhouse, and Gilson and tackle ready to lift cod end aboard. Aluminium fish scoop stuck in grab rail.

only items bought for the model. As can be seen from the photographs of the model most of the paintwork consists of varnish. I use standard good quality varnish, as most of my models are finished in this way.

Above: *Sulair II* viewed from aft.

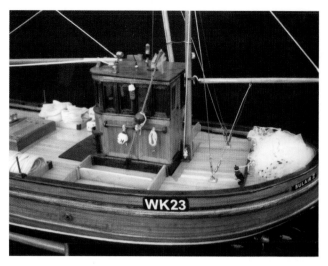

Above: Port quarter view showing dan and buoy used to mark the end of the seine net rope, plus the rail roller stored at the port side of the net platform. This would be inserted into one of the holes seen in the rail when fishing.

The fish boxes on deck are made from 1mm pine strips, the ropes are ordinary parcel string lightly coated with glue, wrapped around a former then arranged to suit whichever side of the boat they are to be worked from, or skipper's preference. The net was made from fine gauze, the floats are the ball ends of dressmakers pins drilled through, with a fake footrope and two bridles added to make it look authentic. *Sulair* is the Gaelic word for the solan goose (gannet). The name and number were taken from a lobster boat I once owned.

MV *EASTWARD*
Scale: ½in = 1ft
Length: 56ft

This model represents the step between the rundown of the seine net method of fishing and the adoption of trawling by the inshore boats of Scotland.

Eastward has been fitted out as a seiner/trawler. From the end of the 1950s companies such as Mastra and Jensen were turning out the type of winch seen on the model. With this type of rig a boat could change from trawling to seine net fishing with very little effort, the removal of the after gallows being the biggest job. With this layout a boat could work the seine net on the clean ground in the summer months and switch to trawling for the winter. Seine net fishing needed a big area of clean bottom with no snags, whereas the trawl rig equipped with bobbins and later hoppers could work on much harder ground. With fish getting scarcer on the clean ground and with a market opening up for prawns a lot of the boats went over to trawling only.

Eastward is built with a centre board incorporating the keel, stem and stern, with the frames slotted into it, 5mm ply being used. The first four frames fore and aft are full frames. In the midship section every second frame is set in from deck level.

The hull is planked with 6mm x 2mm strips cut from Venetian blind wood strips. The deck is planked in pine, 5mm x 2mm. The deck planks were cut from 8mm tongue and groove cladding. The mast was turned from 15mm beading and the gilsons, derricks, etc., were turned out of dowelling.

The Mastra winch and Beccles coiler were made using data from photographs and what I could remember, with the handy poppet/press studs used to make the V-pulleys and tension wheels (painted red on the end of the coiler). There were no plans or drawings for any of the topside fittings, such as wheelhouse, winch, fish pounds, hatches etc. Again, they were all made based on details from photographs and memory.

The hull lines came from a drawing for the MV *Provider* KY201 built for the Storr family in Whitby by Millers, St Monance, Fife. The single sheet drawing had been rescued from a skip by the Anstruther fishing museum staff. I altered the stern a little just making it slightly finer on the quarter and turned in slightly from the horizontal. The *Provider* had what was called the Queen Mary bow; this is quite a full flared bow. On the model I reduced the flare slightly and made the stem a bit finer.

The wheelhouse was made of beech veneer the sides being made separate from the extended windows part. The sides were panelled before being set up as this made sanding down the inlaid area easier. The wheelhouse was made up off the model then fitted minus the roof. The inside was fitted with Mk12 Decca Navigator, track plotter, Atlas radar, KH echo sounder, overhead compass, clock, single-side band radio, Sailor VHF radio, Gardner engine controls, seat locker and deck gratings. The galley is equipped with a coal stove with two pans on it, a small work top, rack with salt, sauce, etc, and row of oilskins hanging on the after bulkhead.

Above: Finished model of *Eastward* viewed from starboard side.

The boxed-in exhaust from the engine comes up through the wheelhouse. I tried to make the wheelhouse like those made by Herd and Mackenzie at that time.

The trawldoors are made from veneer with a short length of electric flex cut lengthways and pushed on to represent the bottom shoes. The net is from bird feeder netting with dressmakers pinheads (coloured ones) drilled through and laced on to button thread to make the headrope. The codend lacer is tied up and the coil of rope on top of the net is called the dog rope and is used to lift the codend aboard. The anchor is

Above left: Port side of finished model.

Above right: showing style of wheelhouse made popular in the 1960s by boatyards like Herd and Mackenzie of Buckie.

Above: Starboard quarter view. **Below:** Forward view of wheelhouse showing Simpson fishwasher, and trawl Gilson, the seine net Gilsons are mounted on top of the galley casing.

Above: Port side of wheelhouse showing inlaid panels, and tackle for port Gilson, with old box-type inflatable liferaft on wheelhouse roof.
Below: Combination winch coupled with Beccles coiler. This enables the boat to use both seine net and trawl methods of fishing.

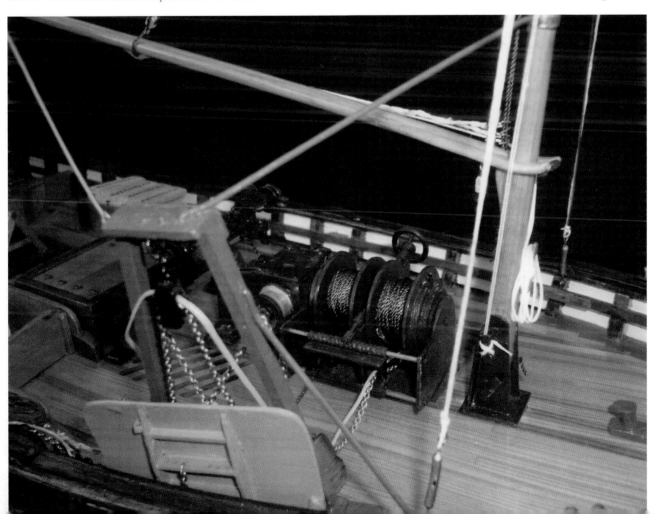

carved from a piece of ebony. The lights are made from scrap bits of brass. The bottle screws (turnbuckles) on the rigging are again made out of copper single-strand electric wire.

Under the waterline the rudder and after end are equipped with anodes with the transducer for the echo sounder fitted further forward. Outlets and inlets for the engine and pumps are fitted in the hull. The usual fuel points, bilge pump and ice scuttles are fitted on the deck.

Items bought for this model include the propeller, some double blocks, and two portholes plus the lettering for the name, numbers, etc.

The name *Eastward* comes from a boat skippered by my grandfather in the 1920s. The number WK210 comes from a boat an uncle had in the 1940s/1950s. Photographs show the colour scheme of the model.

Left: Showing forward trawl door and Mastra type combination winch.

Above: Midship area showing Simpson fishwasher, guide rollers for seine net working. Deck wash hose coiled on wheelhouse front.

IV BEN ALISKY

Scale: 3ft = 1in

Length: 72ft

By the time boats were rigged exclusively for trawling like this one, it is still an ex-seine net hull converted; most of the new boats coming from the Scottish yards were being built solely for trawling.

This model was made from the same basic hull plans (Harold Underhill) as the *Sulair II*. The original plans were for a 46ft hull at ½in = 1ft, and I altered this to become a 72ft hull at ⅓in = 1ft. I had to reduce the beam slightly to get the 20ft 4in beam to which many of this class of boat were built. I also raised the hull by another two planks. The hull is planked with 5mm x 2mm and the deck with 4mm x 2mm strips from Venetian blinds. The deck planking was painted with flat black on both edges before being fitted to resemble caulking. As in the other models the deck planks were joggled into the margin board. Masts, etc., were tuned out of 15mm square bead and dowelling.

The winch as shown on this model is as near authentic as my research could get, but the hydraulic drive motor and controls are based on memory. Probably there should be a hatch where the old belt drive came through the deck before the conversion to hydraulic power. The first time I show this model anywhere near the north-east coast of Scotland, I will probably be put right, notwithstanding the amount of enquiries I have made in that same area for information on this type of winch.

The wheelhouse was again made of beech veneer. The sides and lower front are made separate from the extended top window section. The panelling on the model is made up of squares of oak in the centres with 1mm strips of a black wood set around the outside. Mahogany was then used for the broad bands. The window frames are all made of mahogany, being glazed on the inside. The wheelhouse is

Above: Port quarter of *Ben Alisky*. Note rudder fitted with anodes. The propellor was one of the few fittings purchased for the model.

Above: The trawl gear would be worked from this starboard side.

Left: Starboard side of wheelhouse with after trawl gallows, seine net Gilson on casing top and liferafts.

Right: Port side of the wheelhouse with inlaid panels, oak centre with black 1mm strip of mahogany for the outer bands. The lighter wood above is beech veneer.

Below: Wheelhouse front showing Simpson type fish washer.

fitted out with a Decca Mk21 navigator, track plotter, radar, echo-sounder, main wireless, Sailor VHF, clock, overhead compass, Gardner engine controls and seat locker. The galley has a gas cooker, small work top and rack for oilskins.

All the usual fuel oil points and bilge pump port plus ice scuttles are fitted on deck.

All the lights on this model have been turned out of ash (the broom handle). The fittings on the wheelhouse top are the standard fittings for the time, i.e. DF aerial, radar scanner, searchlight, compass housing, life rafts and engine exhaust.

Trawl doors, nets, etc., are made as in the *Eastward* model, as are the anodes, transducer and the engine cooling water and bilge pump/deck wash inlets and outlets.

The contraption seen in front of the wheelhouses on

Above: Fore deck, showing joggled deck planking and small hatch into the fore locker.

both the *Eastward* and *Ben Alisky* is for washing the gutted fish, the fish being selected and gutted into the baskets like the one in the washer, then washed, before being sent down into the hold.

Parts bought for this model include the propeller, small stanchions, portholes, some double blocks, and the lettering for the white part of the numbers, name, etc.

The anchor was made out of ebony.

The name *Ben Alisky* is purely fictional and came about as I had run out of the letter 'r' in the lettering, so I chose the first Ben/glen or river I came to on the map of Caithness without the letter 'r'.

Above: Trawl winch would have been belt driven originally, but the one on the model has been converted to hydraulic drive.

Below: Showing deck layout.

Modeller's Draught

FPV *VIGILANT (III)*

by J. Pottinger

The authority of the Scottish Fisheries Protection Agency (SFPA) covered the extensive coastline of Scotland from 3 miles north of Berwick-on-Tweed northwards and then south again to the Solway Firth on the west coast, including Orkney and Shetland and the solitary fastness of Rockall in the Atlantic Ocean, an expanse that has necessitated a series of purpose-built vessels to carry out the various designated duties.

The department's origins go back to 1882 when the Fishery Board for Scotland took over the powers previously assigned to the Commissioners for the British White Herring Fishery. They had been invested with power in 1808 to regulate the sea fisheries, and initially Royal Navy vessels were assigned to maintain law and order on the various fishing grounds.

Over the years the pressure on the ever-reducing scope of fishing grounds and implementation of various conservation orders, restrictions implemented through the much derided Common Fisheries Policy following the UK joining the EU, appear to have been based more on political considerations than a response to any practical applications and have resulted in a much widening of the scope of policing responsibilities than the original remit.

Inevitably this trend for policing over the years has resulted in the commissioning of ever more sophisticated and complex vessels since the early auxiliary sail and powered ships. In 1933 the Board conducted a review which resulted in the construction of ten protective vessels comprising three classes, including those being suitable for all purposes, others for local waters and the remainder for sheltered waters.

One of the vessels entering the fleet following this review was the *Vigilant (III)*, a fast twin-screw motor vessel designed as far as possible to resemble a near water trawler, the ruse including a tall steamer like funnel, dummy towing gallows, registration numbers, and trawl winch, with the boarding launch stowed out of sight inside the bulwarks in a special lowered section of the deck forward of the wheelhouse. It is doubtful if much of this deception was effective as fishermen soon became familiar with her silhouette and took evasive action accordingly.

The *Vigilant* was completed at Dumbarton by W. Denny & Bros Ltd., and had the following particulars:

Length overall: 144ft.
Beam: 23ft.
Gross tonnage: 203.
Engines: 2 x Sulzer 8-cyl. Diesels, total bhp = 1,500.
Speed: 14 knots.

She was re-engined in 1971 when two Lister Blackstone 6-cylinder diesels each of 810bhp were installed, a new shortened funnel fitted and numerous modifications were effected over the years to reflect the changing conditions of operations and manning.

As early as August 1939 she was requisitioned by the Royal Navy for service as an examination vessel on the Clyde lower reaches. By July 1941 she was re-assigned as an accommodation vessel to the Campbeltown Rescue Tug Base. In April 1943 she was renamed *IXION* and in the following May reallocated as a target towing vessel at Larne.

A change of duties in August of same year saw her as a reserve vessel at Portsmouth and at the end of the year was designated for special service at Nore Command. It was not until April 1946 that she was finally paid off and returned to the Department. She resumed service in February 1947 and took her original name. In 1980 she was renamed *Vigilant II* to allow naming of a new vessel and was finally sold out of service in 1982 to Sheridan Trading Incorporated S.A. Panama for £18,000, and was renamed *Vigilant*.

THE MODEL

Given the relatively fine lines and small beam and displacement I would recommend that the plan be scaled up to ensure adequate stability if built as a working model. Note that I have indicated a modified waterline on the lines plan than that as shown on the general arrangement which will give greater freeboard.

It will be observed that the deck line forward does not

follow the line of the top of the bulwark but instead has a much reduced sheer forward of the bridge, this helps to hide the boarding launch which is also nested in a lowered section between the winch and foremast.

Another unusual feature is that there was an additional steering position at aft end of the galley deckhouse; this can be seen on section A-A, and where the steering wheel can be fitted over a spindle supported by an open frame, the wheel is shown in stowed position when not in use. The steering engine is inside the casing just below the skylight, which is in fact not over the engine room as is the norm but is in the position as would be found on a similar trawler, with diesel engines, the engine room being much shorter and are under the funnel where the boiler would be sited on a steam trawler.

The remainder of the details will be self evident from the drawings.

Above: *Vigilant* on trials, it would appear that the funnel has had an additional extension on top. (Courtesy Scott Horsburgh, Scottish Government)

Colour scheme as built.
Black: hull, funnel, winch, gallows, bollards, etc.
Red: hull underbody.
Varnished wood: wheelhouse.
Buff: masts and spars, lower bridge, casing and galley deckhouse, boarding launch and lifeboat, ventilators.
Later all grey apart from wheelhouse.

Below: *Vigilant* after conversion berthed in James Watt Dock, Greenock. This shows the shortened funnel and extended forecastle in addition to numerous additions and alterations from new.

This page: (top) View of foredeck and wheelhouse side, the recess in the foredeck has now been covered over and used as a paint store, etc. (bottom) View of forecastle showing pattern of the shell plate rivets; the horizontal line of rivets between the two rubbing strakes indicates the line of the beam shelf supporting the deck beams.

Opposite: (top left) After side of galley deckhouse showing emergency steering position with steering wheel in housed position, and will fit on the black spindle protruding through the plate when in use. (top right) This shows the fine lines forward and curve of whaleback. (bottom) Stem and electric windlass on forecastle, also shown is the curve of the whaleback with margin plate and planked deck.

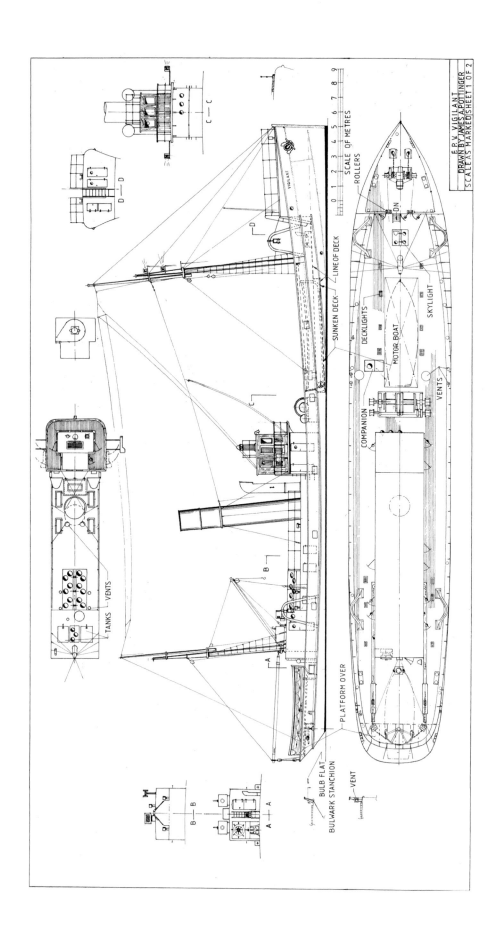

F.P.V. VIGILANT
DRAWN BY JAMES A. POTTINGER
SCALE AS MARKED | SHEET 1 OF 2

SCALE OF METRES

ROLLERS

SUNKEN DECK

LINE OF DECK

DECKLIGHTS

SKYLIGHT

MOTOR BOAT

VENTS

COMPANION

PLATFORM OVER

BULB FLAT

BULWARK STANCHION

VENT

TANKS   VENTS

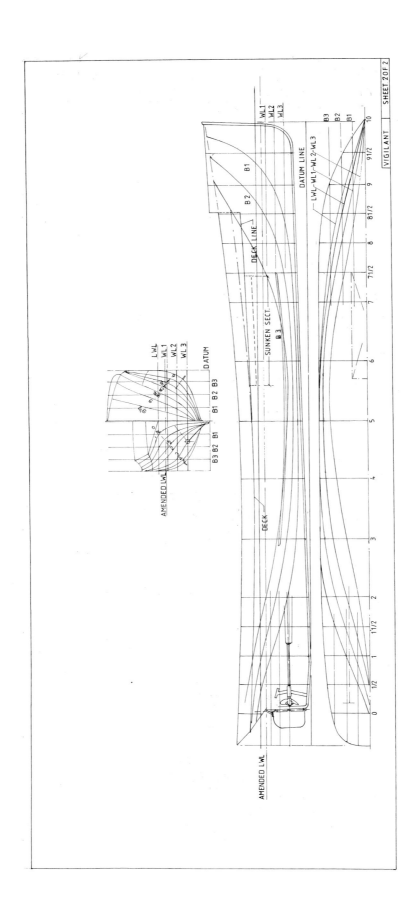

Sengokubune

SHIPS OF THE JAPANESE COASTAL TRADE

by Douglas Brooks

Above: *Michinokumaru* at sea.

Several years ago I was standing on a beach on the small island of Naoshima, located in the Inland Sea region of Japan. My wife and I were there to visit several museums and a sculpture park. It was a beautiful, warm spring day, and while we were enjoying several large sculptures placed on the beach, we could not help but notice the volume of ship traffic passing the island. The number of small freighters plying the sea lanes was a veritable maritime highway. At any one moment, looking east and west, we could probably count over a dozen ships making their way in the inter-island trade between Japan's five main islands.

Japan has been largely overlooked as a historical maritime power. In part this is due to timing; the Edo era, a 250-year period of conscious exclusion from the outside world (1603–1868) coincided with the great era of European exploration and navigation. Had it not been for the Shogunate's desire to withdraw from the world, Japan might well have become Asia's most dominant explorer. Prior to the Edo era Japanese ships were carrying on a regular trade with the kingdoms of China, Korea and the Ryukyus (present day Okinawa).

Anyone who has visited Japan and traveled beyond its cities, knows the interior of the country is divided by steep mountain ranges while most rivers are barely navigable for more than a few miles from the sea. The shogunate's edict forbidding foreign travel, known as the Sakoku, was not intended to stop coastwise trade. The country would have ground to a halt without it. Japan's maritime reputation, prior to the modern era, rests on countless thousands of coastal cargo ships transporting cotton, soy sauce, sake, rice and other essential goods.

The vessels that developed during the Edo era to carry these goods were known variously as *bezaisen*, *kitamaesen*, and *higakkikaisen*. Each name has a regional flavor, but all these vessels can be described as *sengokubune*, literally 'thousand koku ship', a koku being an ancient measure of rice (a koku being the amount of rice needed to feed one adult for one year, or about 150 kilograms).

While scholars seem certain that the Japanese ships which sailed to mainland Asia before the Edo era were round-bottomed, carvel planked and with outboard rudders, the construction of sengokubune mirrored the techniques of Japanese small boat construction. By and large traditional Japanese boats are hard chine hulls, with very thick planking and little if any internal framing such as ribs. In many designs hulls are framed only with horizontal beams tenoned into the planking. The keel of the Japanese small boat is not a vertical timber but a thick, horizontal plank. Larger planks are made up of several boards, and are edge-nailed together using flat iron nails, the heads of which are recessed in shallow mortises and plugged or covered.

Sengokubune featured heavy boxed keels and hard chine hulls, with a garboard wing plank and a near vertical sheer plank. These wide panels were made up of several thick planks which were edge nailed and stapled together. A series of athwartship beams, their ends protruding through the

This page and overleaf: These photographs show *Michinoku-maru* during her construction in the shipyard of the Michinoku Traditional Wooden Boat Museum, Aomori City, Japan.

Above: The shipwright, Mr Tomenshin Niinuma, at his home in Ofunato, Japan.

hull, braced the planking at the chine, while lower beams acted like floor timbers.

The end of the Edo era ushered Japan's first great leap of modernization, as the new Meiji Government sought to catch up to the West's advanced technology. Where earlier shoguns had mandated where a vessel might sail the Meiji Government began putting restrictions on building traditional ship types like *sengokubune*. As a result, the coastal traders of the Edo era disappeared. The last *sengokubune* were built as late as the early twentieth century; not a single original example survives.

In 2001 I met Mr Tomenoshin Niinuma, a shipwright living on Japan's main island in Iwate Prefecture, on the northern Pacific coast. I was in Japan putting together a project to work with several traditional boat builders in order to document their work, and Niinuma was one of several boat builders I met. Before we sat down to talk he took me to the Ofunato harbor to show me *Kesenmaru*, the first Japanese sailing trader built in almost one hundred years. Niinuma had built her, after extensive research, for Japan Expo, and she was launched in 1992.

Niinuma faced considerable obstacles in designing the ship. While many drawings of *sengokubune* survive, traditionally Japanese shipwrights and boat builders maintained many secrets and very often what drawings do exist are incomplete. My research has shown that many boat builders in Japan work even today with no drawings whatsoever, relying on memorized dimensions or secret ratios. Furthermore, very little scholarship had been done looking at how these boats were built. Niinuma considered the challenge of building *Kesenmaru* to be the culmination of his career, and while he was vindicated by the ship's seaworthiness, eventually his design was criticized by maritime historians.

Since *Kesenmaru*, Niinuma has gone on to build three more replica *sengokubune*. He has relied on the same team of local shipwrights that built his first ship. His second and third ships are static museum displays, on Sado Island in the Sea of Japan and at the maritime museum in Osaka (although the Osaka ship underwent extensive sea trials before being placed inside the museum). The design of the Osaka ship was a collaboration with a team of scholars and there is unanimous agreement that the result, *Naniwamaru*, is the most authentic design. Niinuma's most recent ship, *Michinokumaru*, was launched in 2005 and is sailed every summer by the Michinoku Traditional Wooden Boat Museum in Aomori City.

Several years ago I attended the annual exhibition of Japan's ship modeling society, which took place in the Itoya Gallery in downtown Tokyo. The ships on display would be familiar to modelers in the West: galleons, clipper ships, famous warships from the age of sail and later ocean liners. There wasn't a single *sengokubune*, however, a vessel that a little more than one hundred years earlier would have crowded the wharves that lay just a short walk from the gallery. One explanation for this omission is that ship modeling as a pastime is primarily a western import to Japan, and Japan's model-makers are drawn to the very same subjects as western counterparts. No doubt another reason is that modelers everywhere celebrate precision and accuracy, and the *sengokubune* is shrouded in the mists of a forgotten history.

ABOUT DOUGLAS BROOKS

My work is focussed on the appreciation and continued use of traditional wooden boats, and the preservation and sharing of the skills and knowledge needed to build wooden boats. These include American and English boat types, as well as the small boats of Japan. I have worked independently, building custom boats and designing and directing museum boat building projects. I have built traditional boats for private clients and museums across the United States and Japan.

I first traveled to Japan in 1990. There I met several boat builders, one of whom would later become my first teacher. My research in Japan has led to five apprenticeships with boat builders since 1996, building six types of traditional Japanese boats. Most recently I worked with one of the last boat builders of Okinawa. I have published numerous articles on my research and am currently working on a book on traditional Japanese boat building. For more information about my work, research and publications, please visit www.douglasbrooksboatbuilding.com.

Stella Polaris and *Rose*

TWO NORWEGIAN MOTOR SHIPS

by Robert A. Wilson F.R.S.A.

During the summer of 2008, I felt like a change in ship modelling and taking out my old shipbuilding journals I began to search for a pair of good-looking ships of any nationality as subjects. I particularly wanted white hulls because I have always found them notoriously difficult to model satisfactorily, and felt like the challenge. The pair I finally chose were both Norwegian motor ships. The first was the cruise ship *Stella Polaris* of 1927 and the second was the fruit carrier *Rose* of 1938.

Both were to be waterline models and would be built to the same scale of 1:384 (1in = 32ft). I was drawn to the *Stella*

Polaris after seeing a TV documentary covering a round-the-world voyage in the ship between the wars. The film was in good quality colour and showed the ship in many beautiful settings. The *Stella Polaris* was built in 1927 as a cruising yacht for the Bergen Line of Norway by Gotaverken, Gothenburg, Sweden. Details of the Stella Polaris are:

Length overall: 446ft.
Length between perpendiculars: 360ft.
Breadth: 50ft 6in.

Below: The finished model of *Stella Polaris*.

Depth: 30ft.
Gross Tonnage: 5,020.
Machinery: diesel engines, twin screw.
Service speed: 15.75 knots.

The plan was found in the March 1927 issue of *The Motor Ship* journal. This vessel had a very long and successful career spanning seventy-nine years. She sank off the coast of Japan in 2006 while under tow to China for a refit. There was no one on board at the time, so no lives were lost.

The *Rose* was chosen because I liked her clean lines and general appearance. This ship was completed in 1938 and the details are:

Length overall: 334ft 2in.
Breadth: 45ft 6in.
Depth: 28ft 10in.
Gross tonnage: 3,063.
Machinery: Diesel engine, single screw.
Service speed: 16 knots.

The *Rose* did not have a very long life, but it was very eventful. In 1939, she was sold to Germany and renamed *Alstertor*. She was immediately re-fitted as a supply ship for German warships and commerce raiders operating in the Atlantic. Running the blockade early in the war, the *Alstertor* was soon on station supplying the needs of a number of famous ships including *Bismarck*, *Nordmark*, *Herzogin*, *Kormoran*, *Pinguin* and others. On 22 June 1941 the *Alstertor* was spotted by HMS *Marsdale* and a Catalina aircraft, but contact was lost. The following day, she was intercepted by the destroyers *Faulkner*, *Foresight*, *Forester*, *Fury* and *Foxhound* of the 8th Destroyer Flotilla. Seeing that escape was impossible, the *Alstertor*'s crew set scuttling charges and abandoned ship. She sank in position 41°12′North, 13°10′West. The destroyers rescued everyone from the boats, including seventy-eight Allied prisoners from the British steamers *Trafalgar* and *Rabaul*.

The submarine *P33*, also on the lookout for the *Alstertor*, was informed of the outcome to the chase and directed to continue her passage to Gibraltar. I did not discover this short, but interesting history until the model was under construction.

The plans for the *Rose* were found in the February 1938 issue of *Shipbuilding and Shipping Record*. The chosen scale gave the *Stella Polaris* model an overall length of 13.9in and the *Rose* 10.4in.

Above: The completed stern glued and bolted in position.

STELLA POLARIS

The hull was cut and roughly shaped using spare plan copies as templates. The ship had a small deck down aft below the promenade deck, used for mooring purposes. It was necessary to fit this before the promenade deck was glued in position.

The *Stella Polaris* had a clipper bow in the fashion of an iron or steel-hulled sailing ship. The bowsprit, however, served very little purpose other than adding to the aesthetic appearance of the ship. It was just a short steel spike, stayed into the hull and supporting only two stays leading up to the foremast. The clipper bow was cut from sheet brass using a jeweller's saw. A piece of brass rod was used for the bowsprit. This was tapered in a hand-held electric drill. The rod projecting from the drill chuck was laid across the almost-closed jaws of a small steel vice. With the drill running on 6 volts

instead of 12 volts, a taper was soon formed by holding a smooth file on the top and moving it up and down the bowsprit, applying great pressure towards the end of the rod. I use this method on any spars that require a taper. It is illustrated in *Model Shipwright* 128, page 12. It is not a difficult process, but it is very important to run the drill on a slower speed than normal. Using it on high speed can cause the workpiece to whip round and even fly out of the drill. Because of this, and the amount of brass dust produced whilst tapering, it is essential to wear protective goggles and a dust mask.

The counter stern was made using two thin brass templates as shown on pages 38 and 39 of *Model Shipwright* 142. I reinforced the glue with a nut and bolt, countersunk at top and bottom. I cut a 'V' in the top and bottom brass shim templates to maximise the area of bare wood to ensure a good glue bond. The brass areas were given a coat of a good quality contact adhesive. A vertical slot was then cut in the stern to take the stern insert. Because the shim templates are so thin, cutting the slot does not harm the small hobby bandsaw blade. After the stern insert has been fitted, the stern may be carved with very great accuracy using a sharp scalpel. The edges of the shim templates provide good reference points during carving. Any gaps seen in the rough stern may be filled with chemical metal (plastic padding), available at automobile suppliers or DIY stores.

The small lower poop deck was planked with scored thin marine plywood, and the projecting part of the accommodation, the mooring equipment and the bulwarks fitted.

Above: The stern insert glued in place.

DECKS

As one might expect in a high-class cruise ship, all the decks, without exception were planked as were the tops of the upper accommodation blocks. I always use ¹/₃₂in marine plywood for this as I do not like the decks to be too white.

They may be scored by hand. But I have been using a home-made scoring device for some years now. This was

Below: The hull of *Stella Polaris* being fitted out.

described in detail in *Model Shipwright* 127 pages 50 and 51. Basically, this is a wooden board with a bar across the top. A large plastic set square with an old steel ruler glued to one edge, can be slid across the board and the parallel scores made manually with a scalpel. The sheet to be scored is clamped firmly under the top bar. The set square is moved by turning a handle on a long threaded rod that moves the set square to the left after each score. An extra refinement was to add a micrometer to the board so that a precise width

Above: Starboard quarter view of *Stella Polaris*.

could be guaranteed for each scored plank. This device was made in 2004 and is one of my most useful home-made modelling aids.

The plating of the hull was done using paper masking tape. Care has to be taken when making a model of a ship with a white hull as every blemish or inaccuracy tends to show up with great clarity. In earlier models, I used black-painted teleprinter tape punchings for portholes and stuck them on the hulls. I have since discarded that method in favour of drilled portholes. In order to get the lines of ports to follow the hull sheer, I use the simple depth jig shown on page 30 of *Model Shipwright* 133. After three years of use, I still find this simple jig most effective for positioning portholes. Their ports were drilled before the hull was painted. I still hand-paint black or dark-coloured hulls, but for white hulls I use matt white primer aerosol spray from automobile stores. The main disadvantages of using spray paints are the need to mask off those areas that are not to be painted at this stage, and also the fumes that are created. When spraying, I always wait for a fine day and do it outside, and always wear a respirator. Several coats are usually required. When the painting is to my satisfaction, I run the drill into each porthole to clean it up.

The superstructure of the *Stella Polaris* was simple and with few fittings. There was a small step at the forward end of the boat deck. This was to increase the between deck height for the music saloon below.

The bridge had wooden bulwarks with covered-in cabs at the wings. I prepared and coloured the wooden bulwark panels on the computer, reduced them to the required size and printed them on self-adhesive film. This was stuck on both sides of thin plasticard sheet and used for the bulwarks and cabs. A perfectly good alternative method (if a computer is not available) is to obtain a sheet of fine 'V' groove plasticard sheet from a model shop and cut it with the grooves running vertically to form the bulwarks. When I use this method, I spray the bulwarks with Russet Brown car spray before fitting them to the model. Where they are cut at the ends, the white plasticard is exposed, and this must be touched up with a brush, using spray paint that has been sprayed on an old tin lid. Spray paint dries very quickly, but there is normally time to cover the exposed ends before the paint becomes unusable.

The wheelhouse was also made using computer-produced panels. A very good alternative is to cut a slice of mahogany across the grain. The end grain is then on the top and bottom of the wheelhouse and the vertical grain runs up all four sides that can then be varnished. The doors were mass-produced on the computer and stuck on. Alternatively, they may be made from shiny brown paper (cut from a picture in an old magazine).

The side rails were made in the same manner as in the

Braemar Castle shown on page 49 of *Model Shipwright* 144. After I had fitted them, I decided that the vertical deck to deck stanchions between the promenade deck and the boat deck were not thick enough (they were too narrow), so I faced them with wider strips of plasticard. The after deck was completely covered by awning spars.

I made the rails as shown in the *Braemar Castle* article, leaving the extensions on as shown on page 50 of *Model Shipwright* 144. The centre horizontal ridge support for the awnings spars was fitted separately fore and aft. Each of the cross pieces (rafters) I made of wire sprayed white before fitting and glued between the centre ridge spar and the awning side stanchion.

I have not described the construction of the funnel as the method used is included in the description of the *Rose* (see later).

The *Stella Polaris* did not have a great amount of detail in the form of fittings and machinery about the decks, nor much rigging.

MACHINERY

On the forecastle was a windlass for handling the anchors, the usual outfit of bollards and fairleads, and at the after end a ladder each side down to the promenade deck. Two winches were fitted in the forward well deck to operate with the two derricks serving the small hatch, and an electric capstan on the lower mooring deck aft, plus some bollards. All these were made from thin brass rod in the same manner as the deck machines for the *Rose*, described later.

The seven open boats were made using a small home-made vacuum box, fully described and illustrated in *Model Shipwright* 129. This device is powered by connecting the hose of a standard domestic vacuum cleaner to it. A plug of a wooden boat is supported on a thin sheet of perforated wood and a sheet of thin plasticard is placed above it and clamped in position around the sides. The plasticard is heated using a small hobby heat gun and when the vacuum cleaner is switched on, it sucks the softened plasticard down over the plug. The fitting out of similar boats was described in *Model Shipwright* 144. The davits were made from lengths of copper wire bent to shape, also described in that same article. The two motor launches were rather easier to produce. The hulls were cut from thick pieces of plasticard sheet and shaped with a scalpel and wet and dry paper of various grades. The small cabins were cut from thin plasticard, shaped, and glued to the hulls. The windows were small black squares produced on the computer and printed on self-adhesive film.

There was a certain amount of fancy scrollwork around the bow. This was applied (by my wife) using a fine black pen and high quality acrylic gold paint. The name was prepared on the computer and reduced to the size required. It was then printed on self-adhesive matt film and stuck in position on the hull.

MS *ROSE*

Although the *Rose* was built only eleven years after the *Stella Polaris*, she had a much more modern look. The former ship was definitely based on much earlier designs; more akin to the large, elegant steam yachts of the late nineteenth and early twentieth centuries where beauty of form was a very important factor, especially when carrying passengers. The *Rose*, on the other hand, was built with the sole purpose of carrying cargo. Yet even so, she had clean, attractive lines and a nicely balanced profile, well ahead of her time. If she had survived into the 1960s, she would not have looked unduly old-fashioned even then.

Because of the very simple hull form, the initial shaping was quite simple when compared to the more complex form of *Stella Polaris*. The only point of note in the early stages of construction is that a solid bulwark was fitted each side from the after end of the raised forecastle to the after end on the accommodation. This was made from 1/64in marine plywood glued on its edge along the deck. I used contact adhesive for the initial fitting, but ran superglue over the join for added strength. To add even greater strength to these delicate parts, I added reinforcing strips along the inside of the bulwarks where they would be out of view once the boat deck was fitted.

After the lower section of accommodation and the boat deck had been added, I made and fitted the side stanchions. In this model I decided to etch them from 0.002in brass shim. This can be a hit and miss affair if insufficient care is taken. I have found that the brass must be perfectly clean without any trace of grease on it. In order to facilitate this, I sellotape the brass to a piece of card and give it a good cleaning with brass polish. Next, I rule the lines of the stanchions on it using a fine black marker pen normally used for writing titles on blank CD disks. I always rule a lot more than I need in case they do not all etch properly. The lines do provide a certain resistance to the etching fluid, but in order to make certain, I cover them with thin strips of high quality 'invisible' tape. To obtain the strips, I stick a length of it on a scrap piece of acrylic and blacken it with a thick fibre marking pen. The blacking is simply to make it more visible. Narrow strips are cut from it and stuck over the ruled lines.

I obtain etching crystals from an electronic components supplier. Protective goggles, gloves, etc., must always be worn when handling this corrosive material. If it does get in contact with the skin, it must be washed off immediately. Once the surface of the brass is prepared, it is necessary to paint the back to prevent the etching fluid working on the other side. Spray enamel car paint is best for this as it dries quickly. I use a bright colour so that when the etching is complete, it shows up against the black lines.

I prepare the etchings outside using an old washing-up bowl in which I place a house brick. The etching, secured to a small piece of glass (using short lengths of plastic slide binders), is placed in a plastic container on top of the brick. The glass is to ensure the brass etching remains beneath the surface of the etching fluid. The bowl is filled with hot water to just over the level of the brick. The etching fluid is then poured into the plastic container until it just covers the brass (more than that is unnecessary). The purpose of the brick is to provide a firm base for the etching dish and also to help the water in the bowl to maintain its heat during the etching process. If it is cold, it will still etch, but it will take much longer to complete.

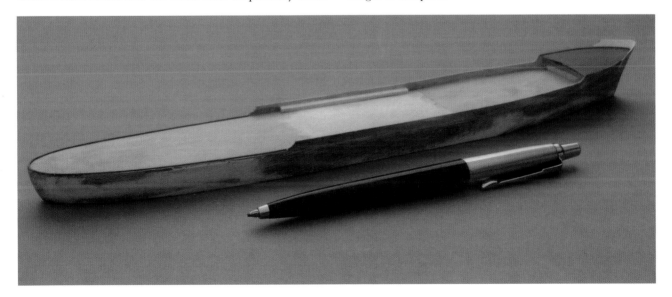

Above: *Rose*: the bulwarks were reinforced on the inside in way of the accommodation.

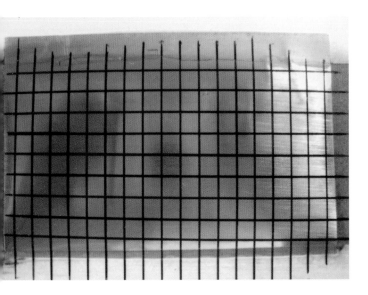

Above: The side stanchions ruled out on the brass shim.

Above: Etchings partly completed.

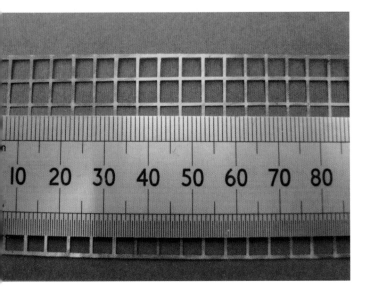

Above: Showing the completed etchings.

Above: The distorted oval funnel.

The backing colour usually starts to show through after about half an hour, and the whole process is usually complete within two hours. Wash the complete etching thoroughly and immerse it in white spirit to remove the paint from the back. The invisible tape strips will usually float free of their own accord after a few minutes in the white spirit. If they do not, they may be peeled off with tweezers.

I cut off the stanchions from the network leaving only the upper horizontal brass strip with the bottom end of each vertical unsupported, as these will rest on the bulwarks below with a very slight overlap. The upper edge is glued along the edge of the boat deck with contact adhesive, and the whole job is made neater by sticking a strip of thin white plasticard over the top edge. The stanchions are, of course, spray-painted white before sticking on the hull.

The funnel, like the one on the *Stella Polaris* was oval, but slightly more complex because the forward curve is greater than the after one in *Rose*, whilst they are both the same in *Stella Polaris*. I cut the funnel from a piece of brass tube and heated it to a red heat in order to soften it. As soon as it had cooled, I squashed it into a rough oval in a vice. This usually results in the sides becoming distorted.

The two curves can be corrected using two rods selected for the required curvature. The fact that I used a threaded rod in the illustration is of no significance; it had the correct diameter. A solid one would have worked just as well. I slipped the funnel on to the rod and holding the left-hand side of the rod in my left hand, I placed the other end on the solid top of a bench vice. By tapping along the top of the funnel with a hammer, the curve was soon corrected. The same was done with the opposite curve using a different diameter rod. The crushed in side was finally corrected using the same method, but with a flat steel bar instead of a rod. A brass base with a central hole for a fixing screw was soldered to the base of the funnel and spray-painted buff colour. The emblem was drawn out on a large piece of paper, scanned into the computer and coloured with the Photoshop software and then reduced to the required size. Finally, I cloned it and printed the two emblems on to a sheet of white self-adhesive paper. The two emblems were cut out using a sharp scalpel and stuck on each side of the funnel.

The cowl ventilator tops and winch parts were turned from brass rod on a lathe. The fine slots in the winches were made by holding a jeweller's saw on the brass as it was being machined.

The masts and derricks were all made from brass tube and rod. The rigging on a ship like this is relatively simple and was done using black enamelled copper wire.

As the ship had a white hull, the slots in the bulwarks for allowing any water to clear from the decks were quite promi-

nent. I made no attempt to cut these in and they were represented by strips of black film stuck on the hull. Some modellers will not approve of this sort of thing, but when the model is viewed as a whole, I find that it is far neater than cutting them in.

The model of the *Rose* was as attractive in its own way as the *Stella Polaris*, despite being of a completely different type. I showed the ship lying at anchor in a calm sea made from crepe paper as described on page 45 of *Model Shipwright* 142.

ADDENDUM: GLUES

I use various types of glue for miniatures, but have always had trouble with superglue bottle nozzles clogging long before the glue is used. I decided to do something about it and I am pleased to say the problem has now been solved. I took a small brass rod and drilled a 1/16in hole down the centre using a small Unimat lathe. It was then turned into a shape rather like the point of a ball pen, but with a thicker knurled band around the centre. The knurling was an added refinement and can be left off. The top of the superglue bottle was cut down to a level where the end of the brass tip could be pushed into it. As the hole is so small, there is no need to put a stopper on it whilst in use. When I have finished using it, I plug it with the pointed tip cut from a cocktail stick. When I next wish to use it, the stick is usually firmly glued in the tip, but this does not matter. The tip may be twisted out of the bottle with a small pair of pliers. Holding it in a pair of surgical clamp forceps I burn it clean

Below: Correcting the distortion.

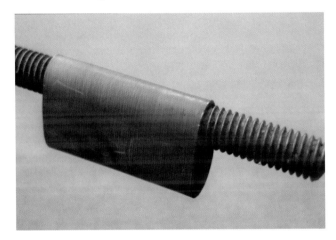

Below: Brass parts for the ventilators and winches.

Below: Corrected funnel shape.

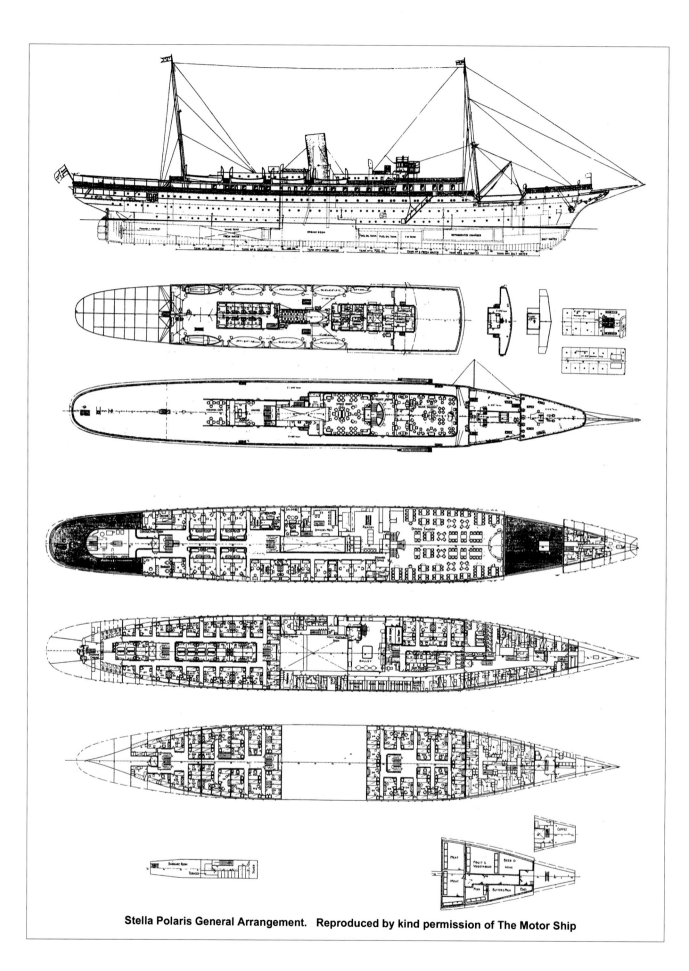

Stella Polaris General Arrangement.   Reproduced by kind permission of The Motor Ship

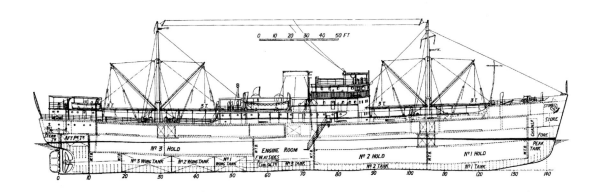

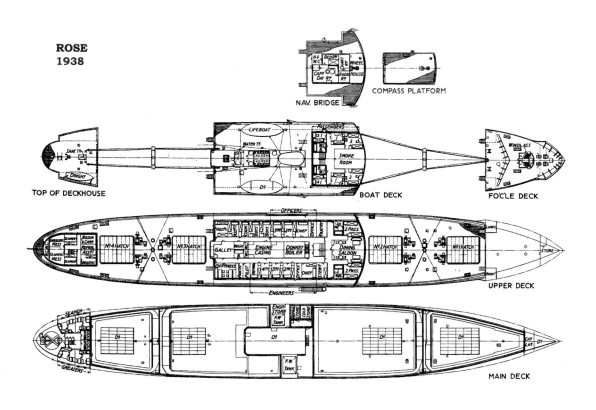

ROSE
1938

Above: The almost completed *Rose* ready to be rigged.

Below left and right: The brass superglue nozzle, and in place in the bottle.

with a small gas blowtorch and plunge it in water to cool it. After it is dried, it may be re-inserted in the bottle for the next glue session. Initially, I made the mistake of burning it clean and replacing it in the bottle at the end of the day. Unfortunately, there must have been some moisture left in the hole and the contents of the bottle went hard overnight. This can be overcome by either making a spare nozzle or making sure that the one left in the bottle is perfectly dry. The only other point is that the part that fits in the bottle should not be too long, or it will be too firmly stuck in the bottle to remove easily.

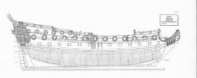
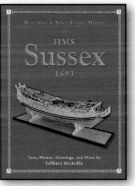

HMS *Roebuck*

A DOCKYARD TYPE MODEL

by Bernard Baldwin

In the last quarter of the eighteenth century, the Royal Navy found itself engaged in a conflict off the east coast of America where unpopular laws and heavy taxes imposed by the British Government had caused a rebellion by the local colonies. The colonialists were waging the war using relatively small lightly armed ships capable of negotiating the shallow waters from Chesapeake Bay and up the eastern seaboard to New York and Long Island. It was quickly realised by the British this was not a situation requiring large ships of the line, more a case for fast, well-armed, handy ships which could harass the enemy among the shoals and shallows of the area.

HMS *Roebuck* was ideally suited for just this type of work. Launched from Chatham Dockyard in April 1774 she was one of the first of a series of twenty-five similar ships, which would be built over the coming years. Armed with twenty 18pdrs on the gun deck, twenty-two 9pdr on the upper deck and two 6pdr on the forecastle she was well equipped to cope with any adversary liable to be encountered in the area. Two rows of gun ports and two apparent tiers of windows across the stern and quarter galleries gave her the appearance, through the inadequate telescopes of the day, of a much larger ship. However, closer examination of the upper tier of windows and galleries would reveal there were no cabins behind them, their lower levels coinciding with the level of the quarter deck; they were indeed quite false and probably intended to deceive any intending aggressor.

In September 1775 *Roebuck* sailed in the company of other ships to assist the North Atlantic Squadron in suppressing the rebellion, and there she stayed for the first six years of her career. That career would include cruises in the North Sea, the Channel and around the Windward Islands, service as a troop carrier and a hospital ship before finally paying off in July 1811.

It is fortunate the draught of the ship is held at the National Maritime Museum, Greenwich, along with, unusually, details of the ships carvings (see *Model Shipwright* 100). The eminent American ship modeller Mr Harold Hann used this information to produce a set of drawings to a scale of ⅛in = 1ft ideally suited to the production of a model. I obtained a copy of these and reduced them, where necessary, to ¹⁄₁₆in = 1ft, (1:192) scale. My previous models had all been built to a scale of 1in = 50ft (1:600) so this was a new venture for me demanding new skills.

THE HULL

The model, which is built in the style of a Dockyard Model but with fully rigged masts and spars, has a hull of pear wood. This was produced by gluing together ¹⁄₁₆in thick wafers of the wood to form a block, wide enough to accommodate the beam and about ¾in (18mm) deeper than the greatest distance from the keel to the highest timberhead in the hull. The wafers are grouped into pairs, a central slot, which would eventually house the keel, being cut in one edge to assist location during assembly. A flat base was prepared with each hull station clearly marked upon it and a firm stop at station No.1, at the bow. Two wooden battens ⅛in x 1¼in (3mm x 32mm) were screwed to the base, parallel to and equidistant from the centreline, with sufficient distance apart to just accommodate the width of the wafer. These and the surface of the base were then rubbed with candle wax to prevent any glue adhering to them. A length of wood longer than the hull and a push fit into the keel slot was used to act as a false keel during assembly. The first pair of wafers was assembled together using two or three spots of PVA glue, slotted onto the false keel and located against the stop, with the keel uppermost, and precisely over the hull centre line. It was important the keel piece remained precisely over the centre line during the whole assembly of the block, otherwise a misaligned hull would be produced. At no time was it allowed to become glued to the wafers. Before each pair was glued into the block it was clearly marked with a number in the centre of its face indicating its correct position along the hull, e.g. 21, 21A, etc.

The nominal ¹⁄₁₆in thick wafers were in fact produced in three different thicknesses, nominal, 10 per cent 0.004in (0.1mm) thicker, and 10 per cent 0.004in thinner than

Above: Port side view of finished model.

nominal. This was to allow for the correction of cumulative errors during assembly. If the wafer pairs began to fall behind or move ahead of their station, thicker or thinner wafers would be used successively to recover the situation. During this phase, longitudinal clamps were used to pull the wafers tightly together and great care taken to ensure they remained perpendicular to the centreline and the keel piece exactly over the centre. With all 58 perpendicular wafers pairs in place and the glue dry, the block was secured to the base by two woodscrews and the stop removed.

Wafers for the cant frames could now be fitted. These are the same basic wafer pairs but split vertically along the centre line and tapered from the outside to the centre. They are used at the bow and stern where the hull curves sharply into the stem and sternpost and reduce the amount of bevelling that would occur on the outer edge of a perpendicular frame. Figure 1 shows the general arrangement. With the glue thoroughly dry, the side battens could be removed and with the base plate acting as a reference plane, the block carved to shape using chisels, sandpaper and the normal card templates. The finished hull block was then sandpapered to the surface finish that would be required on the completed model. No further sandpapering would be possible after the frames had been reassembled. The rising floor

line at bow and stern, the lower and upper lines of the main wale, the line of the frame heads and the cut off line were all pencilled onto the block using card templates. The cut off line is the point at which all the frames would eventually be cut through in order to remove the partially finished hull from the base. The two battens used previously were shaped to fit tightly around the hull block at its junction with the base, before being secured to the base plate. These would form the location points during the reassembly so it was important they were in contact with every wafer. After removal from the base plate, the block was dismantled by progressively immersing one end in cellulose thinners until the adhesive was loosened and the wafer could be removed, an operation carried out in the open air for health and safety reasons. As each wafer pair was taken off, the legibility of the station numbers was checked, before it was laid out, in sequence, on a flat board to dry.

After two days all traces of the thinners had evaporated. Adhesive was applied to the areas indicated in Figure 2 and using the keel slot and the location points to align them correctly, the wafers were joined together again into pairs. To transform these into frames that would ultimately form the hull it was necessary to remove material from the centre. The depth of each frame varies as it progresses from the frame head, where it is the same in depth as in thickness, i.e. square, to a maximum at the keel slot. A line, to indicate this variation and define that part of the wafer to be removed, was drawn in. Material was removed using chain drilling, dental burrs and a scalpel, with an area approximately ½in above the location points and the full distance between them left in place to stabilise each assembly and to provide an area for the frame identification number to be rewritten. To generate the gaps between the futtocks it was necessary to remove a different portion of each frame pair. On frame 21 clean cuts were made at the rising floor line and at the lower line of the main wale and the portion between them removed, there being no adhesive at this point they came away cleanly. Similarly on frame 21A, a portion between the upper main wale line and a point ⅛in (3mm) above the cut off line was removed. With all the wafers similarly treated and converted into frames, the final assembly could commence. Frames 21 and 21A were fitted back onto the base exactly on the correct station line, this time being glued at the location points and adjusted carefully to ensure they were perpendicular to the centre line in both horizontal and vertical planes. When the glue was dry, frames 22 and 22A could be fitted using the keel slot and location points to ensure correct alignment. With all the 58 perpendicular frames fixed in place, the keel, stem and stern-post were added before fitting the cant frames.

Construction continued with the fitting of the main wale, cut from African Blackwood, the gun wale from Cherry wood and ancillary planking from Castello Box. Transom pieces were fitted, greatly stabilising the stern frames, before the gun ports were cut and framed. The whole structure was now stable, and although still quite delicate, it was possible to sever the frames at the cut off lines and remove the hull from its base. The assembly could now be fixed to temporary cradles and a few deck beams fitted at the upper deck level to prevent damage during work on the orlop and the gun decks.

THE REST OF THE MODEL

The foregoing is intended to be a simplified account of the construction of the hull, other problems were encountered en-route, all proved interesting and satisfying to overcome; but isn't that part of the pleasure of scratch-building? However, it is not a project I would recommend to an inexperienced modeller. Methods that are more conventional were used for the rest of the model. Decks were laid, using holly planks 0.030in (0.75mm) wide by 0.010in (0.25mm) thick, over carlings and deck beams of pear wood. The figurehead, a female figure wielding a spear, was carved from boxwood while the spear shaft was made from copper wire. Ranged across the stern are a number of carved figures; the head and shoulders of a female, a dog, a deer with antlers, four angels and a spear-wielding hunter on each quarter. Too small to

Above: Amidships showing the ship's boats; note the capstan beneath.

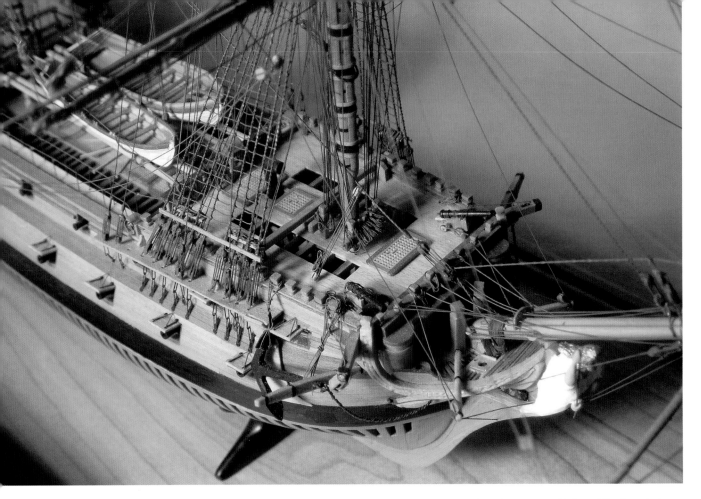

Above: The forecastle with its two 6pdr, the belayed ropes and the galley chimney, behind the shrouds.   **Below:** The fore chains.

Above: The rising floor line at the bow.　　　**Below:** The rising floor line at the stern.

chisels. The use of a false stern board allowed the carving tools to cut into the board and a little behind the figures giving a better impression of relief. After gilding, they were floated off the false board using methylated spirits to soften the PVA adhesive, and then glued into position on the model.

Guns were turned from African Blackwood, which I find a reasonable substitute for Ebony and somewhat less expensive. Those on the gun deck, although unseen in the finished model, are mounted on carriages, complete with tackle, not as silly as it may sound, as they were used to practice the technique before making those on the upper deck, which can be seen. A 29ft pinnace and a 30ft launch were clinker built around a carved wooden plug over which cling film was stretched to prevent the glue sticking to it. The launch has a gun mounting in the bow and the pinnace is decorated around the stern as was the custom of the day.

Masts and spars were turned from Castello Box, a wood similar to lemonwood that has a nice buff colour and turns very well. Main and fore masts are fished and banded and all three stepped on the keel. Annealed nickel/chrome wire

Above: The port quarter gallery.

carve individually, their outlines were cut from boxwood, glued onto a false stern board of African Blackwood before being carved to shape using dental burrs and miniature

0.006in diameter (0.15mm) was used for both standing and running rigging. The annealing was carried out by holding 12in (300mm) lengths between two pairs of pliers, and passing the wire through a candle flame whilst applying slight tension. The result is a length of wire, fairly straight, dull grey in colour and ready to be painted. It holds catenary well, puts no tension on the masts, and is unaffected by humidity. A single strand served for running rigging, two strands twisted together for shrouds, and three strands twisted together for the main and fore stays and the anchor cable: hawser or cable laid cable as appropriate. Canadian Maple was used for the case, the glass being fitted into grooves in the frame pieces and the whole finished with matt polyurethane varnish.

The model took about 1,300 hours, spread over four years, to complete and was awarded the President's Cup and a gold medal at the Society of Model Shipwrights exhibition 2006, a gold medal and The Maze Challenge Cup at the Model Engineering Exhibition at Ascot in 2007.

Below: The figurehead.

REFERENCES

Goodwin, Peter, *Construction and Fitting of the Sailing Man of War 1650–1850*, Conway, 1997.

Hahn, Harold H., *Ships of the American Revolution and their Models*, US Naval Institute Press, 1988.

Lavery, Brian, *Arming and Fitting of English Ships of War*, Conway, 1988.

Lees, James, *Masting and Rigging of English Ships of War 1625-1860*, Conway, 1979.

Marquardt, Karl Heinz, *Eighteenth-Century Rigs and Rigging*, Conway, 1992.

Model Shipwright 100, article by Elizabeth Tucker, Conway.

Top: The main and mizzen fighting tops.
Abovet: The foremast and spars.

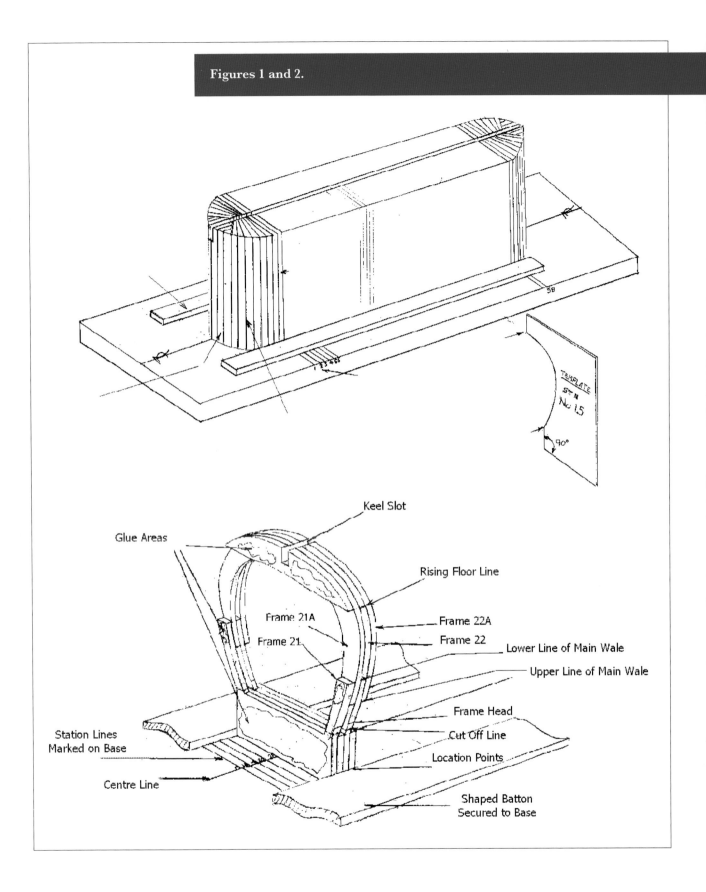

TEMPLATE
STN
No 15

90°

Keel Slot

Glue Areas

Rising Floor Line

Frame 21A

Frame 22A

Frame 21

Frame 22

Lower Line of Main Wale

Upper Line of Main Wale

Frame Head

Station Lines
Marked on Base

Cut Off Line

Location Points

Centre Line

Shaped Batton
Secured to Base

Book News

***Britain's Historic Ships: A Complete Guide to the
Ships that Shaped a Nation***
Paul Brown
Conway, 2009
Hardback, 208 pages, 116 photos and 5 paintings
ISBN 978-1-84486-093-7
£20

I am naturally suspicious of something that claims to be a
'complete' anything and with over a thousand vessels currently on the National Register of Historic Vessel (and the
latest certificate at the time of writing being number 2,316)
this book would have to be a lot bigger than it actually is if it
were truly the complete guide to Britain's historic ships that is
claimed.

The clue of course is in the sub title; the author has made
his selection on the basis of each vessel somehow shaping the
nation, a judgement in some cases a little subjective, but very
obvious for the most part. He has then subdivided the book
into chapters covering specific periods and types, with coverage of several exemplars given in some detail with notes on
additional vessels that fit under the chosen heading. Many of
the ships selected by the author will be well known and are
covered by a variety of off-the-shelf models, from highly
detailed plank-on-frame models to the plastic kits that were
amongst the earliest in the famous Airfix range. The author
has included replicas in some chapters; for example the
chapter entitled 'The Sailing Navy' includes short pieces on
the replicas Golden Hinde, Matthew and Grand Turk.

Other chapters, 'Coastal Steamers and Harbour Craft'
for example, are a collection of short notes on a range of
such vessels and it is in the selection of some of these, and the
omission of others, that one might question the author's logic
a little. Why for example has the *Medway Queen* been ignored,
whereas *Wingfield Castle* is included? Perhaps it's because the
Medway Queen was only a pile of rescued materiel at the time

the author made his selection, but surely her exploits at
Dunkirk 'shaped a nation'?

The format does make for an excellent introduction to the
topic, with useful histories alongside each of the selected
vessels, but the addition of a few line drawings, even if only
of the profiles of the more important ships, would have
increased the interest to a prospective modeller. There are
numerous sources for such plans, although I have to admit to
having so far failed to find a source of drawings for HMS
Caroline. Where the ship histories include reference to their
current situation the entry may perforce be out of date in
some cases; again HMS *Caroline* springs to mind, her service
with the RNR now formally at an end and her future yet to
be decided. In other areas the necessary glossing has left the
reader with a slightly incomplete picture; for example the
author appears to perpetuate the myth that *Turbinia* was a
complete surprise to the Admiralty.

While it can be seen as a worthy attempt to encapsulate a
very diverse topic, I must confess to feeling a little disap-
pointed, although I did come across a couple of things that
were new to me, and I especially liked W. L. Wylie's painting
of *Victory* being restored in 1925. Having carried out work of
one sort or another in connection with some twenty-two of
the vessels listed (and actually served briefly on one, HMS
Bristol!), I didn't get the sort of buzz I would have hoped for
from a new book; one which could have built on existing
knowledge rather than just regurgitating well-known facts.

All together the author has indexed fifty-four named
vessels and six classes, with a full list of the then Core Collection and Designated Lists from the National Register as an
appendix. There is a glossary of terminology, bibliography
and a list of useful websites to complete the work. (Note:
Further details of the heritage fleet, the National Register of
Historic Vessels, are available on the National Historic Ships
web site: www.nationalhistoricships.org.uk, including the
reclassification of the Core Collection and Designated Lists
into a combined National Historic Fleet.)

An interesting book, but it can only be recommended as
an introduction to the subject.

Wyn Davies

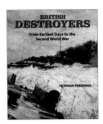

British Destroyers: From Earliest Days to the Second World War

Norman Friedman
Seaforth Publishing, Barnsley, 2010
Hardback, 320 pages, 300 drawings and photographs
ISBN 978-1-84832-049-9
£45

In effect a prequel to his book on British destroyers and frigates since the Second World War (reviewed in *Shipwright* 2010), but focusing purely on the destroyers and the torpedo-boats that preceded them and from which they were derived, this is another huge, highly impressive, though perhaps slightly overwhelming volume from Norman Friedman. It covers, in great detail, the underlying concepts behind the individual classes, the design processes, the weapons and propulsion systems, and the ships' changing roles over the course of sixty-odd years of unprecedented change. It should be noted that while the many modifications that took place during the two World Wars also receive due attention, other aspects of the story such as construction, careers and fates get little mention. Overall, despite this slightly one-sided coverage (which presumably reflects the author's areas of interest and expertise) it is an invaluable book for the naval historian, while for the modeller it also has much to offer.

The obvious comparison has to be with the earlier sequel (so to speak) and one clear problem with that volume was the occasionally debatable quality of the reproduction of the line drawings. This is something of which the publisher was evidently aware, and has addressed here with notable success – the bulk of the drawings (again mostly deck plans and out-board profiles) being reproduced at universally excellent quality. A.D. Baker III, who drew most of them, provides a short but interesting introduction to this aspect of the book: an unusual and welcome departure. (Indeed this reviewer, being of an artistic disposition, would have been happy had there been more about this.) It should also be noted that the drawings were all done in the conventional fashion, using pens, ink and drafting film, and with just a little help from a friend with a computer, and then only in terms of enhancing poor quality originals for reference purposes.

Slightly less welcome is the return to conventional current practice whereby individual footnotes are dispensed with and replaced by 22½ very solid pages of notes near the end of the book. However, British Destroyers is a jam-packed read anyway, and placing these alongside the very dense text and the frequently pretty hefty picture captions might well have resulted in something totally indigestible.

The very numerous photographs are generally well chosen and well reproduced, though they are nearly all straightforward ship portraits, with few detail or on-board views. This is rather a pity, especially when there are sections going into considerable detail about subjects like bridge layout or the fitting of various bits of equipment onto the quarterdeck, and yet these are barely illustrated.

This book is bound to be compared with David Lyon's *The Earliest Destroyers* (Chatham Publishing, 1996), which covers a considerable part of the same subject in a not dis-similar fashion. From a modeller's point of view Lyon's book has the immense advantage of a separate set of fold-out plans of the destroyer *Velox* of 1904, together with a series of detailed cut-away drawings of HMS *Havoc* of 1895. On the other hand the numerous reproductions of official plans from the National Maritime Museum's collection are either too small and indistinct to be of much use, or if they are reproduced at a reasonable size then a section of the detail is lost down the gutter of the book. Probably anyone seriously considering making a model of any of these early ships would best be advised to get hold of both titles.

There are a few minor mistakes here and there (together with one absolute clunker!) and it must be said that reading it can sometimes be seriously heavy going, both due to the author's rather dry style of writing and to the sheer quantity of information that he is presenting. On the other hand, it should be noted that it is also a very handsome book. It is interesting to read that the inter-war 'standard' destroyers of the A-I classes, so often criticised both at the time and subsequently for being much smaller than those being built at the same time for other navies (in particular France and Japan), originally came in for a good deal of adverse comment for being too big!

(From a personal point of view this reviewer warms to the author's continued reference to the establishment which we are now supposed to call The National Archives as The Public Record Office: just how much public money was wasted on this pointless, confusing exercise in rebranding of an establishment that was just fine as it was but which just happens to now be facing serious financial problems?)

Stephen Dent

British Warships 1860-1906: A Photographic Record

Nicholas Dingle
Pen & Sword Maritime, 2009
Hardback, 208 pages, 165 photos
ISBN 978-1-84415-980-2
£35

Like the author I enjoy looking at old photographs, and this book is full of them. The author's stated intent is to bring the pictures held in The National Archives (formerly the Public Record Office) to a wider audience. This book contains photographs from the files of the Naval Construction Department held at Kew and with these he has arguably succeeded in his intent.

The result is a collection of 165 period photographs covering a time of tremendous technological change in the Royal Navy, when it was moving away from the sailing fleet to a recognisably modern mechanically propelled fleet: by no means a smoothly continuous process.

The book is divided into five main periods with an introductory text covering the developments during that time. While the author's main thrust is the pictures, this text sets the scene well, with no obvious glaring errors or omissions.

The photographs themselves are superb and cover the full range of ship types, from 'battleships' to the lowly gunboat. As the author notes there are one or two vessels that apparently slipped through the net, he specifically mentions *Prometheus*, but the coverage is such that you would have to have a very specialist interest indeed not to find something of value here. Unfortunately the reproduction is a little patchy in places, but this presumably reflects the quality of the original material.

The best photographs are obviously directly from glass plate negatives which were capable of recording the finest detail. Each photo is printed at least half page in this generously sized (240mm x 260mm) book and this allows a good deal of the detail to be seen. I suspect it would be asking too much from an already quite expensive book to have one picture to a page. The more important vessels typically do get a page to themselves, often showing some amazing details, for example the bow shot of HMS *Drake*, also on the cover, reveals such detail as the hinged hawse pipe cover, the lanyard to open it before anchoring and a series of ladder rungs down the ship's side to open it manually if the rope breaks.

Each photograph is accompanied by an informative caption giving career and technical details and the ship's final disposition. It is slightly surprising to learn how many of these Victorian ships actually survived until after the Second World War, presumably hulked and unrecognisable. Knowing how costly it is to restore and preserve large ships it is probably as well that we only retained HMS *Warrior*!

If there is a complaint about this book it's a something of a double edged sword. The author has made little attempt to identify the backgrounds of the photographs and this will leave me, and possibly many others, with several more hours of enjoyment just trying to identify where the ships were when photographed.

All in all, a fascinating collection of very detailed photographs which should keep the Victorian and Edwardian naval enthusiast busy for some time in distilling all the details they hold. Perhaps not perfect, but thoroughly recommended none the less.

W. B. Davies

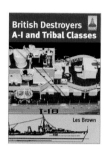 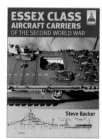

British Destroyers: A-I and Tribal Classes – ShipCraft 11
Les Brown
ISBN 978-1-84832-023-9.

Essex Class Aircraft Carriers of the Second World War – ShipCraft 12
Steve Backer
ISBN 978-1-84832-018-5.

New Orleans Class Cruisers – ShipCraft 13
Lester Abbey
ISBN 978-1-84832-041-3.

Yamato Class Battleships – ShipCraft 14
Steve Wiper
ISBN 978-1-84832-045-1.

All 2009 Seaforth Publishing, Barnsley, 2009
Soft covers, 64 pages, 295mm x 210mm, numerous black & white and colour photographs and line drawings.
£14.99 each

Seaforth Publishing's well-established 'ShipCraft' series will need little introduction to many readers. Aimed principally at the modelling community, each volume focuses either on a specific class or slightly broader grouping of warships. Adopting a largely standardised structure, the books provide both a description of the characteristics and history of the full-sized originals, as well as an overview of the model kits and associated aftermarket products available to represent them. Benefiting from high-quality production values and featuring a detailed design that has steadily improved over time, each edition manages to fit a lot of information into just 64 pages. The series is steadily expanding year-by-year, with the four books now subject to review encompassing those released during 2009.

While there are some variations in the contents of the various editions, each book opens with a design history of the class under consideration. This is typically followed by an overview of career highlights. Attention then switches away from the originals to a review of the strengths and weaknesses of the various kits and accessories available to the modeller. The following 'Modelmakers' Showcase' is possibly the centrepiece of each volume. This displays a range of completed models that have been built to museum-standard levels of quality in full colour as an inspiration towards what can be achieved. Subsequent chapters aid this process through the provision of information on camouflage schemes and detailed changes in appearance, supplemented by profile and plan drawings. The visual material provided is particularly useful, often focusing down to specific design deviations. A concluding one-page list of reference material points the modeller in the direction of any necessary additional research.

The main challenge the 'ShipCraft' brand faces is the difficulty inherent in adapting a relatively rigid format to describe warship groupings of different size and standardisation. This can work well or not so well depending on the subject, as clearly demonstrated by the four books published in 2009.

Steve Backer's *Essex Class Aircraft Carriers* and Lester Abbey's *New Orleans Class Cruisers* are among the better editions in the series. They describe ships that played a key part in securing the US Navy's ultimate victory in the Pacific campaign. Both were reasonably numerous classes built to broadly homogenous blueprints but which still exhibited considerable variations in detail. This allows the two authors to provide a thorough description of their chosen ships' design origins and a summary of their overall significance, while leaving sufficient space for specific differences to be explained. For example, the seven members of the *New Orleans* class were initially constructed as three sub-classes but with as many as five different sub-groupings. These are all clearly set out in the text.

In similar fashion, the kits produced to represent various Essex and New Orleans members are all compared to the detailed appearance of the originals. Errors such as the incorporation of a long H IVB catapult on the starboard side of Dragon's 1:700 scale model of *Essex*, the shorter H II model was fitted at the time represented, are noted as appropriate. As an aside, it is disappointing that model producers continue to make so many mistakes in the details of their products in spite of the considerable technical advances achieved in the manufacture of injection-moulded kits in recent years. As observed by Mr Abbey, only two of the seven individual 1:700 models of *New Orleans* cruisers

recently developed by Trumpeter are fully accurate.

The two books on US Navy subjects are not without their limitations. For example, shortage of space means that coverage of the *Essex* class is solely focused on the wartime period, while colour profiles of the carriers' camouflage schemes are set out in just two pages, covering only six ships. Details of operational careers provide only the broadest of outlines and, particularly in the case of the *New Orleans* class, sometimes seem to omit relevant information. Nevertheless, both are essential aids to the modeller wanting to produce accurate representations of the ships concerned.

The other two 'ShipCraft' volumes reviewed here do not quite match up to the standards achieved by Mr Backer and Mr Abbey. Steve Wiper's *Yamato Class Battleships* provides a sound overview of a famous warship class. The fact that only two individual warships are described means that design and career histories receive more thorough coverage than in other editions in the series. However, the book appears to suffer from a lack of photographic material of its original subjects. As such, its content seems to have been slightly stretched to fill the space available. The 3½ colour pages devoted to images from the 'Men of the Yamato' movie set are a particularly clear case of making a virtue out of a necessity.

Les Brown's description of the British A-I and Tribal class destroyers suffers from the opposite problem of squeezing too much material into the space available. This stretches the format beyond acceptable limits. Although containing an extensive range of photographs and illustrations that are presented in an attractive manner, there is insufficient space to do the different designs full justice; an impression of superficial coverage results. This image is exacerbated by a number of errors, most notably the captioning of a rare full-page colour view of *Hesperus* (H57) as sister-ship *Harvester* (H19). Other captions are also suspect, for example the reference to *Ardent* serving on Russian convoys during 1939–40.

In conclusion, the latest ShipCraft volumes represent good examples of the strengths and weaknesses of a series that provides valuable references to the ship modeller at a reasonable price. While overall quality is steadily improving, further attention to both structure and accuracy of the series would provide the modeller with an even better product.

Conrad Waters

The Spanish Convoy of 1750 – Heaven's Hammer and International Diplomacy

James A. Lewis

University Press of Florida, 2009

157 pages, ISBN 978-0-8130-3358-7

£53.95

'If historians want a larger audience, only a narrative well told and researched offers such a prospect. This is what I have attempted to do in this short book.' So writes Lewis in the preface to his account of seven ships of a Spanish convoy, or flota, whose voyage from Havana to Cadiz ended after seven days when on 25 August 1750 they ran into a ferocious hurricane, 'Heaven's Hammer', off the coast of Georgia. The ships, all (including the escorting warship *Galga*) with valuable cargoes, were forced to run before the storm and ended up scattered across the coast of North Carolina and up to Delaware; a coastline in the hands of hostile British colonialists for whom the badly damaged ships represented an opportunity for self-enrichment. This involved everything from deserting sailors carrying off the silver to colonial corruption, opportunism by locals and plain piracy. The book is very much about the increasingly desperate attempts of the Spanish to hold onto what they could of their treasure and to track down what had been looted. It ends in the present century with the US Supreme Court ruling that the remains of the *Galga* belong to the Kingdom of Spain.

Lewis' diligent and original historical research is superb. While the text runs to just 102 pages, a further forty pages of notes and bibliography shed further light on this complex story involving seven ships and the context surrounding their voyage. Records in Spain, Britain and the USA have been carefully combed and interpreted. The author also demolishes some of the old myths that, for want of proper scholarship, have grown up, perhaps most famously that horses escaped from the *Galga* and became the progenitors of the ponies of Chincoteague.

It is as narrative that the book is less successful. The story is complicated, with a very large cast of characters interacting with one another in several places, and 102 pages is not long enough for so much detail. It is rather easy for the attention to wander as the brain is assailed with so many new names and so much coming and going, and it is hard to find a character to hold onto. Comparisons with Jack Beeching's similarly complex and equally well researched *The Galleys at Lepanto* spring to mind. Beeching's text is perhaps three times as long and, while he does not include end notes, he weaves in quotations from the original sources, fleshes out the characters and generally carries the reader along.

The other caveat, for the general reader and for the public library, is the price. £53.95 reflects the level of scholarship, but puts the book beyond the typical book-buyer.

Jean Hood

The First HMS Invincible (1747-58): Her Excavations (1980-1991)

John M Bingeman
Oxbow Books, 2010
Hardback, 198 pages, 379 illustrations and photographs, 6 line drawings of deck plans and a further 46 illustrations on the accompanying CD
ISBN 978-1-84217-393-0
£40

At first glance this book has almost enough in it to rival the information published on the *Mary Rose*, albeit this is from a much better documented period of naval history. Indeed it is a very detailed exposition of the underwater archaeology of the wreck of the titular vessel from a site not that far from where the *Mary Rose* lay for so long. The book also includes a complete list of all the artefacts recovered over eleven years on a CD inside the back cover, together with some additional illustrations (numbered from 400 for some reason).

Oddly enough the actual birth place of the *L'Invincible*, as she was christened by her French builders, was the Royal Dockyard of Rochefort, which is once more echoing to the sound of the shipwright's tools as a replica of *L'Hermione*, a frigate of 1778 and supposedly Lafayette's favourite ship, is under construction using traditional techniques.

Invincible herself also has a special place in history as the first of the 74's, a type destined to become the most useful class of sailing warship during the Napoleonic Wars. Despite this she succumbed rather quickly to the Royal Navy which, in turn, was not slow to appreciate her virtues, so much so she became the model for the class within the RN.

As a book to consult on individual items this volume will be very useful. After a forward by Dr Margaret Rule, who kindly acted as the author's archaeological advisor, it starts with a brief history of the ship herself up to the point of her loss, with a particularly interesting section thereafter on the attempts to recover her. It then continues with chapters devoted to publicity, staffing the excavation and artefact policy, then the survey, excavations and conservation. These three chapters are followed by three totally devoted to the artefacts. While largely descriptive of the finds themselves, this format does not necessarily make for a flowing read, consisting as it does mainly of a number of short paragraphs on individual artefacts grouped under the appropriate chapter headings, with occasional bits of additional narrative scattered in between.

The book concludes with an appendix from the Admiralty records of all the work done to the ship (with costs in many cases!) whilst in service with the RN and a second on the army buttons found in the wreck. This latter formed a study in itself!

The author, who consistently refers to himself as the licensee of the shipwreck, expects this to be the last voluntary underwater excavation on this scale, and the volume of work this excavation has clearly entailed suggest he may well be right. He was fortunate in being in a position, as a serving naval officer, to draw on a large pool of potential volunteers from with the RN; such a large pool is unlikely to be available within the Navy today.

The author is to be congratulated on publishing his work and for the details on the many artefacts found, some of which now reside at Chatham Historic Dockyard on public display. And while it doesn't actually rival the *Mary Rose* reports in the volume of retrieved artefacts, nor does it replace Jean Boudriot's seminal work on the design of the 74, it is a very accessible book for anyone looking for the details of an eighteenth-century warship and its components.

[Editor's Note: John Bingeman examined some of the Invincible artefacts in his article 'HMS Invincible (1747-58): archaeology provides 250-year-old technical details' in Shipwright 2010]

Wyn Davies

BB Kongô Class & CV Unryû class
Hans Lengerer
Modelhobby, Katowice, Poland, 2010
Hardback, 188 pages, illustrated with b&w photographs, plans and pen drawings
ISBN 978-83-60041-42-0
£46.99

This book is Volume 3 of the 'Japanese Warship at War' series; compared with Vols 1 and 2, photograph captions have been extended and text and drawings added. It is a unit of one of several interlocking series by Lengerer, an acknowledged expert on the Imperial Japanese Navy also noted for his on-line monographs, 'Contributions to the History of Imperial Japanese Navy Warships'. The *Kongô* class is allocated about three-quarters of the book, the *Unryû* class the balance; there are 183 drawings and 92 photographs of the former, and 35 and 31 respectively of the latter. Although the above title appears on the book's cover, the headings inside define its scope more exactly: 'Illustrated Record of the Transition of the Superstructures of BB *Kongô* class...after the Second Modernisation Refitting. Introduction to CV *Unryû* Class.'

The four *Kongôs* began life as battlecruisers, but after major reconstructions, which augmented deck armour, doubled horsepower and extended hulls aft, they entered the Second World War as high-speed (30+ knots) battleships. Two were sunk in 'Ironbottom Sound', Guadalcanal, one succumbed to American submarine torpedoes and one sur-

vived the war badly damaged. There is a very detailed loose sheet of drawings of *Kongô* as built by Vickers, and ten sections of *Haruna* in 1944 from original material. Most of the remaining drawings provide a thorough, well-drawn record of the extensive and much-altered pagoda-type bridge structures, and of changes to bow, stern and bulges. The text comes in part from Lengerer's monographs and admirably complements the drawings, although faults can be found with the translation.

Six *Unryûs*, of modified *Hiryû* type, were laid down in 1942–3 out of a total of 15 (later 13) planned, but only three were completed: *Unryû* herself was torpedoed by a US submarine, while *Amagi* and *Katsuragi* were sunk or badly damaged in port by US air attack. All surviving hulls were scrapped after the war. A good selection of drawings is included, for *Unryû* a large elevation, longitudinal section and flight deck plan and for *Katsuragi* smaller reproductions of general arrangement drawings and enlargements of bridge details. Further photographs of the class were published in Vols 1 and 2, and more will follow in Vol. 4 with drawings rarely seen before; of particular importance in this volume is the publication of the official data book of *Katsuragi* in slightly abbreviated form.

The author intends supplements to both classes, again with text and illustrations, to provide very complete descriptions, and notes that other aspects of the ships will be covered in the 'Technical and Operational History of Imperial Japanese Warships' series. The comprehensive drawings will greatly assist the model-maker, but the book is expensive.

Ian Sturton

Sailing into the Past
Jenny Bennett (Ed.)
Seaforth Publishing, 2009
Hardback, 192 pages, profusely illustrated with photographs, paintings, explanatory drawings and ship's lines.
ISBN 978-1-84832-013-0
£25

This imaginative, well-informed, and highly readable book offers a new perspective on traditional shipbuilding techniques by describing the experience of replicating them and evaluating the performance of the resulting vessels in an objective and very frank manner.

Essentially *Sailing into the Past* covers the research, construction, and the sea-going characteristics of ten wooden-hulled replica sailing craft, classified as being 'Ancient and Medieval Ships' and those of 'The Age of Discovery'. They range from a Greek Trireme and the Roskilde Viking Ships, a thirteenth-century European Caravel, and Japan's coastal trading craft to the more familiar eighteenth-century square-riggers; it culminates in the gripping appraisal of an ill-fated reproduction Baltimore Clipper that endorses the more rigorous approach prescribed in earlier chapters.

Individual chapters have been contributed by authors with a specific interest and personal involvement in the projects described; each has considerable professional credibility in their own right and the ability to communicate their knowledge. Using thirteen different authors may suggest a slightly disjointed 'magazine style' publication, however this is a collaborative endeavour and their inputs have been skilfully integrated such that the chronography evolves smoothly with some back-references and a common phraseology.

Introductory chapters set the scene for the selection and quality of replica vessels described in this book which, in the editor's words, 'are representative of a new breed: a breed founded in solid research that has been assembled over many decades and is still growing'.

The distinction between building a 'floating hypothesis' such as a fourteenth-century Bremen Cog, based upon incomplete evidence, as a form of archaeological experiment and the construction of a thoroughly documented replica such as the delightful little schooner HMS *Sultana* is well made; as is the case for their contribution in evaluating different aspects of our maritime past.

The objective measurement, and comparison, of a sailing vessel's performance is clearly explained as are the benefits of being able to use today's low-cost GPS equipment to debunk the optimistic assessments of windward performance and tacking-angles obtained by previous 'wind on the cheek' or even masthead sensors; the results obtained certainly enhanced my respect for the determination of those who had to work these little vessels in a seaway. While on this topic the comparison of boat speed in knots with an apparent wind-speed measured in metres per second in a later chapter seemed rather unconventional but it presumably derives from using different generations of measuring equipment.

The early chapters emphasise the utility of scale models for the development of a hypothesis in the absence of data, as an aid to plausible construction techniques, and for both air-tunnel and water-tank evaluations before a replica is built. In fact many *Shipwright* readers will find that their own experiences of researching, inferring dimensions from objects such as a barrel, and then creating a ship model from incomplete data parallel the projects recounted in this book such that it becomes almost irrelevant that these are actually full-size vessels being described.

Subsequent chapters provide an absorbing insight into the evolution of maritime technology such that the reader is enticed into discovering how, why, and the implications of the following stage; and while some readers may have in-depth knowledge of a particular type of craft or period very few of us will be familiar with the diversity of vessels covered in this book.

The description of each replica is enhanced by numerous pragmatic insights and observations such as the derivation of the carvel form of construction and the limitations of the clinker style, the practicalities of the 'French' planking technique and a description of the even rarer plank-edge mortice-and-tenon system; a *Shipwright*'s view on the relative merits of steaming or bending planks over an open fire is yet another practical contribution that differentiates this book from the academic.

The challenge of communicating with, and synchronising, three tiers of rowers in a Trireme may not come as too much of a surprise but less obvious were the practical issues of carrying sufficient drinking water to sustain them, and the rapid onset of shipworm infestation.

Similarly less obvious but of interest are the observations on organizing and funding these large projects and then sustaining them financially, their on-going maintenance and obtaining crew members while complying with today's health and safety requirements; the arguments for justifying these and future projects as being educational as well as research tools in a period of austerity are also addressed.

The majority of these chapters are accompanied by good lines' drawings that will be appreciated by *Shipwright*'s readers who are accustomed to comprehending and comparing vessels in this way; in their absence sufficient references are provided for those who wish to carry out further research with a view to building a model. This book alone provides most of the background data, particularly with regards to colour and ornamentation, that would be required to build an accurate static ship model; and I suspect that the descriptions of the vessels' forms of construction and sailing characteristics may tempt a few scale-sail modellers into building a distinctive working version.

Sailing into the Past provides an authoritative, fascinating, and very readable overview of the evolution of the wooden sailing vessel as seen through the experiences of those building and operating modern replicas. The book offers a practical perspective on the construction and seaworthiness of these craft that will appeal to readers with an interest in maritime history in general and to 'period' ship modellers in particular.

Graham Castle